Breadmaking at

Breadmaking at Home

Harold Bagust

ROBERT HALE · LONDON

ISBN 0 7090 5653 2

Robert Hale Limited
Clerkenwell House
Clerkenwell Green
London EC1R 0HT

2 4 6 8 10 9 7 5 3 1

Photoset in North Wales by
Derek Doyle & Associates, Mold, Clwyd.
Printed in Great Britain by
St Edmundsbury Press Ltd, Bury St Edmunds, Suffolk.
Bound by WBC Book Manufacturers Limited,
Bridgend, Mid-Glamorgan.

Contents

Acknowledgements

My thanks are due in no small measure to family and friends, many of whom have tested and opined on the results of my efforts over the years; to Sean Cocks and personnel of Cannington College Department of Nutrition for checking the manuscript for technical errors; to members of the faculty of Southampton University for general assistance and advice; to numerous bakers, millers and farmers for their unstinting assistance and suggestions; to my illustrators Julie Williams and Kate Harwood; and finally to my wife Audrey, without whose criticism and tolerance protracted over more than four years, this book could not have been completed.

Recipes

Introduction

It could be argued that sufficient books on bread have been published to cover every possible aspect of its production, and there is no doubt that the subject has been widely exploited in the Press, on radio and television. My reason for adding another volume to the range is a simple one – I have yet to discover a book written entirely for the beginner which covers all the basic points required to produce a high-quality loaf at the first attempt.

How many books, for instance, warn against over-rising? Yet this is the cause of many initial failures. How many acknowledge that yeast will rise without the addition of sugar, or that the crispness of the crust can be altered by varying the fat content of the mix?

I began baking bread over thirty years ago, reading every book I could find and every magazine article on the subject. I rapidly came to the conclusion that the great majority of the authors had never made a loaf of bread in their lives, relying upon recipes they had discovered in other publications and repeating the errors found therein. Rye bread is an outstanding example: it is almost impossible to produce an edible loaf simply by substituting rye flour for wheat, and any author who says otherwise has obviously no practical experience of making rye bread.

Bread baking is not a precise science requiring critical measurement of the ingredients and exact temperatures but if the basic rules detailed in the following pages are followed an edible loaf will be produced every time, and as confidence grows the cook can experiment with variations without courting disaster.

At the tender age of eight I was taken for a holiday to an aunt who owned a small general shop in the rural district of Stourbridge in Worcestershire. It was the first of several holidays in what was then a small country town served by trams and buses from nearby Dudley Port and Birmingham. The town centre consisted of a handful of shops clustered around a tiny Woolworth's store with a frontage of about twenty feet and a depth of little more in yards, proudly displaying the legend '3d and 6d Store – Nothing over 6d'.

My aunt's shop at 33 Whitton Street, now demolished I am told, sold everything from candles to cooked meats, paraffin, pins, sweets, saucepans – and bread baked daily in the bakehouse behind the shop. The actual shop area was only some twenty feet square and stocked with goods from floor to ceiling. In front of the counter was a row of biscuit tins stacked ten wide and three high, each measuring about 10 x 10 x 10 inches and having a glass panel in the lid through which the contents could be seen. In a corner was a sack of beans and one of dried peas usually with the cat asleep in one or other. The bakehouse was the same width as the shop but at least three times the length to accommodate a large solid pine table, bins of flour, a lead-lined chest wherein the dough was placed to rise, and of course the massive coal-fired oven

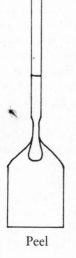

which produced about 200 loaves every weekday morning and double the quantity on Saturdays.

Her day started at 4 a.m. when she began manipulating the dough in the huge lead-lined coffer then, after lighting the fire under the brick-built oven, back to bed for an hour or so to await the second 'rise', then kneading and pummelling the dough into the warm tins before setting them into the oven with the aid of wooden peels (a type of shovel) with handles over six feet long. By the time we came down to breakfast at 8 a.m. the whole house was filled with the aroma of fresh baked bread – the best I have ever tasted.

Later that day, usually about 4 p.m., she would mix the dough for the next day's bread, putting it into the lead-lined vat to mature and rise overnight. (We had no fears about lead in the diet in those days.)

Of course I was too young to understand Aunt Violet's methods, but I certainly appreciated the quality of her bread and made myself rather unpopular at home after the holidays comparing the inferior London bread with the Stourbridge

Peel

product. In all other respects she was an appalling cook; her cakes were terrible and her Sunday joint was either burned to a cinder or almost raw, but to my mind her bread made up for all her shortcomings, and over the years I have found this to be not at all unusual. Many of the bakers of excellent bread seem to fail when it comes to cakes and other items, and vice versa. There was a baker in the Cotswold village where I lived for some years who made the most delicious jam doughnuts and Danish pastries but whose bread was a total disaster, and in the Welsh country town of Machynlleth the bread from one of the local bakeries was so good that I had a loaf mailed to me once a week until the postal service became so erratic that it was often a week old before it reached me, yet the cakes from the same bakery were quite poor.

For many years Aunt Violet's bread remained nothing more than a boyhood memory, and although the bread we ate in London was inferior by comparison it was all that was available and nobody among my acquaintances ever considered making their own, probably because in the days before the advent of modern labour-saving devices they just did not have the time. But in many country areas before the war bread was still baked in the home and there were quite a number of cottages with a bread oven. However, recipes and methods had been handed down from mother to daughter over the centuries and so the quality varied. Most villages and every town had its bakery, and again the quality of the product depended upon the skill and application of the baker or his staff. The large multiple bakeries were not established in England until about the mid-thirties when the millionaires suddenly realized that big money could be made by mass-producing one of the basic foods coupled with the power of advertising.

The general quality did improve somewhat in the 1930s when there was an influx of displaced Jews from Europe, some of whom were excellent bakers and set up in business especially in the Willesden, Golders Green and Swiss Cottage areas of London, though few of their businesses survived the war. Even so they never quite reached the quality of bread I remembered from my childhood although some of their pastries and cakes were marvellous.

Memory is notorious for playing tricks, and I began to think that perhaps the quality of Aunt Violet's bread was a figment of my imagination until one day in 1938 (in my teens) during a cycling tour of Devon I came into the village of Bow, near Crediton, at about 4 p.m. on a glorious summer day.

In those days nearly all country bakers had a small room at the back of the shop where they served teas, and so my fiancée and I were provided with a pot of tea, several thick slices of fresh bread, a dish of butter, one of strawberry jam and a small plate of cakes. The waitress, the baker's young daughter, informed us that if we needed more we had only to ask.

We did not bother with the cakes but stuffed ourselves with bread and home-made jam until we could eat no more, and I knew without a doubt that Aunt Violet's bread had been no dream, for the Bow baker's bread was quite equal to it. The set price for a 'Plain Tea' in those days was 6d, or 7d (about 3p) with clotted cream – it would have been sacrilege to put cream on that bread, and between us we must have consumed nearly two loaves. (On a recent journey my route took me through the village of Bow and I called at the shop still much as I remembered it from more than fifty years ago although the village itself has spread a little. The baker has long since died and the business is now run by his daughter, the waitress who served us back in 1938. Unfortunately she had been unable to continue with the bread-baking side of the business, but assured me that the oven is still there at the rear of the premises together with some of the machinery her father used.)

During the war years and for some time after there was no opportunity to search for good bakers, one ate whatever bread one could get, usually after queueing for long periods, and the wartime bread was made from an assortment of flours, potatoes and various other ingredients which could be shaped into a loaf. Nonetheless, wartime bread was far superior to the modern tasteless 'plastic' breads, ready-sliced from supermarkets, butchers', petrol stations and other outlets, much of which resembles damp cottonwool in both appearance and flavour. It is very sad to realize that for a great proportion of the population this is the only bread they know.

It must have been about 1960 that I decided to try making my own bread with Aunt Violet's memory in mind, and began reading books and magazine articles on the subject, besides listening to advice on BBC *Woman's Hour*. I must have read dozens of books that have been written about bread and tried out hundreds of recipes suggested – often with disastrous results as my family will testify. I am still horrified at some of the recipes and methods suggested by contemporary authors and cooks and am convinced that in many cases their advice, if followed, can only result in home breadmaking being abandoned for ever by most housewives. One of the few exceptions is Elizabeth David whose book *English Bread and Yeast Cookery* first published in 1977 is a mine of common-sense information.

Housewives have been making their own bread for centuries past; true we have no means of assessing the quality, but presumably it was acceptable to their families if only as trenchers upon which to place the meat. Today failure can be almost completely eliminated if a few basic rules are followed and, after several years of trial and error, I feel bound to encourage the baking of a decent loaf by explaining the general principles and offering a few basic recipes in a manner which can be followed by the rawest of beginners. In my experience very few people are concerned with the fine details of bread production – the chemical content and reactions does not interest them any more than the biological history of the yeast used – the quality of the loaf is all that matters: does it look good, does it taste good, is the crust and crumb as I like it, is it wholesome and free from artificial and possibly dangerous 'improvers' and additives?

I read somewhere that bakers in the distant past had a test for good bread: the crumb from a newly baked loaf was formed into a ball then thrown down on to the floor – if it bounced it was good bread. Try this with modern 'plastic' bread; you will find it has about as much bounce in it as a lead balloon. The publication *Food Fit to Eat* (financed by the industry) defines bread as 'a delicate lattice of gluten throughout which starch and carbon dioxide gas is dispersed ... an effect initiated by water'. A more accurate description of modern factory bread would perhaps be 'a volume of water droplets suspended in a thin latticework of chemicals with a minimum of wheat protein'.

This book does not purport to offer a large number of recipes, it is intended to be a handbook and guide for beginners so that the usual initial disasters can be avoided. In my experience books listing hundreds of recipes usually offer the least guidance – the details are intentionally condensed to enable the largest quantity to be included, totally ignoring the quality of the information contained in the recipes and skipping many of the essential details. How many times have you heard someone say 'Oh yes, I did try baking bread once but it was a disaster, even though I followed the recipe exactly.'

Before attempting any of the recipes please read all the preliminary pages first so that you have understood the basic principles. A certain amount of repetition in the recipes is intentional. There is nothing more annoying when halfway through the proceedings to read 'prepare the dough according to the instructions on page so and so' – by now your hands are plastered in wet dough and in no fit state to begin turning pages.

Measurements and temperatures are given in both imperial and metric figures but I have ignored the American 'cups' because they are so imprecise as to be quite misleading. One cookbook currently on sale in this country states '1 lb of flour will make between 3 and 4½ cups, depending on variety used' – a 50% margin of error! Nearly all my American friends now weigh out their ingredients so they will have no difficulty in following the recipes.

Breadmaking is not an art it is an acquired skill and, like most other skills, the more you practise the better the result. If you follow the instructions carefully your very first loaf will be a vast improvement on any factory bread, but as you continue to bake you will begin to appreciate the finer points and your loaves will progress from being 'excellent' to 'superb' as you get the feel of the dough.

Home-baked bread is more expensive than factory bread but this is offset by the knowledge that you will be eating a pure product, not a chemical sponge derived from a little adulterated flour suspended in water.

A home-baked loaf taken straight from the oven has one major fault: it cries out to be eaten. One slice leads to another and within minutes the loaf has disappeared. In our village it became known that I normally bake on Saturdays, and during the summer we are overwhelmed with gifts from the locals each Saturday morning – lettuces, onions, carrots, tomatoes, etc. Unfortunately my oven is not large enough to bake more than about five loaves at a time so we have to ration out the favours – four loaves for the family, one for the village. When you start baking keep very quiet about it or you are liable to be inundated with visitors!

Harold Bagust
Holcombe Rogus, 1995

1

The Truth About Flour and Bread

All that glisters is not gold: It was some time before I came to realize the tremendous difference in flour quality and how it can affect the bread produced from it. You have only to look at the packets of wholemeal flour on the supermarket shelves to find that the sell-by date allows for a shelf life sometimes in excess of two years, yet it is widely believed among nutrition experts that most wholemeal flour produced by the big millers deteriorates rapidly after about three months although some stoneground flour will often still be good at three *years* old.

I began to investigate the possibility of purchasing flour from local mills where I could be reasonably certain of the quality and age of the product, and, with a lot of help from mill owners, museums and tourist associations, have been able to assemble a list of independent flour mills scattered around the country, most of which are actually producing flour, and those that are not, expect to be doing so in the near future. The list which follows later in the book is in county order to make it easy to find the mill nearest to you. Don't miss the opportunity to bake with fresh flour – even if you have to get it by mail order and pay the exorbitant postal charges.

I have been unable to visit every one of the mills listed, nor can I claim to have tested all their flours, however, it has been possible to sample nearly half of them with excellent results. Each is different; Mapledurham is finer than Dunster for instance, and Dunster is slightly coarser than Otter, but every one is pure unadulterated 100% wholemeal with nothing added and nothing taken away. My advice is to try as many as you can whenever you can. The mill descriptions have been supplied by the owners and the details approved by them before printing, but you are advised to telephone to confirm opening times before making a special journey.

During these investigations I have visited the mill at Hele between Ilfracombe and Combe Martin in North Devon and was fortunate to meet the proprietor Chris Lovell who is a leading expert on flour and milling and has written three papers on the subject – *The Truth About Bread, The Truth About Flour* and *Further Revelations*. Those who regard bread as a type of pallet used solely to convey a portion of baked beans or cheese from plate to mouth will have no interest in reading them, but to most people who are concerned about what goes into their daily bread, they will be a revelation indeed. The following paragraphs are based upon Mr Lovell's words and included with his full permission. Copies of his original manuscript can be obtained from Hele Mill at a nominal charge.

The Truth About Bread

The regulations governing flour are not the same as those governing bread; for example, although only four additives may be present in wholemeal flour (sodium metabisulphite, sulphur dioxide, caramel and *alpha*-amylases), wholemeal bread may contain almost all the vast array of chemical additives permitted in white flour.

Small bakers have always claimed that there is no money in bread, so do we then assume that the large multiple bakeries are run entirely for the benefit of the public? Of course not, they exist only to make a profit for the shareholders and directors. No public company has a duty in law to anyone but its shareholders; if it markets a new product it does so only to increase its market share of sales and therefore its profit. Socialism? Communism? No, just plain fact, what some of our politicians call 'market forces'. Unfortunately we, the public, are deliberately duped time and time again, and persuaded by intensive advertising to buy rubbish disguised as high quality, often with the active connivance of government departments and ministers.

The commercial baker, being no different to any other entrepreneur, wishes to increase his profit margin, and therefore is interested in making his bread as quickly as possible with the minimum of expense. To achieve this he requires a flour which presents exactly the same characteristics in every sack, and he has a battery of chemicals that he can add. In a modern bakery using the high speed Chorleywood Process this uniformity is even more important.

Most bakers prefer their flour to be produced from wheat grown on the vast prairies of North America and Canada where the hard grain is of consistent quality and has a high gluten content that makes the bread rise well; and before the war it is true to say that British-grown grain was suitable mainly for animal feed. New strains of wheat now mean that flour can be produced here from home-grown wheat, and the chemical content of the soils can vary from field to field and even from different parts of the same field. But in fact much imported grain is still used.

These variations plus the retention of varying amounts of the wheatgerm is what makes flour flavours different. But variable flours cause problems for bakers because their use requires more time, effort and expense – such variation is avoided and a chemically stabilized flour used instead. This is why the usual wholemeal loaf purchased from a multiple baker or supermarket is almost as well risen as their white bread, tastes very little different from a white loaf, and bears almost no relationship to a home-baked loaf made from the flour ground by a small mill that produces genuine stoneground wholemeal flour. Unfortunately the vast majority of the population has only tasted this 'factory wholemeal' and from the limited space allocated to it on supermarket shelves, it is obvious that it appeals to few.

Incidentally, many small bakers exist on money borrowed from the large millers conditional upon them using only their flour – a similar system to the tied houses in the brewery trade, which explains why flour purchases from a baker makes bread which is seldom better than that on general sale.

This state of affairs is summed up in the following quotations:

'Eleven million tasteless, branless, germless and synthetically adulterated loaves are consumed daily in this country.'

Sunday Times 18.12.77

'British bread is the most chemically treated in Western Europe.'

Report of the Technology Assessment
Consumer Council 1974

Loaves

There is an infinite number of local names applied to loaves of different shapes, but they must now carry an indication of the type of flour from which they are made. Apart from wholemeal, brown and white there is wheatgerm that has added *processed* wheatgerm of not less than 10%, and soda if sodium hydrogen carbonate is an ingredient.

Pay no attention to words such as 'windmill' or 'water-mill' attached to the names of bread, they do not indicate that the flour has been produced in either a wind or water-mill, and even if they did it would have no bearing upon the nature of the flour; wind and water are merely power sources! Furthermore, flour is often made in a mill other than that indicated on the bag, and in the case of supermarket own brands the source is never disclosed.

There are some names of bread which require explanation:

Hovis. This was originally made from flour with not less than 10% added *processed* wheatgerm, and could thus be classed under the heading of 'wheatgerm bread'. For decades Hovis advertised their bread as being made with added wheatgerm but not mentioning the fact that it was made from white flour.

Richard Smith patented his flour about 1885 soon after the new roller mills were introduced into this country. They produced a pure white flour from which all the bran had been extracted, bran at that time being considered suitable only for animal feed. The removal of the wheatgerm during the milling was an added advantage to the miller and baker since it was liable to turn rancid in storage, but its omission made the flour deficient in nutrient content.

Smith separated the wheatgerm from the bran and, after processing, blended it with the white flour. It is sometimes said that caramel was added to produce a darker brown loaf, but a light-brown crumb would result anyway as the bread was baked. It was never claimed to be wholemeal although many people regarded it as such.

The family millers, S. Fitton & Sons of Macclesfield, manufactured Hovis flour under license and, although they were never bakers themselves, maintained a rigid control over bakers producing Hovis bread and biscuits. The recipe and technical advice was supplied together with the embossed tins in which the Hovis loaves had to be baked; thus a Hovis loaf purchased in Edinburgh would look and taste exactly the same as one from a London or Swansea baker.

The post-war years have seen a great change in Hovis loaves. The small dense loaf with its name proudly displayed along the side has been superseded by a puffed-up, chemicalized replacement – an enlarged, mass-produced loaf made from the same weight of dough.

Modern Hovis bread bears little resemblance to Smith's original patent and is made from a range of flours produced by RHM Foods including wholemeal, white, country grain or granary etc. Tastewise, modern Hovis seems no different to other plastic breads in my opinion, and its water and chemical content is similar if not identical.

Granary bread. This is made from white flour with various additives, one of which is always malted meal or malt extract. The natural look is achieved by scattering a few whole or kibbled grains in the mix; it has nothing to do with wholemeal. However, there is no reason why wholemeal flour cannot be used, and several small mills produce a granary-type flour which is a fine ground wholemeal flour with some kibbled wheat (almost whole grains) added. Malt is seldom an ingredient.

Brown bread. Brown bread is almost invariably made from white flour coloured with caramel, but since the introduction of the 1984 Regulations it must have a minimum crude fibre content of 0.6% which is about a quarter of that found in real wholemeal.

Wholemeal with added bran. This is what it says it is, but wholemeal flour contains a certain proportion of endosperm, wheatgerm and bran. It is a nice point for discussion – if the proportions are altered by adding extra bran can it still be called wholemeal? Moreover, much so-called wholemeal is actually white flour with some of the wheatgerm and bran put back into it (see page 30). If it is taken out and then reintroduced can it be described as 'added'?

Hard and soft wheat. Many people are still under the impression that English wheat is unsuitable for making bread, but this applies only to those bakeries that are equipped to use only the harder foreign wheats. Some are now using a proportion of English wheat, usually because the baker is unaware of the composition of the sacks of flour he purchases from the miller – bakers are only concerned that flour is consistent, rises well, and can hold the maximum amount of water (water being cheaper than flour – so far!). In fact English wheat has been improved enormously in the past forty/fifty years and new strains have been specifically developed for flour production. There is no doubt that excellent bread can now be made using English wheat flour, and all the recipes in this book call for English wheat flour whenever wholemeal is specified.

Aerated bread. In the mid-19th century a Doctor Dauglish patented a system of making dough sealed in a flask and aerated with carbonated water under pressure. It was marketed in England by the Aerated Bread Company (ABC) who established a number of tea-rooms mainly in London and the Home Counties selling light refreshments centred on their bread. The ABC tea-shops preceded the Lyons chain by over thirty years and were very successful until the company was acquired by the giant Allied Bakeries in the 1950s. It is possible that a few of the shops still survive although it is several years since I last saw one. The bread was the forerunner of the modern factory bread and just as fluffy and flavourless although not quite so soggy – it did produce a large loaf from a small amount of dough.

The Truth About Flour

A grain of wheat has three main components:

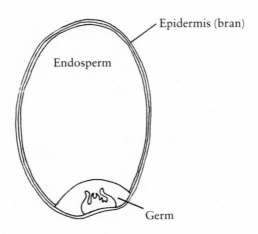

Grain of wheat

1. The flour-yielding part of the grain called the endosperm which is about 85% of the entire grain.
2. The germ – the seed which would ultimately develop into a new plant. This is the very 'life' of the wheat and comprises about 2% of the entire grain.
3. The bran – which is the outer skin or covering of the

grain (there are several distinct layers, each with a different name). The bran forms about 15% of the entire grain.

Types of Flour

The Bread and Flour Regulations 1984 have redefined the names of flour, and have eliminated such terms as '85% Wheatmeal' which few people understood. Now there are just three legal descriptions of flour – 'Wholemeal' or 'Wholemeal Flour', 'Brown Flour' and 'Flour'. These are descriptions of flour, they are not descriptions of bread – an entirely different matter. The term 'Wheatmeal' can no longer be used to describe bread or flour, but apparently it is still legal to use it in reference to biscuits – McVitie's Digestive biscuits are still labelled 'Wheatmeal'.

Wholemeal flour. Legally this is the flour which contains 'the whole of the product derived from the milling of cleaned wheat', in other words, all the components of the grain – all the germ, all the bran and all the endosperm. But in actual fact some of the larger mills remove between 2–5% of the entire grain, and it is not unknown for even a few of the small ones to extract some of the bran for selling separately. Regrettably the Trading Standards Officers turn a blind eye to this practice thus completely invalidating the description '100% Wholemeal Flour' which appears on many flour bags. Not all mills are guilty and few, if any, of those listed in the following pages resort to this subterfuge.

Brown flour. This is flour with a 'crude-fibre content of not less than 0.6%'. The crude-fibre content of genuine wholemeal flour is between 2 and 2.5%, so brown flour has only about a quarter of the crude-fibre found in wholemeal. The legal description makes no mention of the need for any germ at all to be included, so it is usually absent. Brown flour is almost invariably white flour with colouring matter added to darken it, and this is one of the reasons why many people believe erroneously that it is 'almost wholemeal'.

Flour. This is flour which contains less than 0.6% crude-fibre. The legal description says little more than that, but it seldom contains any germ, and has been bleached white – usually with chlorine dioxide. This is a chemical widely used in the textile industry, it is considered too dangerous even to be used for cleaning drains, and its use as an additive to flour is prohibited in many European countries. Bleaching is used not only to whiten the flour but also as a means of rapidly maturing or ageing it in order to make it more suitable for the production of machine-made short-fermentation dough. Chlorine dioxide is known to react with and reduce the amount of vitamin E present in flour.

Wholewheat. This means 'wholemeal'. It is a word wrongly used, causing needless confusion. When grain is milled it becomes 'meal' so it follows that 'wholewheat' should only be used to describe whole grains of wheat before milling. Since the 1984 Regulations the term has been used less and less, probably because this is not a legal description.

Graham flour. Because many American bread books find their way into this country I have included this description although it is seldom marketed under this name in Britain or Australia. It is the equivalent of our wholemeal flour, the name being derived from the nineteenth-century Doctor Sylvester Graham who was responsible for drawing the attention of the American public to the benefits of bread made from flour containing the whole of the wheat grain – information which appears to have been largely disregarded if one surveys the bread section of most supermarkets in the USA today.

Additives (compulsory). All flours, other than 100% wholemeal, must by law have a specified amount of chalk added. This became law following an outbreak of rickets in Dublin in 1940–41. 14 ozs of chalk must be added to each 280 lbs of flour. In addition to the chalk it is compulsory to add specified amounts of iron, thiamin (vitamin B) and nicotinic acid to all flours other than 100% wholemeal. Some consider this little more than a token attempt to compensate for the many items missing from flour that is not 100% wholemeal. The addition of chalk to white flour is regarded as unnecessary by nutritionists today, in fact some think it harmful; its continued use by the baking industry is simply because chalk is cheaper than flour, if it were not so the industry would be pressing the government to remove the regulation.

Other additives. Caramel, *alpha*-amylases, sulphur dioxide and sodium metabisulphite are the only additives permitted in wholemeal flour intended for breadmaking. Several other additives to wholemeal flour are permitted if it is self-raising, or if it is intended to be used for the manufacture of scones, buns, etc. A very great range of additives may be incorporated quite legally into other flours.

In some countries, France in particular, it is illegal to adulterate bread flour with any additives other than ascorbic acid (vitamin C).

Bran. This is the outer woody protective covering of the wheat grain. Since the introduction of roller mills in 1872 millers have been experimenting with different ways of removing it, and have spent millions of pounds on machinery to do so in order to produce a whiter loaf. The bran extracted is usually sold separately or in breakfast cereals at inflated prices.

In the past it was thought that bran was unsuitable for human consumption and was usually fed to animals (possibly one of the reasons why pre-war pork had more flavour), but more recently there has been an almost about-turn of medical opinion which has not gone unnoticed by the big millers and cereal producers. It is now generally agreed that the fibrous nature of bran is beneficial, but to an old-time miller cereals with added bran would have seemed about as sensible as a lawn with added weeds.

Fibre. Shortage of fibre in the diet can be an important cause of constipation, and in many cases an increase in the input of bran can help sufferers. Extra fibre can also assist those suffering from the even worse conditions of colitis, diverticulosis and diverticulitis, as well as several other illnesses.

Although people can often benefit from sprinkling bran on their food, it is not the best way to increase the fibre intake because of its poor water absorption properties. It is as unnatural to eat bran in this way as it is to eat refined foods which cause the need for more fibre in the first instance. Adding fibre to a diet of carbohydrates will not really solve anything, it will simply mask the symptoms caused by eating fibreless foods. The real solution is to change to a wholefood diet using wholemeal instead of white flour, and baking your own bread so you are clear about its ingredients.

Wheatgerm. The wheatgerm is only a tiny fleck, about the size of a pinhead, in a grain of wheat, but it is one of nature's most concentrated sources of protein, iron, fat and all of the B-vitamins. So much controversy has recently centred around the use of bran in the diet (now virtually resolved) that much of the limelight has been diverted away from wheatgerm which is simply nutrition in one of its most concentrated forms.

Its qualities have been known in the athletic world for many years – in 1954 Dr Roger Bannister ate wheatgerm daily before running the first under-four-minute mile. It contains vitamin C, but amazingly, also includes chemical elements which enable the vitamin C in the body to regenerate itself. Vitamin C has been called one of the anti-stress vitamins, but unfortunately it is easily oxidized and would be lost during prolonged storage. It is a great pity that the Food and Bread Regulations do not stipulate a minimum requirement of wheatgerm in flours other than wholemeal, yet permit a range of synthetic additives.

Wheatgerm may be purchased from health food shops and other outlets but is expensive and usually 'stabilized' which virtually means 'killed'. If you eat home-baked wholemeal bread made from flour from any one of the small independent mills it will provide all the wheatgerm required in a normal diet.

Further Revelations

Please note: most of the information in this section has not been easy to obtain, and much of it is sensitive. All statements have been made in good faith but it is possible that some of the references are now out of date or that legislation has changed. It is also possible that practices which were current at the time of writing have been amended or altered but, with few exceptions, the regulations remain much as they were in the 1970s.

The Missing Percentage

After reading *The Truth About Flour* you may wonder why the Trading Standards Inspectorate permits mills to remove a percentage of the ground wheat and yet still call the resulting product 'wholemeal'. The regulations clearly state that wholemeal flour should be 'the whole of the product'. Due to this curious lapse in enforcement it is now necessary to utilize another term to describe wholemeal that has had nothing removed! For the rest of this section the term 'real wholemeal' will be used. It should be particularly noted that the '100%' in '100% wholemeal' is not part of the legal definition, and in the light of the fact that a percentage is often omitted, the 100% can be positively misleading. It is clearly stated in many books that wholemeal as supplied to bakers has had about 5% of the total flour removed.

Why the Inspectorate does not enforce the law remains a mystery, but the reasons for some millers indulging in this practice are understandable if unforgivable.

In the smaller simple mills the flour travels straight from the millstones into bags, but in larger mills it becomes necessary to store it in bins or hoppers; this means that the flour must be moved, usually in an upward direction. Flour is nearly always moved by suction.

The installation of a suction system has many advantages for the mill owner whether individual or company. Apart from transporting the flour with the minimum of manual labour, it also keeps the millstones or rollers cool and prevents a build-up of flour through condensation thereby greatly increasing the output and reducing the fire hazard. Suction systems are usually installed by contractors, and part of the package is a rotary screen at the end of a suction pipe. This consists of a revolving riddle of wire mesh with a screen of such a size that the smaller pieces of flour pass through but larger pieces and any impurities are trapped.

It is very easy for spiders, ants and numerous insects to get into flour, and one of the most troublesome pests is the flour moth against which millers fight a never-ending battle, so it is a great comfort to them to be able to install a screen to eliminate such things from their flour. This would be a sensible and legitimate use of screening because it should remove nothing from the flour except pests and rubbish, but as we shall see the amount extracted when screens are used far exceeds the odd moth or spider and, incidentally, a common method of dealing with flour moths is to pass the flour through a machine that chops them into pieces too small to be seen!

Screening has another advantage for the miller: if the millstones are too dull or incorrectly set the flour that is too coarsely ground can be separated by a screen. Thus a finer flour can be made available by removing the larger pieces of bran. But if part of the bran is removed how can the resultant flour still be classed as wholemeal?

It must be appreciated that not all millers are enthusiasts, or even want to be millers. A farmer might begin by milling his own animal feed, then try making his own flour, find there is a market for it and so decide to expand that side of his business. One of the farm workers could then be given the job of running the mill – an indoor job holding little or no interest for him. Having no interest or aptitude for milling it is unlikely he would bother to read any books on the subject nor feel obliged to pay attention to the finer points of milling such as producing the correct consistency of the flour. He would probably do little more than press buttons on the control panel. It is most likely that the machinery would have been installed by contractors who would be responsible for all the details, and they would almost certainly have installed screening equipment as part of the package. The owner might not even be aware that screens can be removed or the gauge altered, and consequently often between 2% and 5% would be screened out, the screenings being the larger particles of bran. These could then be reground or, more likely, packaged separately and sold as bran at a higher price.

Reconstitution

The foregoing section refers to a few of the medium sized and smaller mills – it is not easy to gain access to the very large mills, and their size makes it impossible to understand exactly what is happening within them unless one is fully acquainted with the process and is able to go where one wishes and stay there for some considerable time. But all large mills employ the gradual reduction process and are set up to produce mainly white flour. The grain passes through rollers which tear it apart, it is then sieved and the larger particles reprocessed through more rollers, then sieved again, rolled again, and so on until a fine powder results. This is a simplified explanation but it covers the general principles of the process.

The germ and the bran are separated out and for many years they were sold as animal feed but these days are more likely to be sold at a far higher profit. When wheat is put through a modern gradual reduction rollermill 100 lb of wheat grain will produce about 70 lb of white flour, about 5 lb of wheatgerm and 15–20 lb of bran inextricably mixed with flour. The rest is lost in dust and evaporation.

Should one of these large mills wish to produce wholemeal flour without installing separate plant or a subsidiary mill, the only way they can proceed is by taking the white flour before it is bleached and adding back the wheatgerm and bran in the same proportions as they were originally. One might call this 'reconstituted wholemeal' and there would seem to be no obvious reason why it should be inferior to real wholemeal. However, since the wheatgerm and bran can be sold at a much higher price than flour and the authorities turn a blind eye to a missing percentage, market forces dominate.

Furthermore, caramel is one of the few additives that can legally be added to wholemeal flour. The main purpose in adding caramel is to produce a deeper brown colour, but the wheatgerm and bran would make the flour a dark colour naturally, so unless something is missing there would seem to be no point in adding caramel – it is not a very desirable additive anyway (see later), and it is illegal to add it to bread in the USA and many European countries.

Stoneground or Roller Ground

The term used by millers for turning grain into flour is 'reduction'. There are three basic methods of reduction:

1. Grinding – between stones or any pair of abrasive surfaces.
2. Attrition – by hitting the wheat with revolving metal hammers.
3. Rolling – tearing the grains apart between steel rollers.

There is nothing intrinsically better about flour properly produced by any of these processes, but recipes in this book specify *stoneground* wholemeal flour because it is more likely to be the genuine article than that produced by the gradual reduction method as described earlier.

It is sometimes stated that roller mills overheat the flour and that this is detrimental. This may have been true in the past when roller milling was in its infancy but it is unlikely to apply today because the whole purpose of the gradual reduction process is to be gradual. However, it must be allowed that mistakes are made and the rollers set too close together or the grain sometimes fed in too fast; the starch quality is then impaired, and if a loaf is made with such a flour it will be found to have almost razor-sharp corners when turned out of the tin.

There is one curious theory still in vogue among some millers that flour stoneground in a mill which is enclosed in wood is better than that which has touched metal and been earthed electrically.

White, Brown and Wholemeal

Legally, brown flour must have at least 0.6% crude fibre in it, and this is contained in the bran – but legally no wheatgerm has to be present. Here again we come up against what could be called 'real brown' and 'brown'. As we have seen, if brown flour is made by the gradual reduction process the wheatgerm will be absent because it has been removed and there is no legal requirement to replace it; therefore most 'brown' flour has caramel added to colour it. However, brown flour produced in a small mill that does not use the gradual reduction process would be wholemeal with some of the bran removed but with most of the germ still in it – 'real' brown flour.

White flour is usually bleached white, but some outlets sell unbleached white flour and the packet will be marked 'unbleached'. (Unless it is so marked it is fair to assume it has been bleached white, and whenever white flour is mentioned in this book it must be assumed to refer to bleached white unless otherwise stated.)

White flour, whether bleached or not, has much removed from it, and the following list shows percentage losses over wholemeal.

Thiamin (vit B1)	77.1%
Riboflavin (vit B2)	80.0%
Niacin	80.8%
Vitamin B6	71.8%
Pantothenic Acid	50.0%

Alpha-Tocopherol (vit E)	86.3%
Calcium	60.0%
Phosphorous	70.9%
Magnesium	84.7%
Potassium	77.0%
Sodium	78.3%
Chromium	40.0%
Manganese	85.8%
Iron	75.6%
Cobalt	88.5%
Copper	67.9%
Zinc	77.7%
Selenium	15.9%
Molybdenum	48.0%

Chemical Revelations

Now that chemicals are being considered and before any further mention is made of them it is necessary to understand something about the science of chemistry. Don't worry, there are not going to be pages of chemical formulae!

Many people, probably most, have no knowledge of chemistry, and their contact with it is limited to a visit to the local pharmacy and perhaps seeing a white-coated compounder in the distance. This mysterious person can sometimes be seen handling clearly labelled jars and bottles and mixing their contents together in minute quantities. Obviously everything is very precise and correct, and the measurements accurate. However, the *science* of chemistry is not a bit like that!

Like other sciences, new discoveries mean that new knowledge is being acquired almost daily; old ideas and concepts are superseded as more information becomes available. Because chemistry is a continually developing science new discoveries are frequently made that render names obsolete; for example, vitamin Bx is the discarded name for para-amino benzoic acid. These changes in nomenclature make it very difficult for the interested but chemically-ignorant layman to understand much of the written information. Sometimes as many as three or four different names are used to describe the same thing, and of course, the older sources use the older names. Unfortunately some of the newer sources also persist in using the old names, especially when the author has copied details from earlier writers.

Further confusion is caused by the use of 'blanket' names, for example nitrogen which is, of course, a gas, but in nutrition all nitrogen-containing substances are loosely referred to as 'nitrogen'. Also, there are no international standards of analysis – or even national ones for that matter. For example, there are three methods of calculating the calorific content of food. There are further differences between methods used in the UK and the USA.

Whereas the results obtained by the three methods of calculating the calorific content of food differ from each other by only a small amount, when it comes to measuring the fibre content of bran there is an enormous difference between the results obtained from the two methods currently used in analysis. In fact the analysts cannot agree even on the name of the product for which they are searching! By one method it is found that wholemeal flour has about 9.6 grams of *dietary* fibre per 100 grams, but by the official method used by the public analyst (as defined in the Regulations) wholemeal has only 2.2 grams of *crude* fibre per 100 grams. The official method is much quicker, but underestimates most of the different components.

This state of confusion is not helped when mistakes are made by those in authority who could be expected to know better. When a new factor was discovered that was claimed to be essential for chick growth, the claimant stated that as nine factors of the B vitamin were already known, the new factors should be called vitamins B10 and B11. In fact the B vitamins had been numbered only up to B6, and B7, B8 and B9 had never existed!

It follows from the above that the confusion increases when one considers all these matters on an international basis. Although there are international agreements on nomenclature, these are not always followed. An example is nicotinic acid which is still sometimes called by its old name of vitamin PP (pellagra-preventative, derived from the fact that a diet deficient in nicotinic acid can result in the disorder pellagra). Nicotinic acid's amide, nicotinamide, has the same biological function and both are known according to international agreement as niacin, but in the USA the old designations niacin and niacinamide are still used.

Someone can always be found to contradict *any* statement – you have only to see the way the powerful tobacco lobby has fought to prove the absence of a link between their product and lung cancer to realize just how market forces work. A note at the commencement of that great work of reference *The Composition of Foods* acknowledges this situation by stating that help and advice was received from many sources – much of it contradictory.

Following this explanation the reader can be forgiven for thinking that chemistry is all very confusing, but this is nothing to the confusion we shall come to later. However, we shall endeavour to make sense out of chaos, and this seems to be the correct moment to discuss the system of E numbers which has been imposed upon us by the EU *in order to make things simpler for us.*

E Numbers

Additives that have been agreed as safe by the EU have been given E numbers, and these can be used for labelling and other purposes instead of listing the chemicals by their full names. The fact that some chemicals have E numbers does not mean that *only* those with E numbers are permitted, there are many additives in use – different ones in different countries – that have no E numbers. The absence of an E number can mean that the chemical is still under consideration by the EU, that it is a permitted additive in Britain, or that it is permitted in some but not all European countries.

The list is constantly under review. Some additives will be found to have numbers in square brackets, these are ones being considered to see if they qualify for an E number (sometimes the square brackets are omitted for reasons which are not apparent); caramel for many years was one of these, yet it is commonly used in the manufacture of brown flour. Incidentally, caramel (E150) is deemed to upset hyperactive children, as is E220 (sulphur dioxide) also in common use, and caramel has been reported to cause bowel problems in some people. The 1987 Food Advisory Committee proposed a maximum caramel content on *certain specified foods*, but the 1984 Regulations place no restriction on its use in flour or bread although it is illegal to add caramel to bread in USA and many European countries.

All food manufactured after 1st January 1986 must carry the E number or actual name of any additive. Words such as 'permitted colouring' are illegal although 'permitted flavouring' is still allowed (surely no manufacturer is likely to use the words 'unpermitted flavouring'!). There are no regulations agreed by the EU regarding the ingredients of flavourings although five are banned in the UK. Flavours make up the largest group of additives that have not been allocated E numbers, and in spite of the fact that the mixtures are often very complex combinations of chemicals, they only have to be listed as 'flavourings'.

Compulsory Additives

The law demands that certain additives must be added to 'enrich' flour sold in Britain. The impression given is that this is a benevolent gesture by the government to provide us with better flour. Let us examine these additives in detail.

There are four items that must be compulsorily added to all flour (Bread and Flour Regulations 1984) other than wholemeal – collectively they are called 'nutrients'.

Calcium (Creta preparata). Calcium carbonate (chalk) was added to the British wartime bread after an outbreak of rickets in Dublin in 1940/41. At that time it was thought that a reduction in the calcium intake caused by the rationing of or the difficulty in obtaining supplies of normal calcium-rich foods such as milk and cheese would result in more children developing rickets, and some adults in developing the bone disease osteomalacia. Since then it has been found that vitamin D deficiency is more likely to be the major cause of these two diseases.

Dr E. Widdowson, whose research played an influential role in the wartime flour enrichment policy, summed up the situation thus: 'When calcium was originally added to flour there were reasons for doing so, but these reasons have now gone.' Nonetheless it is still compulsory for calcium to be added to all flours other than wholemeal. The amount that must be added is so great that there is less calcium in wholemeal than in other flours. Yet calcium propionate (sometimes called calcium propanoate), a commonly used (non-compulsory) additive, destroys the enzymes that enable the body to utilize the calcium in white bread! Its main purpose is as a mould inhibitor, but it has been known to cause a rash among bakery workers and there is a possible link with migraine attacks.

Iron. Iron is added in the belief that the incidence of anaemia due to iron deficiency will be reduced, but recent research has shown that not only is this useless for the purpose but it is potentially harmful. Furthermore, bread enrichment with iron normally takes the form of metallic iron in powdered or reduced states. Neither form is well absorbed by humans; if the body could use inorganic iron, then drinking water from rusty iron pipes would help build red blood cells in anaemic conditions, but we know that this is not so.

Thiamin (vitamin B1). Although thiamin must be added to white flour, about half of it is destroyed by the baking process! The incorporation of sulphur dioxide (a bleaching agent for flour) in foods reduces their thiamin content and can cause problems for sufferers from asthma and kidney and liver disorders. It is also thought to have a bearing on hyperactive children.

Nicotinic acid or Nicotinamide (vitamin B2). This is another synthetic vitamin, and these synthetic vitamins are unable to be used by the human body to the same extent as are natural vitamins. But as is so often the case, there is a contrary opinion that states that there is no difference between the two. (Most synthetic vitamins are coal-tar products, and some coal-tar products are suspected of being carcinogenic.)

By now it must be painfully obvious to the reader that logic has little bearing either on the matter under consideration or, regrettably, on anything that follows! However, so conditioned are we to logic it is often assumed that if certain items are extracted from flour, and if it is considered necessary to replace some of them, then surely as much would be put back as was originally removed. Not so; the quantity of each additive is only about half the amount found naturally in wholemeal flour, except in the case of calcium which, as we have seen, has its own special illogicality.

Additive	Milligrams per 100 grams	
	Amount to be added	Amount in 'real' wholemeal
Iron	1.65 (min)	4.0
Thiamin (B1)	0.24 (min)	0.46
Nicotinic acid (B2) or Nicotinamide	1.60 (min)	5.6
Calcium	235 (min) 390 (max)	35.0

So, the enrichment of flour (another word used is 'fortification') does not raise it anywhere near to the standard of real wholemeal. Over twenty vitamin and mineral elements are greatly reduced when wheat is converted into white flour; only three or four are returned as additives, and then only in small amounts. Moreover, what is added back is either synthetic or inorganic, and is considered by some to be positively harmful, though of course, others will state that they are beneficial. If this is indeed the true situation why must these additives be put into non-wholemeal flour?

The 'enrichment' programme, of course, has been the subject of intense pressure by big business. On 18th July 1940 Mr (later Lord) Boothby stated that the Ministry of Food proposed adding synthetic vitamin B1 to bread. This was most curious: governments in the past had often legislated about bread but never before with the (ostensible) object of enriching it. Mr Boothby went on to say, 'Many Hon. Members know that ... I was chairman of a company which manufactured these vitamins. I ... resigned my seat on the board immediately I was appointed Parliamentary Secretary'. However, he omitted to say that he retained his directorship and shareholding.

Scientists seem to fall into one of two camps – the 'extract and then add' group, and the 'keep the flour whole' side. In the EU only the UK and Denmark make enrichment with nutrients compulsory; other EU countries forbid it.

The industry is always investigating the possibility of using different and cheaper ingredients in the production line, and have recently been experimenting with sugar beet, pea shucks, tomatoes, potatoes, beans, etc. Perhaps one of the most promising so far is the use of coarsely ground wood because it is white, odourless, flavourless, about 80% dietary fibre *and will absorb up to seven times its own weight of water*. It seems that the plastic bread eaters can look forward to an even wetter loaf in the future.

There are many other additives that are not compulsory but are permitted, but before these are considered we must learn more about the baking industry.

The Baking Industry

Although a few small and medium-sized bakeries still exist, most of today's bread is produced in large bread factories. The general public have little idea of the processes involved, so we will now examine the subject and expose the reasons why mass-produced bread is so tasteless, particularly the sliced and wrapped varieties.

For centuries past bread was made entirely by a fermentation process which took between five and twenty-four hours. During this time a modification of the gluten structure of the dough occurs which makes it capable of stretching – this is known as 'dough development'.

It is only since the early part of this century that the availability of fresh yeast has enabled the fermenting time to be radically reduced, since when various attempts have been made to bring about the rapid development of the dough by mechanical means. For many years it has been the dream of the large bakers to acquire a machine capable of extruding a continuous stream of dough which could then be automatically baked, sliced and wrapped.

Such a machine was in fact made – the Oakes Continuous Mixer – so the dream was fulfilled, but in practice it has been found that in most cases it is more suitable to have a machine producing batches of dough in rapid succession than in one continuous stream. The batch system enables the dough mix to be altered more easily than in a continuous system, and it also enables the process to be stopped should any of the succeeding operations develop a mechanical fault. It is not difficult to imagine the chaos if a continuous stream of dough is being extruded whilst the rest of the production line is out of action! Moreover a batch system can be adjusted in size to suit the smaller bakeries and those unable to afford the enormous cost of a continuous system.

Research on mechanical dough development had taken place, rather spasmodically over several decades, but no satisfactory commercial progress had been made until the British Baking Industries Research Association at Chorley-wood in Hertfordshire made a serious concerted attempt at solving the problem, and finally succeeded. It was after the London Bakery Exhibition of 1963 that the Chorleywood Bread Process was accepted by the baking industry, and the large bread factories as we now know them came into being. By 1972 something like 80% of all bread eaten in this country was made by the Chorleywood Bread Process, known as C.B.P.

It consists of mixing ingredients at very high speed combined with meticulously accurate timing. The ingredients must also be meticulously accurate in their chemical consistency and quantity. Some idea of the care needed can be gained from the fact that the timing of the mixing process must be accurate to within about two seconds. Other requirements are a specified level of an oxidizing agent, a critical minimum level of a correctly constituted fat, and a partial vacuum in the mixer. The mixer is operated for only about three minutes, and because the dough development cycle is so short, the rate of water absorption by the flour must be precise and vary as little as possible. The chemical composition of the flour in other respects must also be precisely correct, and this is why 'any old flour' plays havoc with C.B.P. systems.

The advantages of the C.B.P. to the large bakeries are several. The conventional mixing and bulk fermentation stage is replaced by a short period of intensive mixing which lasts only about three minutes as compared with the conventional twenty minutes. After mixing the dough can immediately be divided instead of being left for some time to ferment, thus saving a great amount of floor space. Yet another advantage is that the dough absorbs more water, and water is cheaper than flour. A conventional system uses between 14 and 16 gallons of water to each 280 lb of flour, whereas the C.B.P. uses between 17 and 18 gallons to the same quantity of flour, so between 60% and 63% of a C.B.P. mix is water. This is higher than the permitted limit in

Australia and USA, but in Britain there is no legislation controlling the water content of bread, so the consumer remains unaware. Those bakeries operating the C.B.P. obviously do not consider excessive water detrimental to the quality of the bread but, fortunately for the consumer, the incorporation of too much water in the mix causes stick-ups and brings the plant to a halt.

A further advantage of the C.B.P. to the baker is that as there is no bulk fermentation, less flour solids are lost in the form of gas and alcohol. Also the C.B.P. enables the baker to use a lower percentage of strong and therefore expensive wheat.

A great deal of research went into perfecting the C.B.P. involving the development of new machinery, oxidants and yeasts to deal with the new conditions it imposed.

From the foregoing brief outline of the process it will be seen that it is necessary for bakers to become far more accurate in their measurements, and much more consistent in the chemical constitution of their ingredients. Also they have to have reliable automatic controls for the whole process, for with batches being produced at roughly five-minute intervals (depending upon the size of the mixer installed) it is essential that all subsequent stages be precisely timed. This is necessary not only for the production of a saleable loaf, but to keep all stages of the production line in step with each other.

The sequence of events in a full scale C.B.P. is as follows:

Mix (2–3 minutes); divide the dough (and check-weigh a few pieces); pass the dough through a conical moulder (this gives individual dough pieces some semblance of crumb direction and helps put them into a shape that is easily handled by the final moulder); put dough into first prover for 6–8 minutes (previously this took about 20 minutes); pass the dough through the final moulder where the finished texture and cell formation of the loaf is created; place the dough into tins. The final proving takes between 45 and 59 minutes. The loaves are baked in a continuous oven with the bread moving slowly through it for between 26 and 40 minutes, followed by automatic depanning. Cooling takes about two hours and forty minutes, and finally the bread is automatically sliced and wrapped.

Thus the simple bakery has become an enormously costly

production line – and there are many other things to be synchronized that have not been mentioned above. Smaller bakeries do not need to install the complete system, the high speed mixers can be purchased in a range of sizes from one able to mix only 10 lbs of ingredients to the large machines which can handle 660 lbs in a few minutes. With the smaller mixers it is possible to use less sophisticated ancillary machinery, enabling smaller bakers to change from traditional methods to the Chorleywood process, the high cost of conversion being offset by the saving in time and space, and the increased amount of water that can be incorporated into the mix. Bakeries using C.B.P. are usually called 'plant bakeries'.

About 70% of British bread is made by the very large bakeries, the remaining 30% is divided between about 100 large-scale plant bakeries and some 6000 (non-plant) 'master bakers' – this rather grandiose title merely means that they employ less than about eight people in the bakehouse and have paid their subscription to the Guild of Master Craftsmen – all they have to do is send the fee and they immediately become 'master bakers'. (This applies equally to 'master carpenters', 'master builders', picture-frame makers, potters, chimney sweeps, etc., pay your fee and you become a 'master'.)

From the foregoing it is now possible to begin to appreciate why the white sliced, wrapped loaf has been described as 'cotton wool' and 'plastic bread'. The unwrapped 'freshly-baked' supermarket bread is often little better, it is made by the same method and from the same ingredients, and often supplied to the supermarket ready-moulded and frozen for them to bake in the ovens installed in the shop so that customers are misled by the glorious aroma into thinking the bread has been actually *made* on the premises and so are prepared to pay extra for it.

It has been established beyond doubt that the high speed of production of the C.B.P. profoundly affects the wheat gluten network when compared with a dough mixed by conventional methods, and it would not be inaccurate to state that the actual chemical composition is altered. Also, various chemicals are added to a flour which has not only been bleached but has lost all its germ and most of its bran, and the resulting bread has a much higher water content and lower protein content than old-fashioned bread. Several of the additives declared safe in the past have now been banned for health reasons but many eminent nutritionists are concerned about the long-term effects of many still in use.

In spite of the enormous amount of research into bread and flour, there are some problems that the chemists have been quite unable to solve. Satisfactory bread can be produced from some recipes containing no fats; other flours seem to require excessively high levels of fat to yield a satisfactory bread, but even then the optimum loaf is of poor quality. None of the usual chemical or physical tests seem to uncover any obvious differences in these flours, nor are they from any particular wheat variety.

Permitted Additives

We have already considered the so-called enrichment of flour by compulsory additives, so the reader should not be surprised to learn that some of the permitted additives are called 'improvers'.

Improvers

When freshly milled flour (other than wholemeal) is stored for several weeks it undergoes an ageing effect and produces a stronger and more resilient dough and a bolder loaf – it 'improves' and slowly bleaches naturally. Chemical agents produce these effects instantly.

Bleaching

However many times flour is sieved and rolled in the large mills it is still not white enough for the marketing men so it is bleached to produce 'whiter than white' flour. Several chemicals have been used over the years for bleaching flour. Whenever the safety of these chemicals was queried many eminent scientists stated that they were not dangerous, nonetheless many have been made illegal by the committees appointed to inquire into the matter. One outstanding law case concerned the bleaching of flour by means of traces of nitrogen peroxide – the court learned from a parade of experts that there was no deleterious action on the flour, and that rainwater contained seventy times the quantity of the chemical that was used in bleaching flour, that ham contained five hundred times that amount, and that even human saliva contained thirteen times as much. In spite of this overwhelming evidence of its safety, nitrogen peroxide is no longer permitted for bleaching flour.

Perhaps even more curious is the case of nitrogen trichloride (commonly called agene) which was widely used as a flour bleaching agent for many years. The committee investigating its use reported that: *The committee has been unable to find any evidence that agenized flour is in any way toxic to man. Nevertheless ... the committee feel that the use of agene should be discontinued.* Doubletalk that even politicians would hesitate to use.

One cannot but wonder whether the members of such committees knew in their hearts that the information being provided by the experts was inaccurate. It is obvious that much goes on behind the scenes that never sees the light of day, and the only conclusion possible to a layman is to acknowledge that it is never wise to believe any statement claiming an additive to be harmless.

As long ago as 1927 the Departmental Committee on the Treatment of Flour with Chemical Substances warned against the use of chlorine dioxide. The Bread and Flour Regulations 1960 confirmed this view by recommending that only one bleaching agent be used – benzoyl peroxide (at no more than 50 parts per million), which is a powder. However, behind-the-scenes intrigue and duplicity continues, for in spite of these recommendations, we find the 1984 Regulations *permit* the use of chlorine and chlorine dioxide, which is a gas, banned in other European countries.

Until April 1990 potassium bromate was included in the official list of flour 'improving agents' but: *After consultation ... with such organizations as appear to be representative of interests substantially affected by the said Regulations* (the major millers' and bakers' organizations?) *its use as a flour improver is banned.* Its use in USA has been illegal for years.

It is not the intention to delve deeply into chemistry, so the permitted additives have been listed under different functional headings although several chemicals perform more than one function. Not all additives are permitted in *all* types of bread and flour, some are restricted to specific uses, for example rye bread or soda bread only. Some may not be used in conjunction with others, and many have restrictions on the quantity that can be used. For more information see The Bread and Flour Regulations 1984. All these additives are expensive and have their specific uses which can radically affect the finished product, so there is no point in the baker adding more than necessary.

There is little point in giving the full list of additives under their broad headings until these headings have been explained, so in the following paragraphs the headings are considered individually before the full list appears.

Bleaches and Improvers

Improving does not refer to improving the taste or the nutritional quality of the flour, but to improving its behaviour in the production line when made into dough by machines. L-ascorbic acid (vitamin C) is the only improver permitted by all the original EU countries with the exception of Holland, where five bleaches and improvers are allowed. With our eight or so Britain is still well ahead (or should that be behind?).

Benzoyl peroxide, which is a commonly used bleach, is often given the innocent-sounding title of a 'colour control' and it only bleaches; whereas chlorine dioxide bleaches and also improves. Potassium bromate, which was removed from the list of permitted flour improvers in 1990, is an improver but does not bleach.

Although improvers such as L-ascorbic acid had been used optionally by bakers for many years, they are as essential an ingredient of the C.B.P. as oxidants. They also stabilize the gas cells to enable them to withstand the pressures generated during proving and baking. The detailed chemical reaction brought about by the addition of improvers to flour is a highly complex subject.

Oxidants

These produce a stable, stronger and more elastic gluten network, capable of expanding without rupturing. They are vital to C.B.P. and are listed under improvers.

Emulsifiers and Emulsifying Salts

These help to mix oil (fat) and water to prevent them separating into globules or layers as they would without emulsifiers.

Raising Agents

Self-raising flour contains ingredients that generate carbon dioxide when mixed into a dough and baked. Since there is no yeast fermentation, nor usually much time involved, there is neither ripening of the dough nor mellowing of the gluten; the characteristics of self-raising flour are therefore quite different from those of plain flour.

Bulking Agents

These are normally used in bread for which a slimming claim is made. They pad out the crumb without adding to the calorific or energy value of the bread. Most consist of cellulose or one of its compounds.

Yeast Foods

There is insufficient sugar in flour for yeast to feed upon so more must be added in one form or another if modern mass-production methods are to be employed.

Rope Inhibitors

Rope is a micro-organism (*bacillus mesentericus*) present to some extent in all bakery materials. Rope spores are very common and widely distributed in soil, and can survive the baking process; they can start to reproduce when the temperature returns to the ambient range. Modern hygiene and increased scientific knowledge has resulted in spore counts being reduced to a fraction of those that prevailed thirty years ago, and nowadays it is only when conditions are particularly poor that rapid multiplication of the spores results and an infestation is likely to occur when, for example, the bread is held in a humid atmosphere whilst it is being slowly cooled.

In extreme instances almost the whole of the middle of an infected loaf may become a sticky semi-fluid mass of a brownish colour with an unpleasant smell. The crumb can be pulled out in long threads or 'ropes'.

Mould Inhibitors

A vast number of moulds can grow on bread; they are of many colours – black, white, green, pink and brown. Modern hygiene has reduced their infestation, but calcium propionate is a commonly used mould inhibitor. Unfortunately it also destroys the enzyme that enables the human body to utilize the calcium in white bread.

A rare but interesting form of contamination is due to *erythrobacillus prodigiosus*. Certain virulent but fortunately rare strains are capable of turning bread blood red in about twenty-four hours. Bread thus infected is called 'bleeding bread' in the trade.

Preservatives

Although mould and rope inhibitors are also preservatives, several others are also added.

Buffers

Buffers are chemical substances which can resist considerable changes in the acid/alkali balance of solutions; the scale by which these are measured is called the pH. Buffers maintain the pH at a predetermined level despite the addition of further acid or alkali.

Diastatic Enzymes (Amylases)

An enzyme is a protein substance which acts as a catalyst in chemical changes but which itself remains unchanged at the end of the reaction.

Starch consists of many sugar units linked together in chains. It is naturally present in grain providing a food supply for the growing plant and is broken down into sugar for this purpose by the diastatic group of enzymes called amylases. There are two kinds of amylase – alpha and beta; there is always ample beta-amylase, but the alpha-amylase may not be in sufficient quantities to produce the required amount of sugar, its presence in untreated flour is dependent upon the ripeness of the wheat when harvested.

Australian, and also some American and Russian wheat, is liable to have this shortage; conversely, more and more EU wheat often has an excess of it – there are no chemicals yet available to counteract this.

Proteinases

Proteinase is the old name for endo-peptidases but as some sources continue to use it, it is as well to keep it here.

There are enzymes present in flour that are capable of attacking proteins even though they are themselves also proteins; they are referred to as proteases. They have a mellowing effect upon dough.

Soda

Yeast not only produces gas for the aerating of dough, it also plays an important part in dough ripening. Baking soda, when used in conjunction with an acid, also produces gas but has no such ripening powers. In Ireland, which has a very wet climate and where mainly soft wheat is grown, much of the bread is aerated by means of baking soda and is known as soda bread. Technically this is called 'chemically aerated' bread.

Crumb Softeners

Crumb softeners are also emulsifiers, and assist in retarding crumb firming by inhibiting the release of moisture from soluble starch. The benefits of using them to the baker are: increased volume of bread, a moister, softer and fluffier crumb, a finer and whiter crumb. Crumb softeners are responsible for most factory sliced bread going mouldy rather than stale.

The List of Permitted Additives

The letters F and B after a chemical indicate whether its use is permitted in flour or bread. Alternative names are bracketed after the main name.

Many of these chemicals may be purchased ready-compounded under proprietary names. For example, 'Ambirex' consists of yeast foods, oxidant, fat, and soya flour in the correct proportions. The formulae are kept secret by the manufacturers, and bakers buy them on the strength of their known performance not on their chemical constituents.

Colour

E150   Caramel (F & B). Prohibited in USA.

Chalk
E170   Calcium carbonate (F except wholemeal & B).

Bleach

Benzoyl peroxide (F & B except wholemeal).

Improvers
E220   Sulphur dioxide (F). Should be avoided by
          asthmatics and hyperactive children.
E300   L-ascorbic acid (F except wholemeal & B).
E920   L-Cysteine hydrochloride (F & B except
          wholemeal). Made from animal hair and
          feathers.

Improver (fast acting)
E927   Azodicarbonamide (azoformamide, etc.) (F & B
          except wholemeal).

Improvers and Bleachers
E925   Chlorine (F).
E926   Chlorine dioxide (chlorine peroxide) (F & B
          except wholemeal).

Preservatives
E223   Sodium metabisulphate (disodium pyrosulphite)
          (F except wholemeal). Should be avoided by
          asthmatics and hyperactive children.
E290   Carbon dioxide (B).
E270   Lactic acid (hydroxypropanoic acid) (B).

Rope Inhibitors
E260   Acetic acid (ethanoic acid) (B).
E262   Sodium hydrogen diacetate (dykon) (B).

Mould Inhibitors
E280   Propionic acid (propanoic acid) (B).

E281   Sodium propionate (sodium propanate) (B).
E282   Calcium propionate (calcium propanoate) (B). Source of a rash in bakery workers, possible link with migraine.
E283   Potassium propionate (potassium propanate) (B). Illegal in USA bread production.

Preservative and Buffer (Rye)
E330   Citric acid (B).
E333   *tri*Calcium citrate (B).

Emulsifying Salt (Rye)
E333   *tri*Calcium citrate (B).

Raising agents (for self-raising flour)
E336   mono-Potassium L(+)-tartrate (cream of tartar) (F & B).
E341a   Calcium tetrahydrogen diorthophosphate (acid calcium phosphate or ACP) (B).

Raising agent and Emulsifier
E450a   *di*Sodium dihydrogen diphosphate (tetrasodium pyrophosphate) (F & B).

Bulking Agents (for bread for which a slimming claim is made)
E460   *alpha*-Cellulose (B).
E466   Carboxymethylcellulose sodium salt (carmellose sodium, CMC) (B).

Emulsifiers
E471   Mono- and diglycerides of fatty acids (glyceryl monopalmitate or dipalmitate, etc.) (B).
E472b   Lactic acid esters of mono- and diglycerides of fatty acids (B).
E472c   Citric acid esters of mono- and diglycerides of fatty acids (B).
E472e   Mono- and diacetyltartaric acid esters of mono- and diglycerides of fatty acids (B).
E481   Sodium stearoyl-2-lactylate (B). Illegal in USA.
E482   Calcium stearoyl-2-lactylate (B). Illegal in USA.

Emulsifier and Yeast Food, etc.
E341c   *tri*-Calcium diorthophosphate (tricalcium phosphate) (F except wholemeal & B).

Crumb Softeners and Emulsifiers
E322   Lecithins (phosphotids) (B).
E483   Stearyl tartrate (B).

Raising agents for Soda bread
E500   Sodium hydrogen carbonate (baking soda, sodium bicarbonate) (F & B).
E575   D-Glucono-1,5-lactone (glucono delta-lactone) (F & B).
E541   Sodium aluminium phosphate, acidic (SAP, SALP) (F & B).

Yeast foods
E510   Ammonium chloride (sal ammoniac) (B). Can aggravate liver and kidney disorders by affecting the pH of the urine.
E516   Calcium sulphate (gypsum, plaster of Paris) (F except wholemeal & B).
           Ammonium sulphate (B).

Aerator (for aerated breads)
           Nitrogen (B).

Diastatic enzymes
           alpha-Amylases (proteinases) (F & B).

Buffers
           *di*Ammonium hydrogen orthophosphate (B).
           Ammonium dihydrogen orthophosphate (B).
           Ammonium sulphate (B).

Proteinases
           It is not possible to consider all these items individually here, there would be page after page of contrary opinions.

Other Additives

A number of more or less 'natural' additives may also be added to bread and flour, and some are limited as to the amounts that may be added. These include milk and egg products, liquid or dried egg, rice flour, cracked oat grain, oatmeal, oat flakes, soya bean flour, salt, vinegar, oils and fats, malt extract, malt flour, any soluble carbohydrate sweetening matter, prepared wheat gluten, poppy seeds, sesame seeds, caraway seeds, cracked wheat, cracked or kibbled malted wheat, flaked malted wheat, kibbled malted rye, cracked or kibbled malted barley, starch other than modified starch (high amylose starch).

Soya Bean Oil

Soya bean oil contains about 4% of the natural emulsifier lecithin. The protein and oil factions plus lecithin combine to improve the quality of the crumb in a baked loaf giving it increased softness and resilience.

Saffron

Saffron which adds colour and flavour is obtained from the dried stigmas of the cultivated crocus and the seeds of gardenia.

Caraway

This is strictly not a seed but a fruit, it is mainly used for flavouring.

Malt

Malt, which needs careful handling, can be used as a bread improver only when it is necessary to make up a diastatic deficiency in flour. Malt bread is, of course, an exception.

All the additives that have been mentioned are listed in the Bread and Food Regulations 1984. It is interesting to note that the Regulations do not apply to a certain section of the population – Her Majesty's Forces or visiting forces. No explanation of this is offered.

No attempt has been made herein to advise whether

additives are 'good' or 'bad'. It is all too easy to produce quotes from scientific sources to support both viewpoints. If one begins to examine the additives in detail it is easily possible to get bogged down by the subdivision of a chemical into smaller and smaller components, and by contrary opinions on every single item.

Organic

Organic foods are those grown with the minimum of artificial fertilizers and chemical sprays. However, there is no legal standard or regulation defining the use of the word 'organic', and scientists are not in agreement over how long it takes soil to become organic if it has previously been treated with chemicals – some say five years, others twenty or more.

Grain is usually treated with chemicals before it is sown, but whether organic grain has been so treated is known only to the farmer or the supplier of the grain to him. The natural manures used instead of chemical fertilizers may have come from cattle that have been injected with chemicals, and some of the organic wheat may have been grown in a field adjacent to one that supports a crop grown by inorganic methods, and which could be sprayed from the air or by a powerful machine with a consequent risk of drifting.

A statement is usually made on the packet when it contains flour milled from organic wheat, but it is not unknown for the organic wheat to be mixed with imported hard wheat which is not organically grown. This detail will seldom appear on the packet.

It follows that in buying organic flour one can only hope that everyone involved with its production has been honest and conscientious.

2

Equipment, Ingredients, Methods

Equipment

It is possible to waste an awful lot of money on equipment for breadmaking, but no matter how expensive the tins or basins you buy, the quality of the bread depends mainly upon the ingredients and *you*. It is (or was until recently) possible to purchase an 'automatic' bread-making machine for about £200. All the ingredients were put into the machine together, the power switched on, and a few hours later out came *one loaf*. I am informed by one user that the bread was 'quite acceptable', but so far I have been able to resist the impulse to invest in such an unnecessary luxury.

The first thing you will need is a decent set of scales, preferably those with a pan one one side and a platform for the weights on the other, and although these are quite expensive it is well worth the initial outlay.

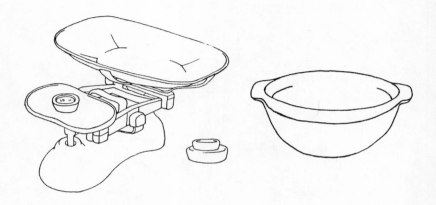

A large mixing bowl will be needed, 12'' (30 cms) diameter at least if 3 lbs (1350g) of flour is to be mixed (the usual quantity for most of the following recipes). I prefer the old-fashioned glazed earthenware type because, being heavy, they are more stable and easy to clean, but glass is almost as good. Plastic is easily cleaned but annoyingly light in use so that you can find yourself chasing the bowl around the table when mixing. Some recipes call for two or more mixing bowls, but one is usually sufficient at the beginning.

If you intend using the overnight fermentation process a plastic bucket of not less than 4 gallons (18 litres) capacity will be needed if the risk of overflowing is to be avoided.

A graduated measuring jug for liquids is essential, marked in either metric or imperial whichever you prefer, and a set of measuring spoons similarly marked. Remember that metric and imperial measurements are not always exact equivalents, so use either one or the other throughout – never mix them.

A hand sprayer (or 'mister') is very useful where the recipe calls for the dough to be dampened. The sprayers sold in garden shops for applying chemicals to attack greenfly are excellent, but do make certain that your spouse has not used it earlier in the greenhouse.

A wooden spoon for stirring and mixing is important. Buy a brand new one and keep it for mixing bread only – wood can hold flavours and aromas for a long time, and if a spoon has been used for savoury recipes it is possible for the taste of onions or perhaps garlic to be transferred to the bread. Keep a separate spoon for use when making highly flavoured savoury breads, and mark it plainly to avoid confusion.

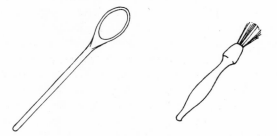

The traditional pastry brush is useful for applying egg-wash or water to glaze baked loaves, but I much prefer a large, very soft flat brush for glazing raw dough, and an ordinary 1 in (2.5 cms) square-cut paintbrush is by far the best for greasing tins, it gets into the corners easier and covers faster. Purchase the best quality brushes you can afford, they will last a lifetime, and the good ones will not shed hairs every time they are used. Buy them new and reserve them specially for cooking purposes.

A large flat surface for kneading (Formica or something similarly easy to clean) which is both sturdy and steady will be needed, at the correct height for your comfort bearing in mind that you could be kneading for fairly long periods. In Victorian times marble was considered to be an acceptable surface for kneading because it was so easy to clean, but because it was very cold (and chilling extends the time taken for the dough to rise) most housewives preferred to use the kitchen table which was made of unvarnished deal and could be scrubbed clean after use.

A brief note about table height; severe back strain can result from using a table at the wrong height for the person kneading. It is important for the surface to be low enough to allow the weight of the body to be brought down on to the dough keeping the arms almost straight, but not so low as to require the back to be unduly bent. It is impossible to give precise figures because some people have long trunks and short legs and others vice versa, but for the average woman of about 5 ft 6 ins the ideal table height would be about 26 ins (for a man of 5 ft 10 in – 30 ins). It is worth spending a little time getting the table height correct for your particular proportions; adjustments can be made either by elevating the table by placing books under the legs, or you can elevate yourself by standing on a couple of telephone directories.

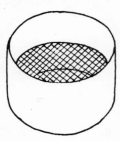

Buy a good quality sieve, the cheap ones soon disintegrate whereas the best can last almost a lifetime. I am still using an old-fashioned hair sieve but it is well past its retirement date and will soon have to be replaced by one of those with a nylon-type mesh. Avoid the wire-mesh sieves if possible, they have a strong tendency to rust and although a certain amount of iron in the diet is good for you, this is not the recommended manner of ingesting it.

Tins: I use 1-lb (450g) tins because my family prefer a small slice, but 2-lb (900g) can be used if you prefer. Make

sure you get the high-sided tins; most of those sold as
non-stick are too shallow and will allow the dough to flop
over the sides as it rises, and in many cases the non-stick
coating deteriorates rapidly after the first few bakings, then
the tins must be greased in the normal way. It is often said
that bread tins should not be washed after use but when
empty returned to the oven for a few minutes on maximum
heat, after which they can be brushed out and stored in a dry
place for future use. I have never been happy with this idea,
after a few bakings the tins become coated with burnt-on
grease which can be transferred to the bread during the next
baking; I much prefer to soak the empty tins in a weak
detergent before scrubbing them thoroughly and drying. This
ensures that they are pristine clean every time they are used.

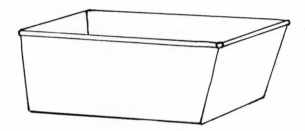

Do not mix non-stick coated tins with ordinary tinplate
ones, the coating on the non-stick tins expedites cooking and
you will find the loaves in these tins burn before the others
are cooked. Because the coating absorbs more heat than the
tinplate, the side crusts of the loaves bake faster than the
crumb so you can normally expect a crisper crust from bread
baked in non-stick tins.

Glass presents different problems – it warms up more
slowly than metal and then holds its heat longer. The effect
on the bread is similar to putting dough into cold tins – the
'spring' is inhibited. It is also more difficult to prevent the
loaves sticking to the glass surface no matter how you grease
or oil it, probably because oven-proof glass is less porous than
tinplate.

Tins can be obtained in a large variety of shapes and sizes
to suit individual needs, but avoid spending vast sums on
shapes you are likely to use only once or twice. I suggest that

until you are more experienced you would do well to keep to the standard rectangular bread tin about 4 x 6 x 3 ins deep (10 x 15 x 8 cms) for the 1-lb (450g) loaf and proportionately larger for 2-lb (900g). If possible get tins with wired top edges; these last much longer than straight-sided ones and will have a greater resistance to twisting and warping. Loose-bottomed cake tins make excellent round loaves so long as the sides are high enough, as do square tins.

Earthenware flowerpots or bowls are excellent for baking bread but use only brand new ones which have been stored under cover and show no signs of algae growing upon them. They must be well greased and baked before use, two or three times for preference or the bread will stick. Plastic pots are useless for this purpose, they will melt in the oven.

A firm, buckle-proof baking-tray will be needed if you intend dispensing with tins. Round loaves, baps, and many other shapes can be tray-baked, and some people prefer the irregular shaped slice to that of a tin-baked loaf although the latter is usually better for sandwich-making.

A wire rack for standing the bread upon to cool after taking it out of the oven is important — loaves cooled on plates or similar surfaces will have soggy bottoms.

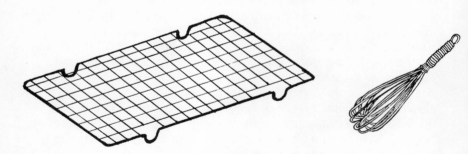

A mechanical whisk or liquidizer is a great help, but the same result can be obtained using a hand whisk or even a fork if you are prepared to allow the extra time.

An egg separator is not essential but it makes life a lot

easier than trying to separate the yolk from the white by tossing it from one cup to another!

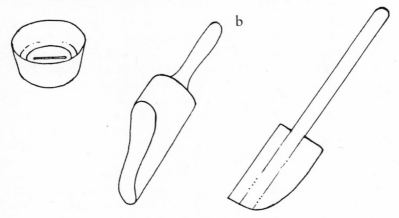

Various small items can be helpful although not essential – a scoop for handling flour and a scraper for getting the last bit of dough out of the bowl. Shaped cutters are not often needed but many cooks like to have them for making rolls and for decorating, and a pair of wooden gauges for

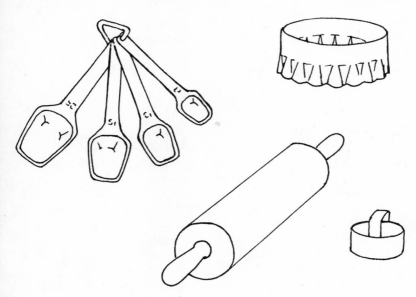

controlling the thickness of pastry dough is a great asset – they should be at least 18 ins (46 cms) long and made from hardwood ¼ x ⅜ in (7 x 10 mm) and can then be used to produce dough of either thickness simply by turning the gauges. Wider gauges (½ in, 13 cms) may be needed for certain recipes including Naan bread.

Ovens: the oven can be the cause of many failures. Few oven thermometers are accurate and in many cases cooking is very uneven, with loaves close to the sides being overcooked while those in the centre are underdone. A lopsided loaf can often be produced by an uneven oven because the heat kills the yeast faster on the side nearest the greater heat, thus inhibiting the spring on that side.

Gas ovens heat up fastest (and lose their heat just as quickly). The modern ones are a great improvement on the older models but they still tend to be hotter around the sides than in the middle.

Electricity is cleaner but the oven can take several minutes to reach the desired temperature; conversely it will continue to hold its heat long after being switched off. On average electricity is about twice the price of gas per unit of heat generated, but unless fan-assisted the heat distribution will be no better than gas. Modern fan-assisted electric ovens heat up much faster and have almost eliminated the problem of hot and cold spots. The ones with a rotating turntable are the most efficient.

Ovens dependent upon bottled gas have all the faults and merits of those fed by town gas (or North sea gas), but running costs are about double those for electricity at the time of writing.

Microwave ovens are not really suitable for breadmaking although some manufacturers think they are. The bread produced is (in my opinion) of poor quality, has a limp crust and poor appearance. Furthermore, unless the timing is very precise the bread will be ruined – a few seconds too long and the crumb will be crisp and dry and suitable only for reducing to breadcrumbs. Compared with the mass-produced sliced bread, a microwaved loaf may be acceptable to some people, but nobody who is prepared to regard *that* as a standard will be bothering to read this book.

Nearly all modern electric ovens are too small for really

efficient baking of bread. Until the mid-1970s it was possible to buy many popular models with an oven at least 18 ins square by 16 ins high but today most manufacturers seem to think that much smaller ovens are required. For a batch of say five small loaves or three larger ones these smaller ovens are just about adequate but it is quite impossible to accommodate a French stick in one, even a reasonable sized baton is a squeeze. The larger ovens are still made in USA and some Continental countries; the former cannot be imported without considerable adjustment to the electrical system, and the latter are very expensive. I still use an ancient Canadian Moffat simply because I cannot find a cooker with an oven of comparable size – we have no mains gas in our village.

Aga cookers, Raeburn, etc. are easily the most efficient fuelwise, and with stable even heat ideal for breadmaking – the nearest thing to the old-fashioned baker's oven. They can be fuelled by oil, gas, electricity or solid fuel with no noticeable difference in the cooking facility, but special care must be taken because the two ovens (if you have a double-oven model) are set at different temperatures – hot and very hot. Check with your instruction manual for the best to use for breadmaking.

Between the wars many houses were equipped with an oven situated above an open fire – a variation of the old kitchen range of the Victorian era, and this is still one of the most efficient for breadmaking after the true bread-oven. Some houses still have them although most have been removed many years ago in the rush to central-heating systems. The oven was large, probably all of 20 ins (51 cms) square and almost as high – and the heat was quite evenly distributed. If you are fortunate enough to possess such a gem, make the most of it, there is no better oven for making bread.

There is an American company who advertise equipment and instructions to enable enthusiasts to build their own brick bread oven either as an extension to the house or as a separate structure in the garden. Some may think this a few thousand pounds well spent but I cannot believe that it will appeal to many in this country.

Built-in oven thermometers are notoriously inaccurate in many cases, but they are usually *consistent* liars so it is easy to adjust your calculations to the required temperature. Free-standing oven thermometers are not always very accurate either – I have had three from a reputable manufacturer, none of which would register above 200°F (100°C, Gas Mark ¼). They were returned and my money refunded without comment, from which one can only assume that this was not an isolated complaint.

My grandmother's method of checking the oven temperature is a rough guide, and if used in conjunction with the built-in thermometer enables a reasonable calculation to be made as to how much to add or subtract from the thermometer reading to reach baking temperatures. Scatter a handful of white flour over the base of a baking tray and place it in the oven pre-heated to 450°F (230°C, Gas Mark 8). Leave for about ten minutes than examine it. If the flour is burnt and smoking the oven is too hot, if it is still pure white it is too cold; it is just right if the flour is an even golden colour. You may have to experiment a few times to get the temperature exactly right, but afterwards you will have a fair idea of how far out your oven thermometer is and can make allowances for it.

It is possible to even out the temperatures in an unevenly heated oven to some extent by the use of ordinary quarry tiles if your oven is large enough. Cover the centre shelf with unglazed quarry tiles which have been well scrubbed, but allow 1 in (2.5 cms) space all round the sides of the oven so that natural convection is not impeded. The tiles must be put into the oven on a high temperature at least an hour before baking begins so that by the time the oven is needed they have absorbed sufficient heat. If the bread is in tins they can be placed on the tiles, if in rounds without tins the dough can be set directly upon the tiles so long as they have been well greased first.

A similar method uses house bricks instead of tiles but these take up much more room and are more awkward to handle although they are just as efficient; it will be necessary to lower the oven shelf to allow for the extra height of the bricks which should always be placed in the oven frog side down.

Whether quarry tiles or bricks are used they should be reserved solely for baking in which case they will seldom need cleaning. In those recipes where steam baking is called for they can be sprayed with water as an additional means of increasing humidity.

If you have an uneven oven but do not wish to bother with either tiles or bricks you will have to move the loaves around in the oven *after* they have baked for at least 15 minutes. If you open the oven door before then there is a risk of the bread collapsing. Moving the loaves around the oven will not alter a lopsided rise but it will ensure the bread is more evenly cooked after springing.

An electric mixer takes some of the hard work out of breadmaking and in most recipes the quality of the product is not impaired. Mixing is much faster and probably more thorough but afterwards it will still usually be necessary to knead the dough in the usual way. The normal domestic mixer (such as a Kenwood Chef) will handle a 3-lb (1350g) mix comfortably but it must be fitted with a dough hook, and these are usually obtainable as supplementary attachments.

In the past great emphasis was placed upon having all utensils warm before starting to make bread; the bowl had to be warmed, the flour set before the fire for several hours before it could be used, the scales scalded and even the correct room temperature was said to be essential for a 'rise' to occur. We now know this to be false. Dough made with good yeast will rise even if kept overnight in a refrigerator. It is true that it will rise more slowly than under warm conditions but eventually it will achieve the same volume and be just as good, in fact there are those who insist that the slower the rise the better the bread. There is no doubt that dough which has taken several hours to rise is more mature than that forced under factory conditions to rise in a few minutes, and even the difference between home-baked wholemeal loaves which have risen for say two hours compared with those produced by a twelve-hour rise is quite noticeable. In most of the following recipes I have allowed for a reasonably short rising-time achieved at normal room temperature or perhaps a little above. 70°F (20°C) is ideal, but a variation of ten degrees either way will not affect the quality of the bread.

If you do not have a truly draughtproof place in which to put the dough for rising, put it into a large cardboard box and seal the lid. This can be re-used many times and is as efficient as any other system.

A very sharp knife is essential if loaves are to be scored or slashed as a form of decoration. If the blade is lightly oiled between cuts it will not 'pull' the raw dough. A single-edged razor blade will serve the same purpose but double-edged blades are dangerous and should be avoided in the kitchen. A surgeon's scalpel with removable blades is ideal and available in art and craft shops.

Apart from the scales, measuring jug, mixing bowl and measuring spoons, most of the foregoing list of equipment can be acquired over a period of time as experience and greater convenience dictates. Even tins can be dispensed with if you are prepared to produce only tray-baked loaves.

Ingredients

If all ingredients and utensils are at room temperature (about 70°F, 20°C) before use the dough will rise faster but it is certainly not essential for good results.

Flour (Wheat). Probably more failures are caused by using the wrong flour than for any other single reason. Ordinary plain flour and self-raising flours are quite unsuitable for breadmaking by the yeast process, and the so-called 'bread flours' vary considerably from brand to brand. Before the war nearly all grain for bread was imported but since then harder wheat varieties have been developed for growing in the English climate and today not only are bread grains grown for the home market but there is a considerable export trade to the Continent.

Over the years I have experimented with most brands of so-called 'strong bread flour' and it is true to say that in general the more expensive the flour the better the quality. However, this must not be taken as an inviolate rule; some of the supermarket brands are quite acceptable although it is true that some are poor, it is a matter of trial and error. I will not list the bad ones because I only try them once and it is possible that the formulae have been improved since the trial. But it is as well to remember that supermarkets stock only fast-selling lines, every inch of shelf space has to yield so much profit, so in general only cheaper 'own brands' or well-advertised household names will be available; for the lesser known (and often better products) the small grocer or health food shops will often be more helpful.

If possible use only strong unbleached white flour specially labelled for breadmaking. Unfortunately this is not so readily available in some districts so it may be necessary to use a bleached product. This will make very little difference to the texture of the finished loaf but, as explained earlier, will contain unwelcome chemicals. When buying wholemeal flour check that it is well within the sell-by date – wholemeal flours usually have a shelf life of about twelve weeks after which they will begin to deteriorate. Brown flour is not wholemeal, neither is granary.

Bread made with strong unbleached white flour will not be as pristine white as shop bread because the latter is made from bleached flour with added improvers but it will be more nutritious. Bread made entirely from wholemeal flour tends to be drier and perhaps a little harsh for most palates, which is the reason why I have mixed a proportion of white with the wholemeal in most of the following recipes. The texture of wholemeal flours varies considerably according to the methods of milling, varieties of wheat used, etc. The flour produced by Mapledurham Mill near Reading, Berkshire is extremely fine and very pale in colour; bread made from this flour is delicately flavoured and has a crumb only slightly tinted. It is ideal for weaning children away from supermarket white bread on to wholemeal, for they often object to the dark colour and strong flavour of most wholemeal loaves. Michelham Priory near Hailsham in Sussex produces a 100% wholemeal flour which is coarser than the Mapledurham product and makes a darker loaf with a slightly stronger flavour. One of the coarsest flours with the strongest flavour is that milled at Dunster near Minehead in Somerset. Again it is 100% wholemeal and yields a rough open crumb with a delicious nutty flavour.

Tastes vary and although my own preference is for a mixture of two-thirds white flour to one-third wholemeal which gives a light spongy crumb with a delicate flavour, you may prefer a different ratio of white to wholemeal flour and as more experience is gained will no doubt adjust the proportions to suit your own preferences – the basic principles are not affected.

Stoneground wholemeal flour produces a coarser textured bread with a stronger flavour whereas the finely roller-milled flours tend to make a denser loaf. Stone milling is a slower process and so the quality of the flour is not impaired by overheating; roller mills run at higher speeds, grind smaller, and are said to destroy some of the natural ingredients which are then often replaced artificially. 'Granary Flour' is a trade name for one of the Rank Hovis McDougall (RHM) products which is a blend of wheatmeal, rye flour and pieces of malted grain with bits of wheat kernel added. Granary loaves bought from bakeries vary considerably although they are supposed to be made to the miller's standard recipe, but it is quite easy to make a granary-type loaf at home if you remember that granary-type flours cannot be sieved satisfactorily.

All-purpose unbleached flour: I have never seen flour so marked in Britain, but for those using American recipes (or books published in USA) an explanation of the labelling is required. There is no exact British equivalent, the nearest would probably be our unbleached strong white bread flour, and its performance is almost the same. It is enriched in much the same way as our strong white bread flour, but the additives are always listed on the bag. In the USA it has no added chalk, and many other fortifying ingredients are also banned by law.

Non-wheat flours: several types of flour other than wheat can be used in breadmaking including potato, maize (corn), rye, oatmeal, barley, etc. Buckwheat is not a type of wheat but the flour from it can still be an ingredient of bread. All the foregoing require special treatment, and in most cases need to be combined with wheat flour before a satisfactory result can be obtained (see the individual recipes for details).

Some foreign recipes call for flours obtainable only in the country of origin – French flour, for instance, is seldom found in Britain; in these cases I have suggested the nearest available substitute, you may be unable to reproduce the foreign bread exactly but you will arrive at a fairly close imitation.

Yeast. Many of my earlier failures were due to the use of so-called fresh yeast from the local baker who, I learned later, was reluctant to assist those making their own bread on the grounds that it would adversely affect his business. The quality and freshness was always in doubt, quite often the yeast would be in the form of dried crumbs which had obviously fallen from the main block, and his two ounces (55g) could vary between one and three ounces (30–85g) because his shop scales were incapable of accurately registering any amount below four ounces (110g).

Yeast is one of the most important ingredients of good bread, far too important to be treated casually. Nowadays I use only the granulated dried yeast which can be purchased in airtight tins or small sealed plastic bags. It is always fresh (if within its sell-by date) and can be precisely measured without difficulty. All the following recipes are based on the use of dried yeast but if you prefer the fresh product (and most health shops are able to supply) it is only necessary to double the prescribed quantity, but do make certain that the yeast is fresh and moist – if it is crusty, brown and dry on the outside it will give nothing but trouble. If your bread is heavy or fails to rise do not assume the problem can be solved by adding more yeast, too much yeast will make the bread taste bitter and unpleasantly 'yeasty'. If the yeast used is fresh (or the granulated dried form) you must look elsewhere for the fault.

Yeast measurements are given in imperial and metric figures, I have avoided using 'a packet' as a form of measurement because packets vary in weight. I have also avoided the use of 'fast-acting' granulated yeasts, marketed under a variety of descriptive names such as 'Speedy Yeast' and 'Time-saving Yeast'. These are expensive and, in my opinion, quite unnecessary if the yeast is set to activate whilst the other ingredients are being measured out. Re-sealable canisters of dried active baking yeast are widely available – brewer's yeast is not suitable for breadmaking.

For the benefit of those suffering from a yeast allergy I have included a few yeast-free recipes. These can never produce a loaf comparable to a yeasted loaf, but they offer an edible alternative when required. The soda breads listed are very good eaten fresh from the oven, but their keeping qualities are practically nil – like French bread, they are horrible a day old.

Fat or oil. Whether fat or oil is used it must be fresh for if rancid the bread will be ruined. In the past I used lard because the best bread I ever tasted was made with lard, but there are many alternatives. Lard has had a bad press in recent years because of the cholesterol scare, but new research has shown this to be exaggerated. Many scientists are convinced that the butter and lard substitutes widely advertised are more harmful than the natural product. It is quite possible to make bread with no fats or oils whatsoever but the inclusion of some kind of lubricant will assist the bread to rise, improve the flavour (in the opinion of most people), make the crumb slightly more moist and extend the keeping qualities.

If unsalted butter is used as a lubricant it should be taken direct from the freezer and grated into the dough *after* it has been mixed, during the first kneading. If it is melted first it will be easier to incorporate into the dough but the bread will not rise so well.

Cooking margarine is another popular alternative but margarine substitutes and fat-free spreads are not suitable being mainly emulsified water and hydrogenated fat which can contain as much as 50% transfatty acids which are thought to increase the risk of heart disease. There was a move in 1984 to make the inclusion of transfat compulsory in the list of ingredients of foodstuffs but this was defeated probably due to pressure from the trade lobbies, and similar pressure on the European Union has resulted in the declaration of transfat being made illegal. Dr Walter Willet of Harvard University has discovered a positive link between the consumption of transfat and heart disease among American adults, and there is now grave concern about its effect upon children who are eating more and more of the stuff in the form of crisps, chocolate, biscuits and numerous fast foods. German margarine contains no transfat but all British margarines and 'fat-reduced spreads' include a percentage of it to solidify the product – without transfat it would be liquid. The long-term effect of transfat in the diet is still unknown but the immediate problems generated by its use are becoming more obvious every day.

A very satisfactory loaf can be produced by using suet.

Vegetable suet is best but you will need to double the quantity compared with other fats. Because it is ready shredded it is easier to rub into the flour, but if it is mixed into the flour *without rubbing* a 'holey' crumb is produced.

A great variety of oils can be substituted for fat including sunflower oil, corn oil, sesame oil and olive oil – each has its own flavour and adherents. If olive oil is preferred use only the top grade (cold pressed, extra virgin is best) and this probably gives the best rise of all the lubricants, and a soft crust. Refined oils in general are almost totally bland and contribute very little to the flavour of the bread – a point in their favour in some cases.

Many plant bakeries are now using a hydrocarbon 'oil' as a cheaper substitute for vegetable oil in the treatment of bread tins to prevent dough sticking, and this has recently been the subject of enquiry by experts concerned with the safety aspect of such practices. Some believe its use is permitted by the Ministry of Agriculture, Fisheries and Food (MAFF) due to pressure from the bakery industry. Yet one more reason to bake your own bread.

Salt. A great deal of fuss has been made in recent years concerning the types of salt most suitable for use when making bread. I use any old salt that happens to be to hand, and have found no difference whatsoever in the bread. Most people find that bread without a certain amount of salt in the recipe is unpalatable; not only does it enhance the flavour of the bread, but it affects the colour and texture of the crumb. All the following recipes call for a reasonable amount of salt, but this can be increased or reduced according to personal preference. Too much salt is not only bad for your health, it leaves a bitter aftertaste in the mouth.

Potassium sulphate can be substituted for salt in the same proportions as salt in the recipes. Some scientists feel that too little potassium in the diet can lead to the development of high blood pressure, others think too much potassium can interfere with normal kidney function, but if you replace the salt in a recipe with an equal amount of potassium you are unlikely to suffer any ill effects unless you are able to consume about a ton of bread each week!

Fruit. When any kind of dried fruit is added to the dough it must first be washed, dried and picked over for stalks and other foreign bodies. Ready-washed currants and sultanas vary in cleanliness from packer to packer as does the water in which they are washed. Take no chances, they cannot be too clean. In the past the fruit from Greece and Turkey has been the most suspect and that from California and Australia the most reliable, but times and regulations change and it is possible that the strict rules governing food products which apply in the USA may have to be observed elsewhere.

Apart from the more commonly used fruits such as currants, sultanas, raisins, etc., many other types of fruit can be utilized in breadmaking, dried apricots, dates, glazed cherries and prunes, for example. They should all be coarsely chopped before being thoroughly mixed into the flour in its dry state. Dried fruit should not be soaked before use, but where fresh fruit is used allowance must be made for the extra liquid content and the fluids called for in the recipe reduced to compensate; canned pineapple, for instance, even when drained will contain over 80% juice.

Vegetables and herbs. Many different kinds of vegetable can be added to dough including potatoes, celery, carrots, onions, garlic, parsnips and pulses. Each requires separate treatment detailed in the recipes. Herbs can be used either fresh or dried, and although the recipes call for dried herbs (because they are more easily available to most people), fresh herbs can be substituted if the quantities are doubled. Tastes vary, and the ingredients have been calculated to give a strength of flavour acceptable to the majority of people. Before increasing or reducing the amounts, I suggest you use the ingredients exactly as listed in the recipe and adjust to your own preferences at the next baking.

Potatoes can be incorporated into the dough either in dry powdered form or freshly mashed. The former is by far the easier method, but the latter gives superior results if a suitable variety of potato can be obtained. There is no doubt that the old Majestic potato is the best for breadmaking, it breaks down well as it cooks and yields a soft, fluffy dry mash which is easily combined with the flour, but Majestic seems to have disappeared from the shops and I have yet to find the perfect substitute. Desiree is probably as good as any of the modern varieties and Wilja is said to be good.

Potatoes for mashing must always be boiled in their skins

or they will absorb additional water and a wet mash will result; for the same reason only potatoes with sound skins should be used. Make sure the eyes of the potato are completely removed after boiling and skinning; the highest proportion of rope spores are found around the eyes, and although rope is seldom seen nowadays in bread there is no point in taking chances.

Milk. When milk is included in a recipe it means whole milk, not skimmed or semi-skimmed unless stated otherwise. Milk must be scalded and cooled before being incorporated into the dough or the rise will be inhibited. Scald does not mean boil – milk is scalded when it is hot enough for a skin to form on the surface; milk which has boiled can adversely affect the dough rising and much of the vitamin-content will have been destroyed.

Pasteurized milk has been heat-treated but not taken to a temperature high enough for breadmaking; it must be scalded just the same.

The inclusion of milk in the mixture produces a softer, slightly denser crumb and a more yielding crust. The bread is more nutritious and will keep longer, the loaves will rise a little higher in the oven and the domes have a slightly deeper brown crust.

Buttermilk. Most soda breads call for the inclusion of buttermilk among the ingredients. This is becoming increasingly difficult to find nowadays, and I have yet to discover a health food shop which sells it; the buttermilk in the only supermarket I have found stocking it turned out to be something akin to a poor quality yogurt. I have substituted natural yogurt in most of the recipes calling for buttermilk and find this almost as good. Here the Irish have the advantage over us – buttermilk is commonly available all over Eire and soda bread is still widely eaten although its popularity seems to be declining, probably because yeasted breads do not deteriorate so rapidly.

Yogurt. Several recipes call for the inclusion of natural yogurt among the ingredients. This can be made from cow or sheep milk with no apparent difference in the flavour of the bread produced. However, goat milk yogurt is said to taint the bread with a strong 'goaty' flavour. I have not tried it myself but am assured that there are people who prefer it.

Whichever type of yogurt you use do make sure it is fresh; stale yogurt can give a strange tint to the crumb and a repulsive flavour.

Soya beans, milk and flour. No other pulse contains as much protein, minerals and vitamins, but its use in bread requires extra care and attention to detail. Soya milk must be not more than a day old or bacteria will begin to multiply at an alarming rate. Soya flour must also be fresh or, if rancid, the bread will be inedible. The best soya flour is yellow and contains all the natural fat-soluble nutrients of the bean.

You are advised to avoid baking with any soya product until you have acquired considerable skill with other less demanding ingredients.

Water. Nearly all mains water now contains a quantity of chlorine and fluoride. The normal very small amounts present have no noticeable effect upon the bread but occasional surges in the concentration can be caused by human error or mechanical faults resulting in the water appearing almost as white as milk. We are assured that this is not harmful to humans but it is certainly detrimental to breadmaking – under these conditions it is best to use bottled (still) water.

Very soft water (and distilled water) produces a slack, sticky dough which does not rise well. To solve this problem dissolve a teaspoonful of sodium bicarbonate in the water. Very hard water can inhibit the action of the yeast; to overcome this alkalinity add a tablespoon of cider vinegar to the water for the main mix – not to the yeast-water.

In days gone by it was usual to use rain water for breadmaking, but this was before the atmosphere was so badly polluted; even so, it must have included a fair amount of bird droppings and other contaminants as it travelled from the roof to the water butt via the eaves and guttering. Today's tap water is probably purer and more reliable, in spite of the fact that city dwellers are often drinking water that has been used several times before.

It has recently been discovered that fish in one of the river estuaries have been affected by oestrogenic pollution of the water coming down from a sewage outfall higher up the river, resulting in the male fish developing female characteristics and being unable to reproduce. We are assured that this cannot affect humans, yet we know the human sperm count has dropped to about 50% of its pre-war level and the reason remains a mystery. Is it not just possible that the extra amounts of contaminated water, incorporated into our foods by modern manufacturing processes could be suspect? Water is used to increase the weight of some frozen poultry and processed foods, and 'plastic' bread is about 60% water at the moment – it is the ambition of the plant bakeries to achieve an even higher percentage if only they can find a machine capable of turning soup into bread!

One Australian bread book states that tap water should never be used for breadmaking as it contains too many chemicals; it recommends sea-water as a healthy substitute – one can only assume that he does not live near Bondi Beach or on the Gold Coast. I would not suggest using sea water from *any* coastal areas known to me in any part of the world – the thought horrifies me.

The terms 'warm' and 'tepid' to describe the temperature of water can be misleading. I have used 'warm' to mean a temperature of between 70° and 80°F (20° and 25°C) in the recipes and eliminated the use of 'tepid'. If you have no thermometer the correct temperature obtains when an elbow immersed in the water feels pleasantly warm.

Sugar and other sweeteners. Where sugar is called for in the recipes either white granulated, soft brown, or demerara can be used except where specified otherwise.

In most cases golden syrup is an acceptable substitute as is molasses. Molasses is a residual product after the pressing of the sugar cane and there are several types, some sweeter than others. As a general guide the darker the colour the less sweet the molasses. All molasses contains a proportion of sulphur which can cause unpleasant side effects on some people; if you or one of your family is allergic to sulphur use golden syrup instead.

Honey can be used instead of sugar but its flavour will vary according to the types of flower which have provided the nectar. The difference will probably be noticed only by the connoisseur but he may object to his bread being carnation-flavoured even if ever so slightly! Some raw honeys can inhibit the yeast action and suppress the rising of the dough so use only pasteurized honey for breadmaking.

Nuts and grains. Several types of nut can be used in breadmaking, some by incorporation into the mix, others to decorate the loaves. Most must first be toasted to avoid discolouring the crumb (freshly chopped walnuts for instance, can give the crumb a pale violet tinge if not toasted before use). There is also a vast range of grains which can be added to the dough, either whole, cracked or kibbled (coarsely crushed), including wheat, oats, sesame seeds, poppy seeds, sunflower seeds, millet, rice, etc. The terms 'cracked' and 'kibbled' are often misapplied to packeted grains. Cracked wheat grains have been crushed and split open by controlled pressure, many of the grains in a packet of cracked wheat will still be whole or nearly so. Kibbled grain has been coarsely ground so that pieces of the kernels perhaps as large as a quarter of the whole seed are still visible but no whole grains remain.

Flavourings. Several kinds of flavouring can be added to bread including coffee, chocolate, lemon, orange, ginger, various spices, etc., and for teabreads the choice is vast. Once you have mastered the principles of breadmaking it is great fun to experiment – but get the basic loaf right first!

In conclusion, it is incorrect to assume that yeast needs sugar (or some kind of sweetener) to activate it; it is quite capable of manufacturing its own sugar (remember it is a living plant) from the starch in the dough or from the mineral content of the water but it will take longer to do so, and in any case most people prefer their bread slightly sweetened although few realize this until they have tasted unsweetened bread.

Many unusual ingredients can be used in breadmaking and I suggest you try them *after* you have mastered the basic principles – a few have been included among the recipes, but this book is chiefly intended as an instruction manual, not a book of gimmicky recipes. A well-baked loaf is more likely to impress your family and friends than one with its crumb layered in shades of red, white and blue!

Methods

Years ago instruction manuals usually detailed fermentation times ranging between four and twenty-four hours according to the type of bread being baked, but with modern yeasts these times can be reduced to more manageable proportions.

Most of the following recipes use quick fermentation methods because they are the more popular with modern home bakers who feel that they lack the time needed for a longer process, but there is no doubt that a twelve-hour rise produces a better loaf and, because the dough can mature overnight, the effort spent is no more than when a shorter rising-time is involved. A dough which matures slowly over twelve, fourteen or sixteen hours produces a better flavoured bread, evenly textured and better risen. Furthermore, a single rise is sufficient so in fact less laborious kneading is required.

Most of the recipes using yeast can easily be adapted to an overnight fermentation simply by mixing as instructed, placing the ball of dough into a large well-greased container, covering with a damp cloth, and setting into a warm place to rise overnight. In the morning (or about twelve hours later) knead the dough for the required number of strokes defined in the recipe, divide, mould to shape and put into the tins to prove. A second rise is unnecessary.

Using a Foodmixer
This is definitely the easiest method and takes less time than hand-mixing. You will probably need a dough hook to fit your machine but I am told that some modern mixers have dispensed with this attachment. Domestic mixers will handle about 3 lbs (1350g) of flour as a maximum, larger industrial mixers are available but these do not come within the scope of this book; all the recipes herein are based upon using little more than 3 lbs (1350g) of flour, some less.

These basic instructions are common to most of the recipes; those where machine-mixing is detrimental are specified.

The onerous task of rubbing the fat into the flour is eliminated when using a machine. Put the sieved flour and salt into the bowl of the machine together with the fat cut into small chunks, start the machine on the lowest speed and in a few minutes the fat will be completely broken down. Finish with a few seconds on the highest speed to obtain even distribution and it is ready to turn into a separate bowl for later use. If you are using a Kenwood Chef it is important to fit the K-beater for breaking down the fat, then changing to the dough hook for the mixing; for other machines refer to the manufacturer's handbook.

Put all the liquid into the machine bowl with the yeast and sugar, stir briefly and wait until the surface is covered in frothy bubbles, then add the flour and any other dry ingredients and mix on the slowest speed until the contents are thoroughly incorporated and the dough is attached to the hook in a ball clear of the sides. If some of the flour remains in the bowl detached from the ball of dough do not add water, scrape the dough off the hook, drop it back into the bowl and start the mixer again on the slow speed. When all the dough is attached to the hook increase the speed to about half the maximum and maintain this for a full two minutes. The dough will now be evenly smooth but not sticky, and can be turned out on to a floured surface for kneading.

If you prefer using oil instead of fat, olive oil is the best without doubt and can be incorporated in the same proportions as fat – if the recipe calls for 2 ozs (55g) of fat 2 fl. ozs (55 ml) of oil will equate but the method must be adjusted slightly.

Sieve the flour and salt together into a bowl and set aside for use later. Put the liquid (water, milk, or a mixture as required in the recipe) into the machine bowl together with the yeast and sugar, stir briefly and put aside until the surface is covered with frothy bubbles. Then add the oil and mix on half speed for about a minute or until a smooth emulsion obtains. Reduce the speed to the minimum and gradually add the flour until it is all in the bowl, then proceed exactly as you would when using solid fat. Whether you use fat or oil makes no difference to the fermentation times.

Mixing by hand

The fat will have to be rubbed into the flour/salt mixture until it resembles fine breadcrumbs with no lumps, then the rest of the ingredients are prepared in the same way as for machine-mixing but stirred in the bowl with a wooden spoon at first, then finished by hand until all are thoroughly incorporated and the dough is evenly mixed. It is then turned out on to a floured surface for kneading.

Oils are very difficult to use when hand-mixing because

they tend to separate from the rest of the liquid resulting in uneven distribution throughout the dough. If you are hand-mixing it is simpler to stay with solid fats but if oil is preferred proceed as follows: put the warm liquid into a large bowl and add the sugar and yeast as detailed in the recipe and set aside to activate. When the surface is covered in frothy bubbles add a tablespoon of the oil together with two tablespoons of flour and whisk thoroughly. Continue to add oil and flour in the same proportions between whiskings until all the oil is in the bowl and the mixture resembles a thin porridge. Gradually add the remainder of the flour, stirring thoroughly between each addition with a wooden spoon. Finish mixing by hand to get even distribution, turn out and knead in the usual manner.

Sponging

Historically, the sponging system of breadmaking was regarded as the only acceptable method. Indeed, it is still sometimes used today, and at least three flour manufacturers detail it upon their bags as the recommended method of making bread. For those who wish to try it, here are the details.

First warm a large bowl, then sieve the flour and salt into it and mix thoroughly. Rub in the fat until the mixture resembles fine breadcrumbs (oil *can* be rubbed in but is very difficult to get evenly distributed, see *Mixing by hand*). Ferment the yeast, sugar and liquid in a separate vessel and set aside until the surface is covered in frothy bubbles. Make a depression in the centre of the flour and pour the yeast liquid into it. Draw a little of the flour from the sides of the bowl and coat the surface of the liquid with it so that it is entirely covered to a depth of about ¼ in (6 mm). Cover with a cloth and set to rest in a warm place. After an hour or so the surface of the bowl will be covered with frothy bubbles, and all the flour can be stirred in with a wooden spoon before finishing by hand. The dough can then be turned out for kneading in the usual way.

Kneading

Kneading is probably the most important part of breadmaking (with very few exceptions which will be specified in the recipes) and can make all the difference between a good and poor crumb. Most books advise 'knead for ten minutes' or some other stated length of time, but to my mind this is too ambiguous; the length of time is not important, it is the number of strokes that defines the requirements of the dough, so throughout the following recipes I have asked the cook to knead for a definite number of strokes. Few cooks will knead at the same rate, some may be quite fast and complete the work at one stint whilst others may prefer to take their time and perhaps have an occasional rest between sessions.

Kneading can be spread over an hour or more if it tires you, but it is important to complete the number of strokes suggested and to perform properly and rhythmically. It is easily the most tiring and time-consuming part of breadmaking which is why so many cooks fail to produce a really good loaf, but if you bake bread every week kneading soon becomes an accepted part of the job and no great hassle. Many cooks play music and knead in time to the rhythm.

Kneading is the process by which the dough is stretched and 'lengthened'; it can be performed in several ways, the most usual of which is to work the dough with both hands, but the same result can be achieved single-handedly or (eventually) by throwing it repetitively against a hard surface such as a table top or even by squeezing it between the fingers. However, the first one is the more usual, and will now be described in detail; it is also the method suggested in all the following recipes which call for kneading.

Take the ball of dough and place it before you on a lightly floured surface; then with the heel of your palms press down on to the dough and away from you at the same time. Rotate the dough a quarter-turn, fold in half by bringing the far edge towards you, then press down and away again. Repeat the quarter-turn and continue for the number of strokes required by the recipe.

Some cooks (and tutors at schools of cookery) knead with one hand only and, if properly performed, this makes no difference to the dough but can result in strained muscles in one arm or the back. It is quite possible to knead a small ball of dough in each hand when making baps or rolls, but otherwise it will be found less stressful for most people to use both hands for kneading.

KNEADING

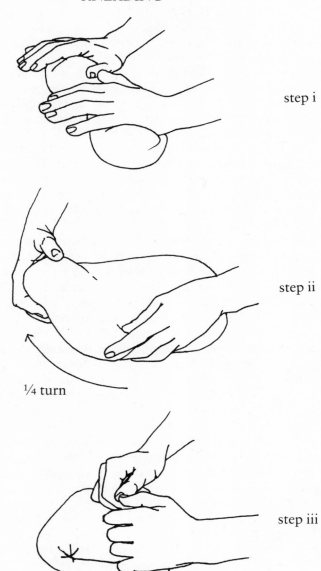

step i

step ii

¼ turn

step iii

Most breads require a total of between 200 and 400 strokes – 200 for the initial kneading followed by a further 100 or 200 after rising, and this can take a good twenty minutes or more. Always utilize your body weight when kneading rather than relying upon the strength in your arms, in this way it will be less tiring.

After 200 strokes the dough will be noticeably different, it will feel smooth and silky and have quite an elastic texture, clammy but not sticky. In fact you may be able to dispense with flouring the table surface and the dough will no longer stick to your hands.

However, if the dough is still sticky too much water has been used in the mix; it can be corrected at this stage by continuing to knead on a floured surface until as much flour has been absorbed as is needed to bring the dough back to the correct condition. Conversely, if the dough is too dry it can be sprayed lightly with water then rekneaded until the water is absorbed. The water content suggested in the recipes must be used only as a guide, it is not possible to accurately forecast the absorption rate of flours, but as a general rule white flour requires less water than wholemeal.

For some recipes the kneading is performed on a dampened surface with moistened hands and this will be detailed in the recipe when required.

To test that the dough is sufficiently kneaded, take the ball of dough in both hands and pull it apart; if it tears easily it needs more kneading, if it pulls out into long strands before breaking it is ready to go into a warm place for rising.

These instructions apply only to yeasted doughs, soda breads are only slightly kneaded if at all (see the recipes for details). Kneading does not affect the dough's ability to rise; rising is controlled by the yeast-content of the dough, temperature and moisture-content. If your dough does not rise, extra kneading will not help it, you must look elsewhere for the fault.

Rising

Form the dough into a ball and return it to the bowl, cover with a dry clean cloth overlaid with a damp one, or a piece of greased polythene, and set to rise in a warm place for between one and two hours or longer according to the temperature. If it is not covered the dough will develop a brittle skin which can result in gritty lumps in the crumb after it is baked, or a 'fly crust' (see Faults section).

The bowl must be large enough to ensure that the risen dough cannot come into contact with the cover. Alternatively it can be put into a large plastic bag to rise but the plastic must be thoroughly greased all over the inside surface or the dough will stick to it and be almost impossible to remove.

The ideal temperature for rising dough is between 70–75°F (20–24°C); below this the time taken will be extended, much above and the yeast will be killed. A slow rise is not detrimental to the bread; some cooks prefer to leave the dough overnight at room temperature so that it is ready for use next morning. You can even keep it in a refrigerator until required – it will continue to rise very slowly, often taking several days to reach maturity. Refrigerated dough must be allowed to return to room temperature before being worked further (this can take several hours), and if you prefer overnight rising be sure to use a large bowl or bucket or the dough could overflow the receptacle during the night.

In some kitchens it is not easy to find a warm, draught-free place but it is an important point. My bread is usually put to rise in the airing cupboard on a shelf above the hot water cylinder – a perfect situation you may think. Not always so however; a child may fling the door open to find a clean pair of socks and forget to close it; a teenager may decide to take the annual bath and drain the tank of all the hot water, or someone can accidentally increase the thermostat setting. The latter can completely ruin the bread but the two former annoyances simply delay the rise and can be coped with.

Draughts which can chill the dough can be avoided by putting the bowl or bag into a large cardboard box and sealing the lid. For those who lack an airing cupboard the same effect can be achieved by putting the cardboard box on an electric blanket (or heated pad) so long as several layers of thick towelling are placed between the heat source and the base of the box and the box is entirely wrapped in two layers of towelling.

When it appears to have doubled in volume and be correctly risen, the dough can be tested by pushing a wet finger into it to a depth of ½ in (1.25 cms). If the hole does not fill or fills very slowly it is ready for the next step; if it fills rapidly it needs a little longer. Over-rising is not a serious fault at this stage.

Some authors insist on the dough being deflated before rekneading, but this is quite unnecessary as a separate operation because it is quite impossible to knead *without* deflating automatically.

Turn the dough out on to a lightly floured surface and begin rekneading immediately according to the number of strokes required by the recipe, then return it to the warm place to rise, covered as before with a damp cloth.

The second rise will take about half the time of the first if conditions are similar, and the dough should be tested after rising in the same way with the dampened finger.

Turn it out again on to the floured surface and knead for the further required strokes then cut into portions as required, mould each roughly to shape, place into warmed, greased tins (or set on to a greased baking tray according to the type of loaf required) and return to the warm place for the final rise which is called the proving. Some books refer to every rise as a prove but this term should be reserved for the final rise after the dough has been put into the tins or other containers.

Some cookers are fitted with warming drawers which are excellent if correctly used. Most have the heating element in the roof and if the dough is not covered during the final proving it will develop a thin skin which will separate from the loaf during baking – a type of 'fly crust'. The temperatures reached by these warming compartments though can be high enough to kill the yeast in the dough so on the whole I do not favour them for proving, a gentle even heat is preferable.

In most cases the tins must be not more than half filled, the dough will then expand to fill as proving progresses. Exceptions to this rule will be dealt with in the appropriate recipes. When the dome of the dough is level with the top of the tin the bread is ready for the oven but if in doubt you can check by making a slight indentation with a *dry* finger (not a poke this time, just a gentle touch), the indentation will slowly fill if the bread is correctly risen.

It is at this stage that the bread can be overproved and

ruined. If the dome stands proud above the top of the tin an inch (2.5 cms) or more it is almost certainly overproved and the result will depend on the degree of overproving to which it has been subjected. Slight overproving, especially if the dough is rather slack, will result in the bread flopping over the sides of the tin and yielding a slice with a 'mushroom' top but still edible; if it has gone further the results can be more spectacular – the loaf looks perfect as it goes into the oven, the dome blows up then suddenly collapses back into the tin; the crumb has the texture of a housebrick and is quite inedible.

Overproved dough can be corrected before it goes into the oven; simply remove it from the tin and reknead for about 20 strokes. Return it to a warm place to re-prove and this time catch it before it has risen too high.

If the temperature for the proving is higher than for the earlier stages (if for instance the dough has been chilled and then proved at 70°F, 20°C) the bread will 'blow' at the top and around the sides but be almost solid in the centre. Conversely, if the dough is warm and then chilled as it proves, the crust will be very tough and rubbery, and the crumb peppered with holes, some of them quite large. A steady even temperature throughout the whole breadmaking process gives the best results.

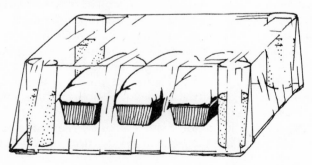

If a soft crust is preferred, the tinned or trayed loaves should be covered as they prove to prevent the formation of a skin but any contact between the loaves and the cover will mark the tops and affect the ultimate appearance. This can be overcome by draping a cover (polythene or fabric) over the loaves but supported by glasses or bottles so that the cover is held well clear of the dough as it rises (see illustration).

As soon as the dough is correctly proved it should be baked, if left for long it will deteriorate and the quality of the bread will suffer. If the loaves cannot be put into the oven within say twenty minutes of being ready don't waste time and effort baking them. If they have stood for a long time destroy them and start again. If a delay of no more than twenty minutes is involved, turn the dough out on to the floured surface, deflate, reknead for 20 strokes before returning to the tins for reproving. The bread will not be quite so good but it will be edible. These times must be used only as a guide – they may vary according to the temperature, recipe and environment.

Freshly made dough can be put into greased plastic bags and stored in a refrigerator for a week or so before being taken out and allowed to return to room temperature before further processing. It is best to refrigerate immediately after the first kneading.

When you have perfected your technique the bread will 'spring' when put into the oven. Don't worry if it doesn't for the first few occasions, it can still be quite acceptable, but a good 'spring' is something to be aimed for. If you have an oven with a glass door it is possible to watch the spring and there can be fewer more satisfactory pastimes. Within minutes the dome of each loaf expands and rises well above the level of the tin and stays there for the rest of the baking; there will be stretch marks where the crust has been thrust up from the sides of the tin and the crumb will be soft and light with air-bubbles evenly distributed throughout. Many cooks *never* achieve a 'spring' with their bread so do not despair if your efforts are not immediately rewarded; if you follow the instructions carefully you will eventually be successful. Bear in mind, however, that bread made from 100% wholemeal flour will not rise as much as that with a proportion of white in the recipe.

Tins and shapes

Square and oblong tins are available, round and oval, terracotta or glass. The container controls the shape of the loaf, not the quality. Bread can be made in almost any shape depending upon the type of slice preferred.

The loaf which is sold in a shop as a 'large tin' or 'sandwich' loaf has been baked in a rectangular container with a lid on top; a 'split tin' is basically the same loaf but baked in an open-topped tin, and the dough has been slashed lengthwise before being put into the oven. Many differently named loaves in bakers' shops are made from the same basic recipe but baked in different shapes – the dough is exactly the same whether the loaf is called a 'bloomer' or a 'Coburg'.

Do not mix types of container in the oven if it can be avoided; bread in a flowerpot, for instance, will take longer to bake than that in a tin or free-standing on a baking sheet, and it follows that a 2-lb (900g) loaf will need longer in the oven than a 1-lb (450g). Loaves must always be baked separately from rolls; the oven cannot be opened to extract the rolls when cooked without adversely affecting the larger loaves.

A large empty fruit-juice can will produce a cylindrical loaf which yields an attractive slice for special occasions. Completely remove the top lid and make certain the tin is washed clean and perfectly dry; thoroughly grease the inside surfaces and make a small hole in the base with the point of a knife or a skewer (it needs to be no larger than ⅛ in); half fill with the prepared dough and set to prove normally. When the dough has risen to the level of the rim bake in the usual way but lower the centre shelf of the oven one step to allow for the height of the tin. Remove from the oven when cooked and allow to rest in the tin for 10 minutes before sliding out on to a wire rack to cool for at least an hour before slicing. If cut across the cylinder of bread a circular slice will result, if sliced with a diagonal cut rather attractive ovals can be produced.

Bread will shrink away from the sides of the tin when cooked if the tin has been greased beforehand and will fall out as soon as the tin is inverted; if it does not, just give it a gentle tap on a hard surface to free it. Always give the loaves a few minutes to rest after removing from the oven before taking them out of the tins to cool on a wire rack but if the loaves are left longer than 10 minutes in the tins the bread will be heavy.

Most vegetable oils, lard or margarine can be used to grease the tins before use, but in the USA many stores sell a product called PAM which is a spray in a pressurized canister; it is the best lubricant I have ever used for bread and cake tins, and if you have the chance of acquiring a few cans there is no better investment of a few dollars. Its British equivalent is a very poor substitute and is best avoided.

If tins are not used and the bread is to be free-standing on a greased baking tray the same basic principles apply but the dough can be moulded into a variety of shapes: rounds, ovals, balls, flat pads (baps) or batons. Many different shapes are described in the following recipes or you can, of course, make your own designs.

A crisper crust will result if the bread is removed from the tins after 30 minutes cooking and baking continued with the loaves out of their tins. If at the same time they are lightly sprayed over with warm water the crust will be even more brittle.

Decoration

Many cooks like the clean, smooth appearance of the rounded dome of a well sprung loaf; others prefer the loaf to carry some kind of decoration.

The simplest way to decorate a loaf is by knife-cuts (slashing) just before the dough goes into the oven, and this can be quite effective. A slit lengthwise down the loaf will open out in the baking to produce the baker's split tin; or you may prefer to make three diagonal slashes across the loaf. A cross made with deep knife-cuts from edge to edge on a round loaf will result in the traditional Coburg shape – or interlocking crescents cut into the surface could make your 'designer' loaf famous.

Cuts can be in straight lines, curves, zig-zags or circles. As you gain experience you will even be able to cut initials in the dough. Another way of decorating a loaf is by additions to the crust; these can be in the form of plaits, knots, bows, etc. They are made from a small piece of the dough, moulded to shape and attached to the loaf with a little milk or water just before it goes into the oven. Some cooks use egg for sticking the ornament to the loaf but if any of the egg runs down it will mark the crust and look horrible.

Extra care in the baking is required if an ornament is attached to the loaf if it is not to burn before the bread is cooked. It may be necessary to turn the loaf upside down in the oven for the last 10 minutes to give the ornament some protection from the heat. Another way is to put a sheet of aluminium foil loosely over the top of the loaf, removing it about 10 minutes before the bread is due to come out of the oven. If your oven has a glass door it is easy to ensure the ornament is not being overcooked; if it has not, ornamental additions to the crust present much more risk, my advice would be to stay with slashing until you get some experience.

Loaves can be decorated with sesame or poppy seeds, caraway, chopped nuts, rolled oats, cracked wheat, etc. Before the final proving, lightly coat the surface of the dough with milk then roll it on a board covered with the selected coating, or sprinkle the coating over the dampened dough by hand, before returning it to the warm, draughtproof place to rise. If using cracked grains, try to get those only slightly crushed or split; those broken down to the consistency of coarse sand will be almost invisible after baking.

Glazing

Glazing is traditional with certain breads, mainly those of continental origin such as rye, but nearly all loaves can be decorated in this manner if desired.

The glaze is best applied with a soft flat brush; the normal pastry brush is too stiff and will mark raw dough and possibly deflate it. The entire exposed surface of the loaf must be covered with the glaze or it will look messy when baked. Details of some types of glaze are listed below.

Apricot jam glaze. Dissolve 2 tablespoons (30ml) apricot jam (without any of the whole fruit) in 2 tablespoons (30ml) hot water. Brush over the top of the loaves as they leave the oven. This glaze is used mainly on tea breads.

Black treacle glaze. A popular glaze in Scandinavia and other parts of northern Europe, not only for tea breads. Mix 1 tablespoon (15ml) black treacle with double the amount of hot (not boiling) water and paint the loaves with the solution as they come out of the oven.

Butter glaze. Brush the loaves with melted butter as they come out of the oven for a matt finish, a medium-brown colour and less crisp crust. A thin coating gives best results.

Cinnamon-honey glaze. Used mainly on tea breads. Melt

1 oz (30g) butter and 2 fl. ozs (55ml) clear honey together, and stir in 1 teaspoon (5g) ground cinnamon. Bring to the boil and simmer for 1 minute. Cool slightly before brushing the loaves with the glaze as they leave the oven.

Coffee glaze. A glaze for rye and similar dark breads; the coffee flavour is barely noticeable after baking. Dissolve 2 teaspoons (10g) instant coffee granules in 2 fl. ozs (55ml) hot water to which has been added 1 teaspoon (5g) sugar. When almost cold strain through muslin and coat the loaves with the solution before baking. The loaves can be reglazed halfway through the baking period if you wish but few cooks feel this to be necessary.

Cornflour glaze. This is the traditional glaze for rye breads but it can be used quite successfully on most types of loaf. Stir 1 teaspoon (5g) cornflour into 4 fl. ozs (110ml) cold water. Bring to the boil and simmer until clear (about 5 minutes). Whilst still quite warm (but not boiling) brush the loaves with the solution at the end of the baking time then return them to the oven for a further 3 minutes.

Egg wash. Beat one egg with the equivalent of half the shell of water, and paint the loaves with the mixture as they leave the oven. If required for tea breads, add 1 teaspoon (5g) caster sugar to the water and dissolve thoroughly before mixing with the egg.

Egg and milk glaze. Thoroughly whisk an egg until it is completely liquidized then add 2 teaspoons (10ml) whole milk and beat until smooth and creamy. Brush over the loaves before they go into the oven.

Honey glaze. Clear honey is best for glazing. Apply by brush immediately the loaves leave the oven. The honey can be warmed if too stiff to apply easily. This glaze remains rather sticky and is used on currant loaves and other tea breads.

Honey and cornflour glaze. A variation of the foregoing glaze. Sir 1 teaspoon (5g) cornflour into 4 fl. ozs (110ml) cold water and bring to the boil. Add 2 teaspoons (10ml) clear honey and simmer until clear – usually about 5 minutes. Brush the glaze on to the bread after it has baked for 30 minutes and again 2 minutes before the end of baking time. This produces a dark, shiny crust.

Lemon glaze. Take the juice of one or two lemons and add to it an equivalent amount of caster sugar. Bring to the boil stirring constantly, cool slightly then paint the loaves with the mixture as they leave the oven. If the mixture is too stiff it can be diluted with a little hot water. Used mainly for lemon-flavoured tea breads.

Milk glaze. This is usually applied to the raw dough just before it goes into the oven, whole milk being used slightly warmed to prevent chilling the dough. If the loaves are then brushed with melted butter as they leave the oven they will acquire a warmer colour and a 'buttery' flavour.

Mottled glaze. Usually applied to tray-baked loaves where a more spectacular effect can be expected. Dissolve ½ teaspoon (2.5g) dried granulated yeast and 1 teaspoon (5g) sugar in 2 fl. ozs (55ml) warm water. Leave to activate until the surface is covered in bubbles (about 10 minutes) then stir 1 oz (30g) cornflour and 1 teaspoon (5ml) olive oil into the yeast liquid. Allow to stand for a further ten minutes or until the surface is again covered in bubbles, then stir briefly and paint the loaves with the glaze just before they go into the oven.

Oil glazes. Several types of oil can be used for glazing including sunflower, corn, olive, etc. Apply as the loaves leave the oven. Results are similar to butter but the flavours are different.

Orange marmalade glaze. Dissolve 2 tablespoons (30ml) orange marmalade (without the peel) in the same quantity of hot water and brush the loaves with the mixture as they leave the oven. Used mainly on tea breads.

Salt-water glaze. The standard glaze for French and Italian breads producing a crisp golden crust. Dissolve 2 teaspoons (10g) salt in ¼ pt (140ml) warm water and brush the loaves with the solution before baking. A second application can be made halfway through the baking time but this is seldom necessary.

Strawberry jam glaze. Dissolve 2 tablespoons (30ml) strawberry jam (without any whole fruit) in 2 tablespoons (30ml) hot water. Brush the loaves with the mixture as they leave the oven. For use on tea breads.

Sugar glaze. Chiefly for use on tea breads. Dissolve 2 ozs sugar in 4 tablespoons (60ml) water, bring to the boil and simmer for 1 minute. Cool slightly then brush the loaves with the glaze as they leave the oven.

Sweet milk glaze. Dissolve 1 tablespoon (15g) caster sugar in 2 tablespoons (30ml) whole milk, heat sufficiently to completely dissolve the sugar but do not boil. Brush the loaves with the glaze about 10 minutes after leaving the oven. A tea bread glaze.

Victorian glaze. This is a variation of the earlier cornflour glaze developed by Victorian bakers to imitate an egg glaze at lower cost. When used on plain crusty bread it is almost indistinguishable. Mix 3 ozs (90g) cornflour with 1 pint (550ml) water, starting with 1 tablespoon (15ml) of the water and adding the rest gradually to produce a thin milky liquid. Bring to the boil, stirring continually until it becomes quite clear. Allow to cool then whisk briskly for 3 minutes or until a smooth creamy paste results. Brush the loaves with the paste before they go into the oven and again halfway through the baking time. When the bread is cooked lightly spray or brush over with clean warm water as it comes out of the oven.

White wine glaze. Dissolve 2 tablespoons sugar in ¼ pt (140ml) white wine, bring to the boil then cool. Brush the loaves with the mixture as they go into the oven and again halfway through the baking time. Effervescent and fortified wines are unsuitable for this purpose but concentrated grape juice can be used.

3

Recipes

All the recipes which follow include every detail required to produce an edible loaf at the first attempt; some are easier to follow than others and the more difficult ones have been noted. Except in a very few instances the *method* is complete on a page or pair of facing pages so it will be unnecessary to turn a page with floury hands to complete a baking, although lack of space may dictate the necessity of putting the list of ingredients and any suggested variations separately. It is essential to read the chosen recipe right through from start to finish before commencing work.

If you begin by making the First Time Loaf several times until you are satisfied with the results, you can then advance to the more elaborate breads with confidence. Once you have perfected baking your own bread you will never willingly return to eating anything else.

For your convenience recipes are roughly graded using a system of stars as follows:

      ★ Easy   ★★ Intermediate   ★★★ Tricky

Begin with the easy ones until you have acquired some experience, but none will be beyond your capabilities within a few bakings.

Always abide by the three golden rules before commencing work:

1. Read the recipe *right through* including the suggested variations (if any).
2. Assemble all equipment and ingredients; in this way you are unlikely to forget anything.
3. Bring all ingredients (especially eggs and milk) up to room temperature or they will chill the mixture.

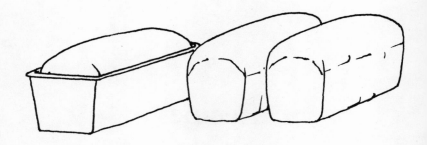

The First Time Loaf

The First Time Loaf★

This is the loaf I baked almost every week when my family was at home. The simple straightforward recipe is the basis for many of the breads which follow. I suggest baking it five or six times without variation before experimenting with other recipes, by which time you will be beginning to get the 'feel' of the dough at its various stages, and be able to dispense with some, but not all, of the testing methods.

Initially there will be slight variations in the bread from each baking although all should be quite edible. Make a note of the difference and, if possible, the reasons for them ('made the mix a little too wet this week' or 'forgot to add the salt'). Practice makes perfect and, given time, everyone can make perfect bread adjusted to their own particular taste.

This recipe produces five 1lb loaves or fewer larger ones with a medium-crisp crust and buoyant, open crumb. It is ideal for toasting, and if frozen will keep for about three months.

INGREDIENTS

1½ pints (825ml) warm water
4 teaspoons (20g) granulated dried yeast
4 teaspoons (20g) sugar
1 lb (450g) stoneground wholemeal flour
2 lb (900g) strong white flour, unbleached if possible
4 teaspoons (20g) salt
2 oz (55g) fresh lard

METHOD

Hand-Mixing. Put the warm water in a bowl and add the yeast and sugar, stir gently for a few seconds, then leave to activate; it is ready for use when the surface is covered with frothy bubbles.

Whilst the yeast is developing sieve the flours and salt together into a large bowl and mix thoroughly. Rub the lard into the flour until the mixture resembles fine breadcrumbs with no lumps; this can take all of 15 minutes but must be done thoroughly.

Make a well in the centre of the flour mixture and pour in the yeast liquid. Mix by hand or wooden spoon until all the ingredients are incorporated to form a stiff, coarse dough – do not add extra water to slacken it.

Turn out on to a floured surface and knead for 300 strokes – this can take 20 minutes or longer but should not be skimped or rushed (quality bread comes from good kneading).

Form the dough into a ball and return it to the bowl, cover with a damp cloth or greased polythene sheet and put it in a warm place to rise. This will take between 1 and 2 hours according to the temperature.

When the dough has doubled in size turn it out on to a lightly floured surface and re-knead for a further 100 strokes. Return it to the bowl, cover as before, then put it back in a warm draughtproof place for the second rise which will take about half the time of the first.

When the dough has again doubled in size turn it out on to the floured surface as before and cut it into five equal portions (or less if you prefer a larger loaf). Gently knead each portion for about 20 strokes then form into smooth torpedo shapes and place each in a greased, pre-warmed tin.

Each portion can be pressed into the tin so that it fits the rectangle better if you wish, but normally the dough will expand to fit the tin naturally and unaided. Tins must not be more than half filled to allow for proving.

Put the loaded tins into a warm draughtfree place for proving which will normally take between 30 and 45 minutes according to temperature. They should be covered with a *dry* cloth – if the cloth is at all damp the rising dough will stick to it.

When the dome of the dough has risen so that it is level with the top of the tin the bread is ready for the oven.

Bake on the centre shelf of an oven pre-heated to 450°F (230°C, Gas Mark 8) for 15 minutes, then reduce the heat to 400°F (200°C, Gas Mark 6) for a further 15 minutes. After a further 15 minutes (45 minutes from the start of baking) take one loaf out of the oven, turn it out of the tin and test by tapping the base with the fingertips: if it sounds hollow it is done, if not it needs a few more minutes baking.

After removing the loaves from the oven, cool for a few

minutes in the tins then de-tin and put them on a wire tray. Do not slice for at least an hour.

Machine Mixing (using a dough hook). Sieve the flours and salt together into the mixer bowl, add the lard chopped into small pieces, and run the machine on the slowest speed (using the K-beater if your machine is a Kenwood Chef) until the fat is completely broken up. Increase the speed to about half the maximum and within minutes the mixture will resemble fine breadcrumbs.

Meanwhile stir the yeast and sugar into the warm water in a separate vessel and set aside to activate. When the surface is covered in frothy bubbles, fit the dough hook, start the machine on the lowest speed and gradually add the liquid to the flour mixture. Continue mixing until all the dough has formed into a ball on the dough hook, then increase the speed to about half maximum and run for a full 2 minutes.

Turn out on to a lightly floured surface and knead for 100 strokes. From then on the method is exactly as for hand-mixing.

VARIATIONS

The ratio of wholemeal to white flour can be varied but a little more water will be required the more wholemeal is included. Bread made solely from wholemeal flour has a flavour that is too strong for many tastes, however, if this is required the white flour can be omitted entirely.

Honey or golden syrup can be substituted for the sugar but excessive sweetening can inhibit the action of the yeast so be miserly with it.

Vegetable oil, butter or margarine can be used instead of lard, but margarine must be block margarine not one of the fat-reduced substitutes; butter is best taken direct from the freezer and grated into the flour.

If olive oil is substituted for the lard it can impart its own distinctive delicate flavour to the bread; most people appreciate it, a few do not.

First Time Rolls★

Home-made rolls are quite different to those purchased in a baker's shop or supermarket. They will be more dense because they have not been blown up with chemical additives, and the bland taste of the mass-produced product will be replaced with a distinctive flavour which varies according to the flour used. This recipe makes about 18 rolls but you can vary the size to suit your own requirements but do weigh out the dough portions – guesswork is all very well when you have some experience, but not to be recommended at first.

Use the same ingredients as for the **First Time Loaf** but reduce the water to 1¼ pints (700ml) to produce a slightly stiffer dough.

Mix and rise exactly as for the loaf but instead of dividing the dough into loaf-size pieces, weigh it out into 3-oz (85g) portions and roll each into a ball either between the palms or with a rotary action on a firm surface (if the surface is too heavily floured the dough will skid rather than roll and be impossible to mould into a sphere).

Space out the balls of dough on a greased baking tray allowing enough room between them for expansion, and set into a warm place to rise. When they have doubled in bulk they can be baked on the centre shelf of an oven pre-heated to 450°F (230°C, Gas Mark 8) for 15–20 minutes. Cool on a wire rack and do not freeze for at least four hours.

Kenwood 4-Hour Softcrust Bread ★

The Kenwood Chef Mixer is said to be among the most widely distributed kitchen gadgets and one of which a great many cooks have some knowledge. This recipe is designed specially for use with a Kenwood fitted with the special dough hook but it can probably be adapted to other mixers quite satisfactorily. From opening a bag of flour to taking the bread from the oven takes almost exactly four hours *if the instructions are followed to the letter* and optimum temperatures maintained.

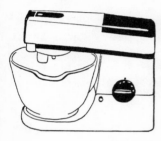

Makes five small loaves or fewer larger; the bread keeps well and can be frozen.

Animal suet can be substituted for the vegetable product but the bread will not rise so well.

Correct temperature throughout is the secret of this recipe. The closer all utensils and ingredients are to 85°F (29°C) the better will be the bread and the more accurate the timing.

INGREDIENTS

4 teaspoons (20g) granulated dried yeast
4 teaspoons (20g) sugar
1¼ pints (700ml) warm water
4 oz (110g) shredded vegetable suet
2 lb (900g) strong unbleached white flour
1 lb (450g) stoneground wholemeal flour
1 tablespoon (15g) salt

METHOD

Dissolve the yeast and sugar in 1 pint (550ml) of the warm water and set aside to activate. It is ready for use when the surface is covered in frothy bubbles.

Melt the vegetable suet in a separate measuring jug.

Sift the flours and salt together into a large warmed bowl.

Pour enough of the remaining warm water into the melted

suet to bring the total amount of liquid up to ½ pint (280ml) and stir well.

Put the yeast liquid into the bowl of the machine and add the suet liquid. Fit the dough hook and run the machine at half speed for 1 minute to emulsify the liquids.

Reduce to the slowest speed then gradually add the flour mixture until all is in the bowl. Continue running at this speed for 5 minutes or until the dough forms a ball on the dough hook – do not add more water.

Increase the speed to half maximum and run for a full 3 minutes (by the clock) before turning the dough out on to a lightly floured surface.

Knead for 50 strokes by which time it will feel soft and silky. It should be fairly slack but not sticky, if it is sticky knead a little more flour into it.

Form into a ball, cover with a damp cloth and place in a warm place to rise until it has doubled in volume. This will take about an hour at 85°F (29°C).

When properly risen bring the dough back to the floured surface, knead for a further 30 strokes, then divide into five equal portions or less if larger loaves are required.

Knead each portion for 20 strokes then form into a ball before elongating slightly into a torpedo shape and placing carefully into its well-greased warm tin, which should be no more than half filled with dough.

Place the loaded tins in a warm draughtproof place, and cover with a dry cloth to prove. They are ready for the oven when the dome of each loaf stands about ¼ in (6mm) above the edge of the tin.

Bake on the centre shelf of an oven pre-heated to 450°F (230°C, Gas Mark 8) for 45 minutes or until the bread sounds hollow when tapped on the base with the fingertips.

Overnight Bread and Rolls⋆

After baking the **First Time Loaf** a few times I suggest you try this overnight recipe. It is just as easy to make but the quality of the bread is superior – no mass-production line can allow sufficient time for the dough to ripen naturally so you are unlikely to taste anything like it from the multiple baker or supermarket.

It was the method widely used by small village bakers before the introduction of the more profitable Chorleywood system, and it can be applied to almost all the yeasted recipes in this book. Many people will find it more convenient to make the dough overnight, and although a minimum of twelve hours is preferable, a longer fermentation is not detrimental up to a maximum of say sixteen hours. No extra effort is called for, it is simply spread over a longer time span.

The recipe makes five small loaves or three larger, the bread keeps well and can be frozen.

INGREDIENTS

1 teaspoon (5g) granulated dried yeast
1 teaspoon (5g) sugar
1¼ pints (700ml) warm water
3 lb (1350g) strong white flour, unbleached if possible
1 teaspoon (5g) salt
2 oz (55g) lard

METHOD

Dissolve the yeast and sugar in the warm water and set aside to activate; it is ready for use when the surface is covered in frothy bubbles.

Sieve the flour and salt together into a large bowl and mix thoroughly.

Rub in the lard until the mixture resembles fine breadcrumbs with no lumps.

Hand-mixing. Make a depression in the centre of the flour and pour the yeast liquid into it. Mix with a wooden spoon until a rough dough results then turn it out on to a lightly floured surface.

Machine-mixing. Fit the dough hook to the machine, pour the yeast liquid into the machine bowl and start it on the lowest speed.

Gradually spoon in the flour mixture until it is all in the bowl, and continue mixing until a rough dough has formed into a ball on the dough hook, then increase the speed to about half the maximum and run for 2 full minutes.

Turn out on to a lightly floured surface.

From then on the methods are identical.

Knead for 200 strokes when the dough should have become smooth and silky. If it is still a bit harsh a little water can be kneaded in, a teaspoon (5ml) at a time – it is seldom that more than a tablespoon (15ml) of extra water will be needed. The dough must never be wet and sticky – but this condition can be corrected by adding more flour as kneading proceeds.

Do not adjust the liquid content until the dough has been kneaded for at least 200 strokes – it changes dramatically as kneading progresses.

Oil a very large bowl, or plastic bucket, making sure the entire inner surface is covered, form the dough into a ball and put it in. Lightly oil the surface of the dough to prevent it drying, cover with a damp cloth and set aside to rise and mature overnight. Any vegetable oil can be used.

Place the dough anywhere where normal room temperatures obtain. If it gets too cold the yeast will work more slowly; even in a refrigerator it will still rise eventually but take days rather than hours.

The following morning turn the dough out on to a floured surface and knead for a further 200 strokes, then divide into five equal portions (less if larger loaves are required) and roll each into a ball between the palms of the hands.

Mould each piece into a torpedo shape and put into warm pre-greased tins. The tins must not be much more than half full.

Cover with a clean *dry* cloth and set in a warm, draughtproof place to prove.

When the dough has increased in volume and the dome of each loaf is level with the top of the tin, bake on the centre shelf of an oven pre-heated to 450°F (230°C, Gas Mark 8) for

15 minutes, then reduce the temperature to 425°F (220°C, Gas Mark 7) for a further 30 minutes.

Remove one loaf from the oven and tap the base with the fingertips; if it sounds hollow the bread is done; if not return it to the oven for a few more minutes. Cool on a wire rack.

VARIATIONS

A proportion of wholemeal flour can be included in the ingredients without much affecting the outcome. If the bread is made entirely of wholemeal flour a little more water may be required and it will not rise so high in the oven.

Margarine can be substituted for the lard but it must be block margarine, low-fat substitutes are not suitable.

Rolls can be made from the same ingredients and by the same method except that the risen dough is weighed out into 3 oz (85g) portions, each portion rolled into a ball, spaced on a lightly greased baking tray, and set to prove in a warm place until doubled in bulk. They are then baked on the centre shelf of an oven pre-heated to 450°F (230°C, Gas Mark 8) for 15–20 minutes.

Note: To produce extra crusty loaves spray them over with clean water just before they go into the oven. Ten minutes before the end of baking time knock them out of the tins and finish baking on a tray so that all surfaces are crisped.

Only one rise is necessary for this bread but the container must be covered with a *damp* cloth. If the cloth dries out, the surface of the dough will be covered with a crust, and the crumb of the bread may then contain small gritty lumps – very unpleasant. The cloth though covering the loaves for proving must be quite dry – the slightest touch of damp will cause it to adhere to the domes of the risen loaves and mark them.

No-Knead Quick Wholemeal Bread★

This bread is a favourite with those in a hurry because the kneading has been totally eliminated. The recipe yields a rather flat-topped, dense loaf which is best eaten within a few hours of baking if the full flavour is to be enjoyed and it is delicious eaten fresh from the oven with a bowl of home-made soup.

It makes a 'hearty' slice which must be cut quite thickly if it is not to disintegrate, has a robust flavour and crisp crust. Although the absence of fat means it will not keep or freeze well, if only half the loaf has been used at the first meal the remaining portion can be stored overnight in the refrigerator if it is wrapped and sealed in clingfilm. Although the crumb may be acceptable the next day, the crust will be rubbery, but if toasted, it is still very good.

The use of black treacle for sweetener yields a very dark crumb and intensifies the flavour. If you prefer a paler crumb use the suggested alternative at the end of the recipe substituting golden syrup for the treacle.

It cannot be tray baked, neither can it be made into rolls, and is best baked in a rectangular 1½ lb tin although a round one can be used if preferred. In either case the tin must be high-sided or the dough will flop over the sides. The recipe makes one loaf.

INGREDIENTS

    2 teaspoons (10ml) black treacle
    ¾ pint (425ml) warm water
    1 teaspoon (5g) granulated dried yeast
    1 lb (450g) stoneground wholemeal flour
    1 teaspoon (5g) salt
    Sesame seeds for decoration (optional)

METHOD

Warm all the ingredients, baking tin and mixing bowl before commencing – this will speed up the process considerably, and pre-heat the oven to 450°F (230°C, Gas Mark 8).

Stir the treacle into the warm water and agitate until

completely dissolved.

Add the yeast and stir for 30 seconds to disperse evenly, then set aside in a warm place to activate. It is ready to use when the surface is covered in frothy bubbles.

Mix the flour and salt together in a large mixing bowl with a wooden spoon, make a well in the centre and pour in the yeast liquid, stirring vigorously until a slack dough is produced, too wet for kneading but just slack enough to drop slowly off the spoon. If necessary a little more warm water can be added but the mixture must be stiffer than a batter mix.

Turn the dough into the warmed, greased tin and set into a warm, draughtproof place to prove. The tin must be no more than three-quarters full, a little less for preference, or the dough will droop over the edges as it rises. When it has risen to the level of the top of the tin it is ready for the oven. Sesame seeds can be sprinkled over the top of the loaf at this point if required, but the bread is very good without. The seeds will stick without prior glazing.

Bake for about 20 minutes on the centre shelf at 450°F (230°C, Gas Mark 8), then reduce the temperature to 425°F (220°C, Gas Mark 7) and bake for a further 25 minutes.

Test by tapping the base of the loaf with the fingertips; if it sounds hollow the bread is done.

Place on a wire rack to cool for at least one hour. If you slice too soon the crumb will pull away from the crust.

VARIATIONS

A mixture of white and wholemeal flours can be used but the texture and flavour of the bread will be quite different.

Golden syrup can be used instead of black treacle but the colour of the crumb will be lighter and the character of the bread radically altered.

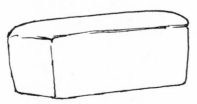

'Sponge' Bread★★

The sponge method of breadmaking was that normally used when every village and hamlet had its own baker, or breadmaking was a regular household duty. As population and demand grew the manufacturing process was speeded up with a consequent reduction in quality.

It is a lengthy process which cannot be hurried but well worth the extra time and effort. The crumb is very even and remains moist longer, and the crust is thinner and less brittle. The subtle flavour cannot be described, all one can say is that it is pleasantly different.

It is not to be recommended as a first attempt at breadmaking, get some experience with the **First Time Loaf** before trying the sponge method, and if your first attempt is not quite up to standard do not despair, try again following the recipe more closely.

There are several minor variations to the method found in old recipes, but the results all seem to be very similar. The following is one that can easily be adapted to match the type of bread required – white, wholemeal or any combination of bread flours.

INGREDIENTS

1¼ pints (700ml) warm water
4 teaspoons (20g) granulated dried yeast
1 tablespoon (15g) sugar
2 lb (900g) strong white flour, unbleached if possible
1 lb (450g) stoneground wholemeal flour
4 oz (110g) fine ground potato flour
1 tablespoon (15g) salt
4 oz (110g) lard

METHOD

Stir the sugar and yeast into the warm water and set aside to activate. It is ready to use when the surface is covered in frothy bubbles.

Sift the flours and salt together into a large bowl and rub in the lard until the mixture resembles fine breadcrumbs. Any lumps of fat in the mixture will result in the crumb having holes in it.

Set aside about 4 oz (110g) of the flour mixture, place the rest into a large container (I use a plastic bucket kept specially for the purpose) and make a well in the centre of the flour. Pour in the yeast liquid and stir carefully with a wooden spoon, drawing some of the flour away from the edges but not so much as to allow the liquid to come into contact with the sides of the vessel.

Continue stirring for a few minutes until you have a sloppy batter surrounded by a narrow area of dry flour, then take the set-aside flour and sprinkle it over the surface of the batter until it is well covered with dry flour.

Cover with a dry cloth and leave overnight to mature. The vessel must be capable of containing at least twice the volume of the mixture to allow for expansion during fermentation – my bucket is of 4-gallon capacity.

Next morning the surface of the flour will be seen to be cracked and the yeast mixture showing through. Take a wooden spoon and stir the mixture thoroughly until it is smooth and even with no dry flour in evidence, then discard the spoon and mix by hand for 10 or 15 minutes until a silky-smooth dough results.

Turn out on to a lightly floured surface and knead for 200 strokes. Form into a ball and place in a pre-warmed bowl large enough to allow for the dough to increase to about double its bulk.

Cover with a dry cloth first, then cover the dry cloth with a damp one, and set aside in a warm place to rise. It will take an hour or more for the dough to double in volume at a temperature of 80°F (27°C) which is the optimum; if the temperature is lower the dough will take longer to rise but this will not adversely affect the quality of the bread whereas a higher temperature may kill the yeast.

When the dough has doubled in bulk turn it out on to a lightly floured surface and knead for a further 200 strokes, then return it to the warmed bowl, cover once more with the dry cloth followed by the damp one, and set again into a warm place for a further rise which will take roughly half the time of the first.

When the dough has again doubled in bulk turn it out on

to the lightly floured surface and knead for 100 strokes then allow to rest for 5 minutes before dividing into five equal portions (or fewer if larger loaves are required).

Mould each piece into the required shape or place in pre-warmed tins, and put into a warm, draughtproof place to prove. This will take about twenty minutes at 80°F (27°C) by which time the dough will have risen in the tins, or expanded on the baking tray to double its volume and is ready for the oven.

The oven should be pre-heated to 450°F (230°C, Gas Mark 8) and the bread placed on the centre shelf. After 15 minutes reduce the temperature to 400°F (200°C, Gas Mark 6) and continue baking for a further 30 minutes. Test the loaves by tapping the base with the fingertips, if the bread sounds hollow it is done. Cool on a wire rack.

The bread can be eaten two hours after it leaves the oven but it is at its best next day. It keeps well and can be frozen when quite cold.

VARIATIONS

As already mentioned, the sponge method can be used with any bread flours with excellent results. Those wishing to avoid the use of lard can substitute olive oil but this needs a slight adjustment to the method as follows:

Using 4 fl.oz (110ml) olive oil, prepare the yeast mixture as usual but reduce the amount of warm water to 1 pint (550ml), set aside to activate. When fully activated, add the olive oil to it and whisk vigorously until a smooth emulsion results (an electric liquidizer is best if you have one).

Prepare the flour mixture as usual but omit the lard. Pour the liquid into the well in the flour and quickly stir with a wooden spoon, gradually incorporating some of the flour from the sides, then coat the surface with the set-aside flour, and proceed according to the method detailed above.

Olive oil produces a softer crust.

Note: The initial mixing is hard work but avoid the temptation to add more water unless absolutely necessary. If, when you are kneading, the dough is sticky, it is too wet; in this case work more flour into the dough as you knead. A dough that is too wet will result in loaves on a baking sheet spreading instead of springing, and those in tins flopping over the sides.

Softcrust Wholemeal Bread★★

Extremely popular among the elderly and the very young, this bread has an excellent flavour as well as a pliable soft crust. I first discovered it in Wigton, Cumberland where it was served with the local home-made rum butter, but I believe the recipe is fairly widespread over the north of England.

The secret lies in the initial slow rise coupled with less yeast than normal. Any attempt to rush it will result in a disappointing loaf.

Although this recipe calls for a mixture of flours, wholemeal alone can be used without a proportion of white flour, but the potato flour is essential. The combination of flours gives a wholemeal crumb which is to the taste of many people who find all-wholemeal too strong and hearty.

The recipe makes five small loaves or fewer larger.

INGREDIENTS

1 teaspoon (5g) granulated dried yeast
1 teaspoon (5g) sugar
1¼ pints (700ml) warm water
2 lb (900g) strong white flour, unbleached if possible
1 lb (450g) stoneground wholemeal flour
3 tablespoons (45g) fine potato flour
2 teaspoons (10g) salt
2 eggs size 3
3 tablespoons (45ml) vegetable oil
1 tablespoon (15ml) warmed pasteurized honey

METHOD

Dissolve the yeast and sugar in the warm water and set aside to activate. It is ready for use when the surface is covered in frothy bubbles – usually about 15 minutes.

Sieve the flours and salt together into a large bowl.

Beat the eggs well in a separate bowl then gradually add the oil followed by the warmed honey. Beat all together thoroughly using an electric beater or liquidizer if possible, to get a smooth mixture.

When the yeast liquid is ready, add it to the eggs and whisk for a few minutes to ensure even dispersal.

Hand-mixing. Make a well in the centre of the flour, pour in the liquid and stir with a wooden spoon until a rather harsh, lumpy dough is obtained. Turn out on to a lightly floured surface for kneading.

Machine-mixing (using a dough hook). Put the liquid mixture into the bowl of the machine and mix on the lowest speed, gradually adding the flours a little at a time until all is in the bowl. When the dough has formed a ball adhering to the dough hook, increase the speed to about half the maximum and continue mixing for one minute, then turn it out on to a lightly floured surface for kneading.

From then on the methods are identical.

Knead for 200 strokes by which time the dough will be soft and silky. It should be not so dry that it crumbles whilst kneading, nor so wet that it is sticky. A little more water can be added if necessary at this stage, or extra flour to absorb excessive moisture.

Water is best added by wetting the hands as kneading progresses or by spraying with a hand spray. Extra flour can be incorporated by dusting the kneading surface as kneading progresses.

Return the dough to the bowl and cover with a damp cloth or greased polythene sheet, place it in a warm, draughtproof place to rise. This can take four or five hours at low temperatures but if the temperature is raised to speed up the rise the bread will be inferior. 80°F (27°C) is ideal but it is not necessary to be precise, the dough is correctly risen when it has doubled in bulk.

Turn it out on to a lightly floured surface and knead for a further 40 strokes. Allow the dough to rest for 10 minutes then divide it into equal portions according to size of loaves required.

Gently knead and form each portion into an elongated ball or torpedo, and place into a pre-greased tin, making sure the tin is no more than half filled.

Cover with a dry cloth and place the loaded tins in a warm, draughtproof place to prove which will take about half the time of the first rise. The bread is ready for the oven when the dome of each loaf has risen level with or just slightly above the rim of the tin.

Pre-heat the oven to 475°F (240°C, Gas Mark 9), place the loaves on the centre shelf and bake for 20 minutes before reducing the temperature to 425°F (220°C, Gas Mark 7). Bake for a further 25 minutes before testing.

Do not over-cook, a total baking time of 45 minutes is adequate for most ovens at the stated temperatures. Not only will a harder crust result from over-cooking but the crumb can become harsh and dry and the entire character of the bread ruined.

Remove the bread from the tins and set on to a wire rack to cool.

VARIATIONS

Golden syrup can be substituted for honey.

If olive oil is used for the vegetable oil it will slightly affect the flavour of the bread, some prefer it, others do not.

Rye Bread★★★

Centuries ago rye was one of the staple grains grown in England together with wheat to form the crop known as 'maslin'; today rye is still widely used in Eastern Europe, Scandinavia and the old USSR, but in England its popularity is mainly among Polish and Jewish communities close to the major cities, although some health food shops and a few bakeries do stock rye bread.

Rye grains are subject to a fungal disease called ergot which can be fatal to humans if it gets into the flour; fortunately it is almost unknown in Britain.

Baking with rye is much more difficult and demanding than with wheat flour and the first requirement is freshness. Rye grains must be freshly ground and after grinding stored in a refrigerator until required for use where the flour will be good for a maximum of six weeks. It must be brought up to room temperature before using. Rye flour is sold by most health food shops but only buy from one with a rapid turnover – if it has stood on the shop shelf for six weeks without refrigeration it will be inferior.

Machine mixing is not recommended for rye bread, it is too fast and if overmixed or overheated the crumb will be short and brittle.

Bread made entirely from rye presents almost insuperable problems to the home baker so I have concentrated upon rye/wheat mixtures which give a better chance of success. The proportions can be varied, and recipes using mostly wheat flour with just a little rye can be handled in the usual way for wheat bread, but if more than about 15% of rye is used special treatment will be required including a slower, gentler mix with the liquid being added gradually and over a longer period of time. Even a very small amount of rye flour added to the wheat will result in a much denser crumb.

Kneading is another area where extra care is important for although rye dough does require kneading, the process must stop when it begins to get sticky, sometimes after only 100 or 150 strokes depending on the ratio of rye to wheat flour. Exact liquid measurement is not possible with rye, it is a matter of getting as much water as possible into the dough before it becomes sticky, adding the water gradually and watching the dough all the time until the required consistency is reached. The more rye in the recipe the more water will be required.

Rye dough must be kept cool or it will ferment – 70°F (21°C) should be regarded as the maximum, lower if you can allow the extra time it will take to rise. The dough is more fragile than wheat dough and must be handled throughout more carefully when kneading and shaping. All manual operations should be performed on a damp surface (not floured) and the hands kept moist to prevent sticking.

Rye takes longer to rise than wheat dough, and because of this there is a risk of under-or over-proving. When correctly proven it will feel spongy and will expand (spring) rapidly when placed in the oven although bread that has been underproven is still quite good although the crumb will be denser.

It is usual to bake rye bread on a baking tray in the form of a torpedo but this presents problems for the beginner because rye bread tends to spread and crack and for this reason I suggest using tins initially. Control of oven temperatures is important; violent variations in temperature will affect the bread, as will hot spots in the oven, and you are advised against opening the oven door for the first half-hour of baking.

Rye bread cannot be hurried; if you begin mixing at 7 a.m. it is quite possible to be baking fourteen hours later if the risings have been slow, but it is the slow rise which gives the best results.

Finally, do make certain the bread is thoroughly cooked – underbaked rye bread is about as palatable as undercooked potatoes!

The recipe makes five small loaves, three large ones, or if you are tray-baking, any size you wish.

INGREDIENTS

1 tablespoon (15g) granulated dried yeast
¼ pint (150ml) warm water
1 lb (450g) rye flour
2 lb (900g) strong white flour, unbleached if possible
1 tablespoon (15g) carob powder
1 tablespoon (15g) salt

Plus, mixed together,
¼ pint (150ml) warm water
2 tablespoons (30ml) golden syrup or pasteurized honey
2 tablespoons (30ml) cider vinegar
2 tablespoons (30ml) vegetable oil

A little extra warm water for kneading.

METHOD

Dissolve the yeast in the warm water. It is ready to use when the surface of the liquid is covered in frothy bubbles. Allow plenty of time because without sugar it will take longer to develop.

Meanwhile sieve the flours, salt and carob powder together into a large bowl and mix thoroughly with a wooden spoon. Make a well in the middle of the bowl and pour in the activated yeast liquid followed by the rest of the liquid ingredients. Mix thoroughly until a stiff, crumbly dough results, more like gravel than dough and prone to falling apart when handling.

Turn out on to a dampened surface and attempt gentle kneading with damp, cool hands. At first it will seem to be almost impossible to knead with bits of dough breaking away at every move, but gradually as more warm water is incorporated from hands and surface the dough will begin to hold together and soften slightly. Knead slowly and gently for 100–150 strokes (rye dough must not be overkneaded) by which time it will begin to feel slightly sticky.

Gently roll the dough into a ball and return it to the bowl for rising in a draughtfree place at a temperature of between 70° and 75°F (21° and 24°C), covering the bowl with a damp cloth or polythene film.

Rye dough must rise slowly so allow at least four hours for it to double in volume at about 70°F (21°C) and as much as six or eight hours at lower temperatures. Any attempt to expedite the rise will ruin the bread.

When the dough has doubled in bulk turn it out on to a dampened surface again and knead gently for another 50 strokes adding water if required, then return it to the bowl for the second rise which will take about half as long as the first.

Again turn it out on to a dampened surface and knead for another 50 strokes, adding more water as before if necessary until a smooth but slightly sticky consistency results. Divide into two, three or more portions according to the required size of loaf and carefully roll each portion into a ball then into a torpedo shape. If traditional tray-baked loaves are required place the portions on a tray, fairly close together to prevent them spreading more than necessary; if to be tin-baked half-fill the warm, greased tins then set to prove covered with a dry cloth in a warm draughtproof place until the dough has risen level with the top of the tins.

Pre-heat the oven to 425°F (220°C, Gas Mark 6) at least an hour before it is needed and place a vessel capable of holding at least one pint of boiling water on the floor of the oven. Rye breads respond to steam with a better flavour and more open texture derived from a higher 'spring'.

The loaves should be sprayed with warm water just before being put into the oven. After 15 minutes reduce the temperature to 400°F (200°C, Gas Mark 6) and by 25°F (13°C, 1 gas setting) every 5 minutes until it is down to 300°F (150°C, Gas Mark 2). The bread will take about an hour to bake, longer if the loaves are large. Once the temperature is down to 300°F (150°C, Gas Mark 2) you can open the oven, re-spray, and move the bread around to compensate for any high or low spots, but this should be a rapid operation done once only.

When the bread appears to be cooked, take one loaf and tap the base with the fingertips; if it sounds hollow and the sides feel crisp when gently squeezed, it is done; if not return all the loaves to the oven upside down (out of their tins) and bake for a further 10 minutes at 350°F (180°C, Gas Mark 4).

Cool the loaves on a wire rack for at least an hour before cutting.

Caution Steam is dangerous and great care must be exercised when opening the oven door or severe scalding can result. Always use oven gloves and keep your face away from the rush of steam which will burst out as the oven is opened. Keep children well away.

VARIATIONS

The ratio of rye to wheat flour can be adjusted to individual taste but remember the greater the rye content the more water will be required, and the denser and darker the crumb.

Caraway, dill or cumin seeds can be added to the flours at the same time as the salt but only small quantities are recommended – try a tablespoon (15g) of either until you discover the strength which suits you.

The traditional glaze on rye loaves is obtained by mixing 1 oz (30g) of cornflour with ½ pint (280ml) boiling water and stirring briskly for 5 minutes until it is quite clear. The crust is brushed with this rather thick liquid just before the loaves are put into the oven and again as they are taken out. If the loaves are to be glazed it is not necessary to spray them with water.

Rye bread has a habit of cracking during baking, especially if the cook has been a little heavy-handed during the kneading. A crack can often be concealed by slashing the surface but this must be done *after* the bread has baked for 35 minutes but as soon after as it is seen to be cracking, and as quickly as possible. The illustration shows such a loaf with the crack disguised.

Peasant's Potato Bread★★

At a time when only the wealthy were able to afford to eat white bread, this was the staple loaf of the labouring classes – or as near as we can get to it using modern ingredients and methods. Of all the recipes using potatoes this is one of the most popular, and probably the easiest to make; the crumb is coarse-textured and rather moist with a well-defined flavour. It is excellent toasted, stores and freezes well. The dough can be baked in tins or on a baking tray – I prefer the latter because it then yields a beautiful oval slice which seems more in keeping with its peasant origins. Makes two small loaves or one large.

INGREDIENTS

½ lb (225g) mashed potato
1 teaspoon (5g) sugar
2 teaspoons (10g) granulated dried yeast
½ pint (280ml) warm water
½ pint (280ml) natural yogurt
1 lb (450g) stoneground wholemeal flour
½ lb (225g) strong white flour, unbleached if possible
1 teaspoon (5g) salt
2 tablespoons (30ml) olive oil

METHOD

Boil the potatoes in their skins. When cool, peel and mash thoroughly making sure no lumps remain. Weigh out exactly ½ lb (225g) *after* mashing.

Dissolve the sugar and yeast in the warm water and set

aside to activate. It is ready for use when the surface is covered in frothy bubbles.

Mix the yogurt into the mashed potato and beat until a smooth batter results.

Sieve the flours and salt together into a large bowl and mix thoroughly.

When the yeast liquid is ready add the olive oil to it and whisk until a smooth emulsion is obtained with no separated globules of oil visible, then add this to the potato batter and beat until it is smooth and creamy.

Pour this liquid into the flour and stir with a wooden spoon until a rather coarse, lumpy dough is obtained. Turn this out on to a firm surface and knead for 200 strokes. The surface may need to be lightly floured to prevent sticking, but keep the flour to a minimum. However, if the dough is *very* sticky you will have to knead more flour into it, a wet dough will be impossible to tray-bake.

Form into a ball and place into a lightly oiled bowl, cover with a dry cloth overlaid with a damp one, and put into a warm place to rise. It is ready to use when it has doubled in bulk – usually between one and two hours according to the temperature.

When ready, turn out again and knead for a further 100 strokes, divide into two equal portions (or leave entire if a large loaf is required), roll each portion into a ball and either set out on a warmed, greased and floured baking tray, or place into warmed, greased tins which should be no more than half full. Cover with a *dry* cloth and put into a warm draughtproof place to prove. The bread is ready for the oven when it has doubled in volume or has risen so that the dome is level with the top edge of the tin.

Bake on the centre shelf of an oven pre-heated to 400°F (200°C, Gas Mark 6) for 45 minutes before testing by tapping the base of a loaf with the fingertips – if it is done it will sound hollow. Cool on a wire rack. Do not slice for at least two hours.

VARIATIONS

The addition of ½ oz (15g) caraway seeds to the flour before the liquids are incorporated appeals to some people but completely alters the character of the bread.

Authentic Peasant's Potato Bread would have used entirely wholemeal flour; the inclusion of a proportion of white flour is optional.

Note: If the potatoes are peeled *before* boiling they will absorb too much water.

The Rothes Loaf★★★

This bread is almost unknown in England, and even in Scotland it was rapidly disappearing from the shops before the First World War. The reason is not difficult to discover; although extremely popular with the buying public it required a great deal of skill in production usually necessitating the attention of the owner/baker himself. The scoring of the loaf before baking can make or mar the appearance of the bread: if the cuts are too deep they will open out too much in the baking, too shallow and they will appear as scars on the crust rather than cuts.

There was still one baker occasionally producing the Rothes Loaf in Elgin until 1942, but this was really a case of a skilled craftsman keeping his hand in in the hope that eventually his son would take over from him. Whether this came to pass I cannot say but the last time I was in Elgin the bakery had vanished.

Success depends upon the dough having just the right water content, and the knife cuts being even and at the correct depth. This is not a recipe where perfect results can be guaranteed but the loaf is always edible even though its appearance may be faulty. Because the absorption rates of flour vary, the amount of water in the ingredients can only be taken as a guide.

The recipe makes about four oval loaves according to size required. The bread keeps well and can be frozen.

INGREDIENTS

1¼ pints (700ml) warm milk and water (mixed)
2 teaspoons (10g) granulated dried yeast

2 teaspoons (10g) sugar
2 lb (900g) strong white flour (unbleached if possible)
1 lb (450g) stoneground wholemeal flour
4 teaspoons (20g) salt
3 oz (90g) lard
1 oz (30g) caraway seeds

METHOD

Dissolve the yeast and sugar in the warm water and milk and set aside to activate; it is ready for use when the surface is covered in frothy bubbles.

Sieve the flours and salt together into a large bowl and rub in the lard until it resembles fine breadcrumbs. Add the caraway seeds and mix in thoroughly.

Make a well in the flour and pour in the yeast liquid, stir with a wooden spoon until a rough dough is produced. It will feel harsh and lumpy at this stage, but do not add more water.

Turn out on to a lightly floured surface and knead for 200 strokes by which time the dough should be soft and silky. If it is sticky knead in more flour; if after 200 strokes it still feels harsh add a teaspoon of warm water and continue kneading until it is absorbed.

Form the dough into a ball and return it to the bowl. Cover with a damp cloth and set to rise in a warm place until it has doubled in bulk; this will take about an hour at 70°F (21°C), longer at lower temperatures.

When properly risen turn the dough out again and knead for a further 200 strokes. Allow to rest for 10 minutes then divide into four equal portions and form each piece into a rounded oval tucking the edges underneath.

Place the loaves on a lightly greased baking tray with sufficient space between each to ensure they cannot touch as they expand, and place uncovered in a warm draughtproof place to prove, which will take about half the time of the first rise if the temperature is the same. The loaves are ready for the oven when they have doubled in bulk.

Pre-heat the oven to 450°F (230°C, Gas Mark 8) and just before placing the loaves in the oven make a series of parallel cuts across the dome of each loaf about ¼ in (6mm) deep using a razor blade or sharp knife. If the blade is dipped in water between each cut it will not drag the dough and the cuts will be sharp and clean.

Bake on the centre shelf of the oven for about 45 minutes or until the loaves sound hollow when tapped on the base with the fingertips. Cool on a wire tray.

VARIATION

Margarine can be substituted for the lard.

Note: If the dough is too slack (contains too much liquid) the bread will spread as it bakes and look more like a large bap when it comes out of the oven.

Rothes bread makes particularly good toast especially when spread with marmalade.

The Dornoch Rumpy★★★

This is a variation on the Rothes Loaf which has suffered the same fate and for similar reasons.

Proceed exactly as for the Rothes Loaf but form the dough into a ball instead of an oval, tucking the edges underneath so that a smooth round dome is produced.

After proving and just before the bread goes into the oven, cut it one way as before, then make more cuts at right angles. Bake exactly as the Rothes Loaf.

German Potato Bread★★

The addition of potatoes to wheat flour has been widespread in northern and eastern European cultures almost since their arrival from America in the sixteenth century.

Why it is relatively unknown in Britain I cannot say, but the following recipe will dispel any doubts about the quality, lightness and keeping qualities of well-made potato bread.

The dough must be made from fresh flour and potatoes that have been carefully peeled to ensure that every eye and blemish, however small, has been removed. The variety *Maris Piper* is one of the best for this purpose because it breaks down and mashes well.

Attention to absolute cleanliness is essential or there is a very small risk of encountering the disease known as 'rope' (*bacillus mesentericus*) which is not destroyed during the baking process but continues to multiply inside the crumb, devouring it until nothing is left but a slimy, hollow crust, invisible until the loaf is sliced. 'Ropy' bread is almost a thing of the past if normal precautions are taken, the main source of infection being stale flour.

Some recipes call for left-over mashed potato to be used but this yields an inferior crumb because of the extra liquid absorbed by mashed potato prepared in the usual way. If you wish to try potato bread begin by preparing the ingredients correctly and you will be rewarded with a loaf which is light and moist, and having a subtle semi-sweet flavour.

In the opinion of many, potato bread makes the best of all toast and is also very good for sandwiches. This recipe makes two large loaves or three small ones.

INGREDIENTS

½ lb (225g) mashed potato (weighed *after* mashing)
1 tablespoon (15g) granulated dried yeast
¼ pint (150ml) warm water
¼ pint (150ml) fresh natural yogurt
2 tablespoons (15ml) pasteurized honey
2 tablespoons (15ml) olive oil (or other vegetable oil)
1 lb (450g) strong white flour (unbleached if possible)
1 lb (450g) stoneground wholemeal flour

2 oz (60g) kibbled wheat grains
1 tablespoon (15g) salt
extra warm water as needed

METHOD

Carefully inspect the potatoes and discard any showing blemishes or damage to the skin where water can penetrate during cooking. Wash them thoroughly and boil in their skins until quite soft, drain and leave for a few minutes to cool before carefully peeling and cutting out all eyes and blemishes. It is essential that only perfect material is used. Mash thoroughly with a potato masher (a fork is not so efficient and will leave lumps) for several minutes until a floury consistency is obtained, then weigh out the ½ lb (225g) required for the recipe.

Dissolve the yeast and honey in the warm water and leave to activate. It is ready for use when the surface is covered in frothy bubbles.

Sieve the flours and salt together into a large bowl, add the kibbled wheat and mix thoroughly.

Hand-mixing. Add the yogurt and oil to the mashed potato. Mix all together until a smooth paste results, then add the yeast liquid and stir with a wooden spoon until thoroughly mixed.

Mix the flours, salt and kibbled wheat in a large bowl and make a well in the centre. Pour in the liquids and stir with a wooden spoon until thoroughly mixed.

If necessary a little extra warm water can be added at this stage but it should be spooned in sparingly, the mixture must not become sticky.

Turn the dough out on to a lightly floured surface for kneading.

Machine-mixing using a dough hook. Place the mashed potato in the mixer bowl, add the yogurt and oil and mix on the lowest speed until all ingredients are thoroughly incorporated. Add the yeast mixture and continue mixing on the lowest speed until a smooth, creamy consistency is obtained.

Gradually add the flour a tablespoon (15g) at a time until it is all in the bowl and continue mixing on the slow speed until it has formed into a ball on the dough hook. If necessary a little extra warm water can be added at this stage if it is felt that the dough is too crumbly to adhere to the dough hook, but be careful it does not become sticky. It should be rather dry and crumbly before the speed is increased to about half the maximum and the machine run for a full two minutes after which the dough can be turned out on to a lightly floured surface for kneading.

From then on the methods are identical.

After kneading for 200 strokes the dough should become soft and pliable, if it is not, a little warm water can be added by moistening the hands and the surface and working it into the dough as kneading continues. The dough needs a total kneading of 400 strokes by which time it will be smooth and elastic but not sticky.

Form it into a ball and return to the bowl, cover with a damp cloth or polythene film and set to rise in a warm, draughtproof place for between one and two hours according to the temperature.

When the dough has doubled in bulk turn it out on to a lightly floured surface and knead for 20 strokes, form into a ball and return it to the bowl for a further rise in the warm, draughtproof place, covering it as before.

When it has again doubled in volume (this will take about half the time of the first rise), turn it out on to the lightly floured surface again, and divide it into equal portions as required.

Each portion should now be kneaded for a further 20 strokes, then formed into a torpedo shape by rolling on the surface before being placed into a warmed and greased tin. Tins must be no more than half filled to allow for proving.

Place the filled tins in a warm, draughtproof place for about 30 minutes or longer according to the temperature – a slow rise is not detrimental to the bread. Cover with a dry cloth.

When the dough has risen to the top edge of the tin it is ready for the oven.

Pre-heat the oven to 350°F (180°C, Gas Mark 4) and bake the bread on the centre shelf for about one hour. Test by taking a loaf out of its tin and tapping the base with the fingertips – if it sounds hollow it is done.

VARIATIONS

The bread can be made entirely of wholemeal or white flour if preferred but if entirely of wholemeal it will probably need a little more water.

Golden syrup can be substituted for the honey.

Loaves can be tray-baked if preferred but more skill is required initially to determine the correct rising at each stage. I recommend using tins for a first attempt.

A light dusting with self-raising flour over the tops of the loaves before they go into the oven gives an attractive finish, or you can decorate with knife cuts in the usual way.

The kibbled wheat can be omitted but the traditional character of the bread will be lost.

Slapdash Bread★

I was given this recipe by an elderly Herefordshire lady who, in her youth, had been employed in the kitchens of a Russian princess who had come to England to escape the horrors of the Russian Revolution. Whether the recipe originated in Russia or England is unknown, but we do know that this was the bread the cook prepared for the staff's consumption – the princess and her family ate white bread prepared by the regular kneading method.

By the time the cook had made the bread for her mistress and prepared breakfast for the family and staff she would have had to begin preparing lunch, and although not alone in the kitchen (at least four other women were employed there) she would have had little spare time for making bread for the staff, so it is quite possible that she devised this recipe to make her workload a little lighter.

Slapdash Bread requires the absolute minimum of time and effort to produce an acceptable loaf. I have adjusted the recipe to use modern ingredients but the basis remains the same as that used over seventy years ago (except that it is unlikely that any white flour would have been included).

The most important part is the mixing and, if this is to be done by hand with a wooden spoon, it can be a tiresome and lengthy business so I recommend using a food mixer fitted with a dough hook. Makes five small loaves or fewer larger.

INGREDIENTS

1¼ pints (700ml) warm water
4 teaspoons (20g) dried granulated yeast
4 teaspoons (20g) sugar
6 tablespoons (90ml) sunflower oil
2 lb (900g) stoneground wholemeal flour
1 lb (450g) strong white flour, unbleached if possible
2 heaped tablespoons (35g) potato flour
1 tablespoon (15g) salt

METHOD

Put the sugar and yeast into the warm water, stir to disperse, then allow to stand until the surface is covered in frothy bubbles. When the liquid is ready, pour it into the bowl of the machine, add the oil and mix on a fairly high speed for a few minutes until it is thoroughly emulsified.

Sieve the flours and salt together. Reduce the mixer speed to slow and gradually spoon the flour into the bowl. Continue mixing slowly until the flour and liquid are thoroughly combined then increase the speed almost to the maximum and run for a full minute.

Turn the dough out on to a floured surface and divide between five small tins or fewer larger. This is a very wet sticky dough and cannot be kneaded. The tins must not be much more than half full or the dough will flop over the edges as it rises, resulting in a mushroom loaf.

Set to rise in a warm, draughtproof place, and watch carefully to see that the dough does not rise too high. When it has risen level with the top of the tins it is ready for baking.

Bake on the centre shelf of an oven pre-heated to 425°F (220°C, Gas Mark 7) for about 45 minutes or until a loaf sounds hollow when tapped on the base with the knuckles, remove from tins and stand loaves on a wire rack to cool.

Slapdash loaves have rather flatter tops than conventional bread, but although the 'doming' is slight a 'spring' is still easily achieved, and the crumb light and open. If the top crust 'sinks' the mixture was too wet – adjust at the next baking.

Ignoring the time allowed for rising and baking, the actual time spent in manual work is less than 15 minutes, and most of that is spent in operating the mixer and weighing out the ingredients.

This bread cannot be tray-baked.

VARIATIONS

The ratio of white to wholemeal flour can be varied to suit individual tastes. Most other vegetable oils can be substituted for sunflower but if you wish to use any solid fat (lard would probably have been used in the past) it must first be melted and added to the warm water at a temperature which will not allow it to coagulate before being emulsified, yet not so hot as to destroy the action of the yeast.

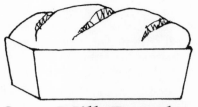

Soya Milk Bread★★

This bread rises exceptionally well to give an open fluffy crumb and a fine dark but softish crust. It keeps well and can be frozen for about two months. Soya milk is obtainable from health food shops and most supermarkets. This recipe makes two large loaves or three small ones.

INGREDIENTS

¾ pint (420ml) fresh soya milk
4 tablespoons (60ml) vegetable oil
2 tablespoons (30ml) pasteurized honey
1 tablespoon (15g) granulated dried yeast
¼ pint (140ml) warm water
1 lb (450g) strong white flour, unbleached if possible
1 lb (450g) stoneground wholemeal flour
2 teaspoons (10g) salt

METHOD

Boil the soya milk and simmer for 2 minutes then cool to lukewarm (about 70°F, 21°C). When the correct temperature is reached stir in half the honey and the oil and whisk vigorously until a creamy smooth emulsion is obtained.

Dissolve the yeast and the rest of the honey in the warm water and set aside to activate; it is ready for use when the surface is covered in frothy bubbles.

Sieve the flours and salt together into a large mixing bowl.

Hand-mixing. Make a well in the centre of the flour, pour in all the liquids and stir with a wooden spoon to mix. Add a little more warm water if necessary to produce a soft dough but it must not become sticky.

Machine-mixing using a dough hook. Put the activated

yeast mixture into the machine bowl and add the soya/honey/oil liquid, mix on the slowest speed and gradually add the flour one tablespoon at a time until it is all in the bowl. When all is thoroughly incorporated increase the speed to near-maximum and run for 2 minutes adding a little more warm water if required to make a soft dough.

From now on the methods are identical.

Turn out the dough on to a lightly floured surface and knead vigorously for 300 strokes (this is one of the few recipes where rapid kneading is important). Form into a ball and put into a warm place to rise. Soya doughs usually rise quite fast, so check after 30 minutes. When the dough has doubled in volume, turn it out on to the lightly floured surface, deflate by pressing with the palms of the hands, and divide into two large portions or three small as required.

Put into warmed, greased tins and return to a warm place for proving, preferably at a slightly higher temperature (80°F, 27°C). Cover with a dry cloth.

When the domes of the loaves are arched above the tins they are ready for the oven. If the tops are then slashed diagonally with a sharp knife the bread will spring higher in the oven and the crumb be more open.

Place the loaves on the centre shelf of an oven pre-heated to 350°F (180°C, Gas Mark 4) and bake for about 45 minutes.

Test in the usual way by tapping the base of a loaf with the fingertips, if it sounds hollow it is done, if not give it a further 10 minutes or so before testing again.

VARIATIONS

Instead of the mixture of white and wholemeal flours either can be used on its own; however all wholemeal will give a strong flavour which rather obscures the delicate soya taste.

2 oz (55g) butter can be used instead of the oil but it will have to be added after kneading has proceeded for 200 strokes. It is then shredded straight from the freezer and worked into the dough as kneading continues. This is not a method I would recommend unless necessary for dietary reasons; it makes a lot of extra work and, if not done thoroughly, can result in a very uneven crumb.

Crusty Cracked Wheat Bread★★

Cracked wheat can be used in several ways to suit individual tastes. In this recipe it is soaked in boiling water for ten minutes before being added to the flour, and this gives a soft, chewy grain content, only just noticeable when eating and nearly invisible in the slice. If you prefer the grains more crunchy, reduce the time they are in soak. You can even do away with the soaking altogether and use them straight from the packet – if you are prepared to risk a few broken teeth! The recipe makes five small loaves or fewer larger with a crisp crust which complements the grains in the crumb. It keeps well, and can be frozen.

INGREDIENTS

12 fl.oz (340ml) boiling water
¼ lb (110g) cracked wheat grains
1 pint (550ml) warm water
2 teaspoons (10g) granulated dried yeast
2 teaspoons (10g) sugar
2 lb (900g) strong white flour, unbleached if possible
½ lb (225g) stoneground wholemeal flour
2 teaspoons (10g) salt
2 oz (55g) lard

METHOD

Pour the boiling water over the cracked wheat and set aside to soak for 10 minutes, then drain and cool.

Dissolve the sugar and yeast in the warm water, stir slightly and set aside to activate. It is ready for use when the surface is covered in frothy bubbles.

Sieve the flours and salt together into a large bowl; rub the lard into the flour until it resembles fine breadcrumbs.

Hand-mixing. Add the cracked wheat to the yeast liquid and pour all into the flour. Mix with a wooden spoon until a rough dough results.

Machine-mixing using a dough hook. Prepare the ingredients as for hand-mixing, then put the yeast liquid into the mixer bowl and add the cracked wheat. Start the machine at its lowest speed and gradually add the flour mixture until it is all in the bowl. Continue mixing until a ball is formed on the dough hook, then increase the speed to about half the maximum and run for a full 2 minutes.

From then on the methods are identical.

Turn the dough out on to a lightly floured surface and knead for 200 strokes by which time it will become smooth and silky.

Form into a ball and set into a warmed bowl. Cover with a damp cloth and put into a warm, draughtproof place to rise which will take about an hour at 70°F (21°C).

When the dough has doubled in volume turn it out and knead for a further 100 strokes. Form into a ball, and again return it to the warm place for the second rise, covering as before.

This second rise will take about half as long as the first at the same temperature. When the dough has again doubled in volume knead for 20 strokes, then divide it into five equal portions (or less if larger loaves are required) and roll each portion into a ball.

Knead each ball for a few strokes, then form into torpedo shapes and half-fill pre-warmed and greased tins, or set out on a greased baking tray.

Put the tins or trays into a warm, draughtproof place to prove. When the dome of each loaf has risen level with the top of the tin, or the trayed loaves have doubled in volume, they are ready for the oven.

Place them on the centre shelf of an oven pre-heated to 450°F (230°C, Gas Mark 8) and bake for 15 minutes, then reduce the temperature to 400°F (200°C, Gas Mark 6) and bake for a further 15 minutes before removing the loaves from their tins. Continue baking for a further 15 minutes without tins to produce the crisp crust. (The tray-baked loaves will be crisp anyway.)

Test by tapping the base of a loaf with the fingertips, if it sounds hollow the bread is done. Cool on a wire rack.

VARIATIONS

The ratio of white to wholemeal flour can be varied to suit individual tastes.

The longer the cracked wheat is soaked the less water will be required in the mix. This recipe is about right for a ten-minute soaking; any longer and you will need to reduce the quantity of warm water to be incorporated, a shorter soaking time may need a little more water. If the dough becomes sticky, add more flour, if it is dry and crumbly (after the first kneading) add more water a teaspoon (5ml) at a time.

Camper's Pan Bread★★★

The advantage of this bread is that it can be baked over almost any kind of fire in a 10-inch frying-pan or any similar vessel. It will not keep but should be eaten whilst still hot, preferably spread with fresh or garlic butter. It is not particularly difficult to make but needs constant attention during cooking to be successful, which is why I have given it three stars.

INGREDIENTS

8 oz (225g) strong white flour, unbleached if possible
5 teaspoons (25g) fresh baking powder (not soda)
2 teaspoons (10g) sugar
1 teaspoon (5g) salt
2 oz (55g) lard
½ pint (280ml) warm water

METHOD

Sieve the flour, baking powder, sugar and salt together into a large bowl, making sure they are thoroughly mixed. Cut the lard into small pieces and rub into the mixture until it resembles fine breadcrumbs. Add the water and mix to a smooth batter.

Grease a 10-in frying-pan (or other suitably heavy vessel) and set it on a low heat.

Pour the mixture into the pan and cook it *slowly* keeping the heat *very* low. The bread will gradually begin to rise. When it has stopped rising (this will take quite a time) examine it to see if it has browned on the bottom; if it has, turn it over in the pan and cook the other side even though it still seems rather wet.

Each side usually needs about 35 minutes to cook but overcooking is preferable to undercooking. If it takes longer the bread will rise better, but if it is not fully risen before the bottom is browned it will be heavy, as it will if baked over a fire that is too hot.

Camper's Pan Bread is delicious eaten with barbecued chicken, sausages, bacon, eggs, fish, etc., or as a substitute for the beefburger bun.

VARIATIONS

Margarine can be substituted for the lard, and a proportion of stoneground wholemeal flour can be included.

Note: Failures with this recipe are usually caused by stale baking powder or cooking over too intense heat. To overcome the latter I set a trivet over the source of heat so that the frying-pan never comes into direct contact with the flame or electric element.

Do ensure that the pan is very thoroughly greased; if the bread sticks it will be impossible to turn it without breaking – and re-grease the pan before cooking the second side.

Nutty Rosemary Bread★

You can mix and chop your own nuts for this recipe, and can then be certain they are fresh. However, I normally use ready-chopped nuts because I can get them from a local delicatessen which has a rapid turnover. Stale chopped nuts can host moulds which, although invisible, can adversely affect the bread.

This is a variation of an old Derbyshire recipe given to me by an elderly lady who had acquired it from her grandmother, Rosemary Milden, so it is probably at least a hundred years old. The delicate aroma, open crumb and slightly nutty texture make it a great favourite with all who have tried it, and it is one of the easiest fancy breads to bake. It also freezes well.

The recipe makes five small loaves or fewer larger, or it will make about eighteen 3-oz rolls.

INGREDIENTS

1½ pints (830ml) warm water
4 teaspoons (20g) granulated dried yeast
4 teaspoons (20g) sugar
2 lb (900g) stoneground wholemeal flour
1 lb (450g) strong white flour, unbleached if possible
¼ lb (110g) potato flour
4 teaspoons (20g) salt
2 oz (55g) dried rosemary (or double quantity fresh)
5 tablespoons (75ml) olive oil
3 oz (90g) fresh chopped mixed nuts

METHOD

Dissolve the yeast and sugar in the warm water and set aside to activate. The mixture is ready for use when the surface is covered in frothy bubbles.

Sift the flours and salt into a large bowl and mix thoroughly. Add the rosemary and mix in.

Slightly warm the olive oil and whisk it into the fermented yeast liquid until it is emulsified – use a liquidizer if you have one.

Gently toast the chopped nuts under a grill until they are a light golden brown, set aside to cool, then mix into the flour.

Hand-mixing. When the yeast liquid is ready add it to the flour in the bowl and mix well with a wooden spoon at first, finishing by hand.

Turn the dough out on to a lightly floured surface and knead for 200 strokes, then form into a ball and place in a large, warm, oiled bowl for its first rise. Cover with a damp cloth and set in a warm place for about an hour or until the dough has doubled in volume.

Machine-mixing using a dough hook. Warm the bowl of the mixer and the dough hook. Pour the fermented yeast liquid and olive oil into the mixer bowl and run the machine at the lowest speed until a smooth emulsion results.

Gradually spoon in the flour mixture and continue mixing until all the ingredients are incorporated and evenly distributed, and have formed a ball on the dough hook. If after five minutes or so some dry flour remains in the bottom of the bowl you can add a teaspoon (5ml) of warm water but the dough must never become sticky.

When all the dough is attached to the hook increase the speed to near maximum and run for a full two minutes.

Turn the dough out on to a lightly floured surface and knead for 200 strokes, then form into a ball and place it into a large, lightly oiled warm bowl for its first rise, covering it with a damp cloth. Place in a warm place for about an hour or until it has doubled in volume.

From then on the methods are identical.

Turn the risen dough out on to a lightly floured surface and knead for a further 200 strokes. If it seems at all sticky work a little more flour into it as you knead. Then once more form it into a ball and return it to the bowl for its second rise in a warm place, covering as before with a damp cloth. The second rise will take about half the time of the first.

When it has again doubled in bulk, turn it out on to the lightly floured surface and knead for a further 40 strokes, then allow to rest for 10 minutes before dividing into five equal portions or three if larger loaves are required. Mould each piece of dough roughly to shape and half-fill warm greased tins, or set on to a greased baking tray.

The loaves must now be put into a warm, draughtproof place to prove, covered with a *dry* cloth. Those in tins will be ready for the oven when the dome of the dough has risen level with the top of the tins, those to be tray-baked will have doubled in volume.

Bake on the centre shelf of an oven pre-heated to 450°F (230°C, Gas Mark 8) for 15 minutes, then reduce the temperature to 400°F (200°C, Gas Mark 6) and bake for a further 30 minutes. Turn out one of the loaves and tap the base with the fingertips – if it sounds hollow the bread is done.

The top crust should be a pale golden colour and the sides about the same. If the sides and base seem too pale, bake upside down for a few more minutes (out of the tins). This recipe produces a fairly soft, pliable crust – if it is hard and crunchy it is overcooked and the crumb will be rather dry.

Cool the bread on a wire rack. It can be eaten two hours after leaving the oven when many people think it is at its best (still slightly warm) especially when combined with a savoury snack such as cheese and pickles, a poached egg, or complementing a home-made soup.

VARIATIONS

The ratio of white to wholemeal flour can be varied.

The correct amount of water to be used is a matter of feel and experience – the greater the wholemeal content the more water will be required and *vice versa*. The quantities listed can only be approximate but will seldom vary by more than a tablespoon (15ml).

The quantity of rosemary can be adjusted to suit individual taste but this recipe produces a pleasant mild aroma which seems to agree with the average palate. Add more or less as you please. The same applies to the nuts.

French Bread ★★★

Breadmaking is a national art in France but very few French housewives now bake their own bread. Even the smallest village will often have more than one bakery and every day at least one will be open for business. Mass-produced plastic bread *can* be found in supermarkets and chain stores, and this is no better or worse than the English product.

French bread is superb when fresh but deteriorates rapidly. It is best eaten within four hours of leaving the oven and no Frenchman ever eats bread a day old which is the reason why French bakers produce a regular succession of small batches throughout the day. The first job every morning is to collect the long baguettes from the bakery, and it seems to the overseas visitor that the entire population of France is on the move soon after daybreak with a supply of loaves under the arm or in the bicycle pannier *en route* to the breakfast table.

Don't expect the same quality of bread from every baker in France; as here, expertise and methods vary slightly from place to place, area to area. Some of the best I have tasted was in the St. Malo and Agen areas, the poorest in Quimper and Audierne. It pays to shop around.

French bread is considered inferior by English bakers because the crumb contains holes, some of them quite large, which make it difficult to spread with butter, but, of course, this is part of the character of the bread. By law all French bread must be made with at least 80% of flour ground from wheat grown in France which has a very low gluten content, and this necessitates a different approach to the whole process. The bread must be steam baked at a lower temperature than most other breads, and since no artificial bleaching of the flour is permitted the colour will be creamy rather than pristine white. Furthermore, no chemical improvers are permitted other than vitamin C (ascorbic acid).

When the bread is first put into the oven it is enveloped in a burst of scalding steam which is injected through pipes and cut off after about fifteen minutes, allowing the bread to rise unhindered by the formation of a crust. The water content is low because soft flour absorbs less water than strong flour.

French flour is almost unobtainable outside France so we have to improvise, but it is still possible to produce a fairly good representation of the real thing by careful attention to detail. Do bear in mind though that this bread deteriorates rapidly – it is best eaten soon after leaving the oven, and does not freeze well.

Several recipes recommend making a dough from strong white flour as for ordinary bread and simply stretching the dough to the length of a French loaf; this will produce a perfectly edible bread but it is not and will taste nothing like French bread. French bread cannot be rushed without spoiling; it is far better to start the dough working overnight so that its first rise is completed in the morning and the process then continued during the day. If you have little spare time French bread should only be attempted at a weekend or during a holiday period; it is very time-consuming and demands a great deal of attention.

Since very few British ovens can accommodate the length of a French baguette this recipe makes four batards.

INGREDIENTS

    4 teaspoons (20g) granulated dried yeast
    ¼ pint (140ml) warm water
    1 lb (450g) strong white flour, unbleached if possible
    2 lb (900g) plain white flour (not self-raising)
    2 teaspoons (10g) salt
    1 pint (550ml) chilled water

METHOD

Dissolve the yeast in the warm water and leave to activate. Note that since no sugar or other sweetener is used the yeast will take longer to ferment. It is ready for use when the surface is covered with frothy bubbles.

Sieve together the flours and salt into a large bowl, add half the cold water to the yeast liquid when it is working well, then pour it into a depression made in the centre of the flour and mix thoroughly with a wooden spoon. Try not to use the hands at this stage to avoid raising the temperature of the dough more than is absolutely necessary. Do not use a mixer for French bread; they overheat the dough, even on the lowest speed.

The dough will now be quite stiff and lumpy. Turn it out

on to a smooth surface and commence kneading, wetting the hands and surface with the remaining water from time to time until all the water is absorbed as kneading continues. Knead for at least 400 strokes but work slowly with frequent breaks so that the dough does not become overheated. If necessary an extra tablespoon of water can be added but be careful not to make it sticky. It should be smooth and silky to the touch.

Return it to the bowl and cover with a dampened cloth (if a greased polythene sheet is used it must not touch the dough at any stage) and place in a cool place to rise (max. temperature 65°F, 19°C) which will usually take four or five hours, possibly more. An increase in temperature will ruin the bread; it is better for the rise to take longer at a lower temperature. It can even be put into the refrigerator overnight.

The dough is correctly risen when a dampened finger pushed into it to a depth of ½ inch (12mm) leaves a depression which fills very slowly. It can now be deflated by turning out on to the working surface and gently pressing all over with the moistened flat of the hands, kneading gently for about 20 strokes before returning to the bowl for a second rise which, at the same temperature, will take two hours or more.

Test again by the same finger method and, when fully risen, turn out on to a lightly floured surface for dividing and shaping. It should now be bouncy, elastic and silky-soft.

BATARDS

For the classic French batard, divide the dough into three or four equal portions (depending upon the size of loaf preferred) and roll them into balls as you gently press to deflate. Fold the edges under and place them, edges underneath, on a lightly floured surface to rest until they are soft again (usually about 15 minutes but if the dough was at all sticky after the last operation they will need a little longer before the stickiness disappears). It is essential to keep them away from draughts – doors and windows opening at this stage can ruin the bread.

When fully soft each portion should be gently rolled by

hand on the working surface until it elongates to about twice as long as wide (longer if you wish). Set to prove in a warm, draught-free place (65°F, 19°C) for about 1 hour or until each loaf has doubled in size.

Whether the bread is baked in tins or on a baking tray it will stick to the surface unless it is greased but if any grease reaches the dough the bread will be ruined. So after thoroughly greasing, remove the surplus, then coat the surface with a fine covering of flour, making certain that every bit of grease is covered. Shake off the surplus flour and the tin or sheet is ready for use.

BAGUETTES

The long thin sticks of bread which form the main ingredient of a French breakfast are made from the same dough as for batards, but simply rolled out longer. When baked they will be approximately three times the diameter of the raw dough so aim to put into the oven unbaked loaves about 1 in or 1½ ins thick.

Special baking tins are obtainable for baguettes but as these are expensive you can make an acceptable alternative with sheets of aluminium baking foil formed into long narrow channels. Set the aluminium channels fairly close together to prevent the dough spreading as it proves (but allow room for expansion), and if you cut the foil generously you will be able to lift the loaves by the foil to prevent distortion. The foil must be liberally coated with flour to prevent sticking, or a floured tea-cloth will serve the same purpose.

The loaves will take an hour or more to prove and are ready for the oven when they have doubled in size. If you attempt to rush them the bread will be rubbery.

BAKING

French bread must be steam baked and there are several ways of achieving this, some more complicated than others. I use the following method with excellent results in an electric oven or Aga but it is near to impossible and very dangerous to try the same system with a gas oven.

You will need a heatproof dish to place in the bottom of the oven to hold about a pint of water; it can be of ovenproof glass, glazed earthenware, iron, etc. The dish will be subjected to considerable stress so avoid using anything valuable in case it breaks.

Pre-heat the oven to 475°F (240°C, Gas Mark 9) with the empty dish in place. Open the oven and half fill the dish with boiling water, quickly close the oven and wait 5 or 10 minutes for the interior to become filled with steam. If yours is a leaky oven it may be necessary to place the dish of water as high as possible in the oven before steam will be generated, or even one dish at the top and another at the bottom.

Take each proven loaf and spray with lukewarm water then quickly slash diagonal cuts down the length with a sharp knife. Open the oven and place the loaves on the centre shelf; spray all over the loaves and the interior walls of the oven before gently closing the door.

At 5-minute intervals open the oven carefully and respray the bread and the oven walls. Do this three times, then reduce the temperature to 350°F (180°C, Gas Mark 4) and bake until the bread is done.

CAUTION. Great care must be exercised when the oven door is opened to spray the bread for steam can cause severe scalding. Ensure that your arms are protected and that you

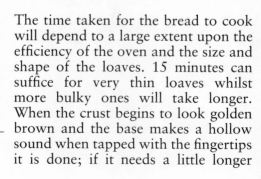

use efficient oven gloves, and that you keep your face well away from the rush of steam that will escape as the oven door is opened. *Children should be kept out of the kitchen.*

The time taken for the bread to cook will depend to a large extent upon the efficiency of the oven and the size and shape of the loaves. 15 minutes can suffice for very thin loaves whilst more bulky ones will take longer. When the crust begins to look golden brown and the base makes a hollow sound when tapped with the fingertips it is done; if it needs a little longer reduce the temperature slightly and remove the dish of water, then check again after 5 minutes.

Although French bread is at its best when eaten still warm from the oven, it should be placed on a wire rack to cool for about 30 minutes before being cut or broken – it will still be warm and crisp but if cut too early the crumb may collapse under the pressure of the knife.

VARIATIONS

The proportions of strong white flour to ordinary plain flour can be varied to suit individual taste, but I strongly recommend a trial period using the above recipe before experimenting.

Note: No fats or sugar are used in the making of French breads and it is essential that no kind of grease or oil comes into contact with the dough. The development of the dough depends upon a long slow rise.

Italian Foccacia★

This popular Italian flat bread can be baked plain or with many interesting additional ingredients. There are numerous recipes all claiming to be authentic; this one includes an assortment of fresh herbs, but dried herbs can be used with only a slight alteration to the flavour. The quantities of herbs have been left for the cook to decide because tastes vary so much – each time you bake Foccacia it can have a different flavour.

INGREDIENTS

1 teaspoon (5g) dried granulated yeast
1 teaspoon (5g) sugar
½ pint (280ml) warm water
1 lb (450g) strong white flour, unbleached if possible
1 teaspoon (5g) salt
4 tablespoons (60g) Parmesan cheese, freshly grated
2 cloves garlic, chopped
Basil, rosemary and sage or herbs of your choice, finely chopped or dried, in amounts to suit your taste, (1 teaspoon (5g) of each is a reasonable guide initially)
5 tablespoons (75ml) olive oil
12 black olives, pitted and chopped
Coarse salt and dried rosemary to finish

METHOD

Dissolve the yeast and sugar in the warm water and stir to activate. It is ready for use when the surface is covered in frothy bubbles.

Sieve the flour and salt together into a large bowl, add the grated cheese, garlic and herbs and mix thoroughly.

When the yeast mixture is ready, add the olive oil and whisk until a smooth emulsion results. Pour the liquid into the flour and mix with a wooden spoon until all the ingredients are evenly assimilated into a rough dough.

Turn the dough out on to a lightly floured surface and knead for 200 strokes by which time it will have become smooth and rather oily but not sticky. If necessary knead in extra flour.

Form the dough into a ball and return it to the bowl, cover with a dry cloth overlaid with a damp one, and put it into a warm place to rise at a temperature between 70° and 80°F (21° and 27°C). This will usually take about an hour.

When the dough has doubled in volume, knead for a further 100 strokes, cover and return to the warm place for another half-hour or so. When it has again doubled in volume knead for 20 strokes then divide into three equal portions.

Shape each piece into an oblong and roll out slightly with a rolling pin until a long oval about ½ in (12mm) thick results.

Set each on to a greased baking sheet and press hard all over the surface with your finger to make dimples.

Cover with a polythene sheet supported so it cannot touch the dough, and put into a warm place to prove for about 30 minutes or until almost doubled in size.

Brush with olive oil ensuring that each dimple is filled with oil, stud the surface with pieces of olive and sprinkle with the rosemary and a little coarse salt, before baking on the centre shelf of an oven pre-heated to 400°F (200°C, Gas Mark 6) for about 20 minutes. The bread should sound hollow when the base is tapped with the fingertips.

Foccacia can be eaten on its own or split and stuffed with tomatoes, peppers, cheese, etc.

VARIATIONS

The same mixture makes an excellent pizza base. After kneading and dividing the dough, form each piece into a ball, then roll out to make a circle of dough slightly smaller than the greased sandwich tin in which it is to be baked. Spread the dough with your chosen topping, cover and leave to rise for about 20 minutes, then bake for 15 to 20 minutes in an oven pre-heated to 425°F (220°C, Gas Mark 7).

Kentucky Corn Bread⋆

This savoury bread is a popular delicacy from the southern states of the USA. Almost every household seems to have its own individual recipe but this one is fairly standard today. Makes one large loaf or two small.

INGREDIENTS

3 oz (80g) maize flour (not cornflour)
4 oz (110g) self-raising flour, unbleached if possible
½ teaspoon (2.5g) salt
2 oz (55g) suet, animal or vegetable, shredded
½ pint (280ml) soya milk
3 eggs, size 3
Small green pepper, chopped
4 oz (110g) mature Cheddar cheese, grated
Small onion, chopped
½ teaspoon (2.5ml) English mustard freshly mixed
Small can sweetcorn, drained
Pepper to taste, black or white

METHOD

Sieve the flours and salt together into a large bowl and add the suet. Mix thoroughly with a wooden spoon. Warm the milk in a saucepan and stir in the flour mixture. Bring to the boil stirring constantly. Separate the eggs.

Remove the pan from the heat and stir in the chopped green pepper, cheese, egg yolks, onion, mustard and sweetcorn. Season to taste with pepper and return to the heat for 2 minutes.

Whisk the egg whites until quite stiff then fold into the mixture with a palette-knife.

Pour the mixture into well-greased loaf tins and bake on the centre shelf of an oven pre-heated to 400°F (200°C, Gas Mark 6) for about 45 minutes.

The bread is done when the top is firm and it has shrunk away from the sides a little. Test by tapping the base with the fingertips – if it sounds hollow remove it from the tin and set on a wire rack to cool.

Good eaten hot or cold with salad, as an accompaniment to a homemade soup, or as a base for poached egg on toast, etc.

Ciabatta★

A rather coarse-textured Italian bread with an uneven crisp crust. The distinctive olive oil flavour makes it good with cheese and as an accompaniment to many savoury dishes. It is easy to make with little kneading – too much kneading will alter the characteristic texture. This recipe makes one traditional divided loaf baked in a rectangular pan.

INGREDIENTS

1 teaspoon (5g) sugar
1 teaspoon (5g) granulated dried yeast
½ pint (280ml) warm water
1 lb (450g) plain white flour (*not* strong bread flour)
1 teaspoon (5g) salt
¼ pint (140ml) warm olive oil

METHOD

Dissolve the yeast and sugar in the warm water and set aside to activate. It is ready to use when the surface is covered in frothy bubbles.

Sieve the flour and salt together into a large warmed bowl.

When the yeast mixture is ready add the warm olive oil and whisk briskly until the oil is completely emulsified to yield a smooth creamy liquid.

Stir the liquid into the flour and, with a wooden spoon, mix just sufficiently to incorporate all the ingredients.

Turn the dough out on to a lightly floured surface and knead gently for 30 strokes, adding more flour if it seems at all sticky. After kneading the dough should still feel and look lumpy and coarse.

Divide the dough into three or more equal portions, shape each into a torpedo shape, and place them side by side in a well-greased oblong pan taking care not to smooth the surfaces – they should look rough.

Brush the tops with olive oil, and set aside in a warm place to prove, covering the loaves with a polythene sheet or dry cloth supported so that it cannot come into contact with the bread as it rises. At a temperature of 70–80°F (21–27°C) it will double in volume and be ready for the oven in about an hour.

Bake on the centre shelf of an oven pre-heated to 400°F (200°C, Gas Mark 6) for about 30 minutes. Test by tapping the base with the fingertips – if it sounds hollow it is done.

The bread should be cooled on a wire rack. The segments are pulled apart to serve (they separate easily) while still warm. If stored, the loaves should be put into a hot oven for a few minutes before pulling apart and serving – always store them whole or the sides where they have been in contact with each other will become dry and flaky.

VARIATIONS

Add two finely chopped cloves of garlic to the flour mixture before adding the liquids. This makes the most superb garlic bread. Use more or less garlic to suit your particular preference.

Before baking   After baking

Quick Dinner Bread★★

This bread is usually baked in a rectangular or circular dish, the size depending upon the thickness of bread required. A pan 10 x 8 ins (26 x 20cms) will produce bread about 1½ins (4cms) thick which is then cut into 2-in (5cms) squares and served still warm from the oven. Although it can be stored and frozen it rather loses its appeal because it tends to dry out quite quickly. Very little kneading is required but careful timing is necessary to have the bread ready exactly when required to accompany the meal.

INGREDIENTS

18 fl. oz (500ml) whole milk
1 teaspoon (5g) sugar
1 tablespoon (15g) granulated dried yeast
1 lb (450g) flour – stoneground wholemeal, strong white flour (unbleached if possible), or any mixture of the two
1 teaspoon (5g) salt
1 teaspoon (5g) ground caraway powder (optional)
1 oz (30g) block margarine (not low-fat spread)

METHOD

Scald the milk, cool to blood heat then add the sugar and yeast. Stir briefly to disperse, then set aside to activate; it is ready to use when the surface is covered in frothy bubbles.

Sieve the flour, salt and caraway powder (if used) into a large bowl and mix thoroughly. Melt the margarine over a low heat.

When the yeast liquid is ready add the melted margarine and whisk vigorously to get even dispersal.

Add the liquid to the flour and beat until a soft slack dough results – if you have a food processor it is ideal for this part of the process.

Turn the dough out into a warm bowl, cover with a damp cloth and stand in a warm place to rise for about 30 minutes or until it has doubled in bulk.

Knead for 50 strokes on a lightly floured surface, form into a ball and gently flatten with a rolling pin roughly into the shape of the dish you intend using. Carefully lay the pad of dough in the pre-warmed and greased dish and make deep cuts in it with a sharp knife to produce 2-in (5cms) squares. If the knife is lightly greased it will not 'pull' the dough.

Cover with a dry cloth and set into a warm, draughtproof place to prove. It is ready for the oven when it has doubled in volume, usually about 30-35 minutes.

Bake on the lower shelf of an oven pre-heated to 400°F (200°C, Gas Mark 6) for between 30 and 40 minutes.

Set to cool in one piece on a wire rack, pull apart just before serving so that the sides of each piece (the kiss crusts) are not beginning to dry.

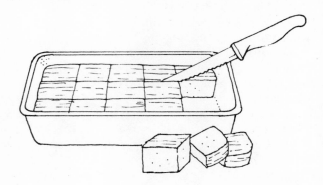

Sourdough Bread★★★

This is a great favourite with our American friends who claim that the best comes from San Francisco, but usually to British palates it is an acquired taste.

There are many different recipes for making sourdough bread, every one calling for a long period of preparation, but the one detailed here is probably the simplest for beginners, and the most likely to yield an acceptable loaf at the first attempt.

Before embarking on sourdough bread I suggest you purchase a ready-made loaf from a baker – if you really hate it there is no point in going ahead. It is not easy to find in Britain, but several local bakeries in Ireland make it regularly, usually in small batches. Having no experience with sourdough, I was instructed in the mysteries by a delightful Irish lady in the county town of Schull in County Cork. If ever you are in the district make a point of sampling Adele Connor's bread – it is baked on the premises and is as good as any I have tasted, wholemeal, white, soda or sourdough.

The Starter

All sourdough recipes require a starter, and this can take between seven and fourteen days to prepare. It is said that the fourteen-day starter produces a loaf with a better flavour than the seven-day, but unless you become a sourdough addict you are unlikely to notice a great difference. No yeast is required for a traditional starter, but I prefer the addition of a little yeast to speed things up. It seems to make very little difference to the bread and certainly reduces the time taken for rising.

INGREDIENTS FOR STARTER

10 oz (280g) stoneground wholemeal flour
½ teaspoon (2.5g) dried granulated yeast
¼ pint (140ml) warm water

METHOD

Mix the flour and yeast granules with enough of the warm

water to make a thick batter in a large glass or ceramic mixing bowl (or rigid plastic) – no metal utensils should come into contact with the starter at any time. It is essential to use a container large enough to allow for considerable expansion – I use a plastic bucket. You can omit the yeast and just make the batter from the flour and water – it will work more slowly but the final result will be the same.

Cover and stand in a warm place (70°F, 21°C is ideal) for twenty-four hours by which time the mixture should have a somewhat crusty surface and smell rather sour. Every morning feed the starter with 2 tablespoons (30g) of flour and the same of warm water, and continue the process for seven days. Watch carefully; if fermentation is too violent and the mixture shows signs of overflowing the container it can be kept in a refrigerator but must be brought back to room temperature before using.

Each time the starter is fed, the extra flour and water must be thoroughly mixed in using a wooden or plastic implement. At no time should salt be added or fermentation will cease.

After feeding the starter for seven days it can be used if you are impatient, but better results will be obtained if the process is continued for a further seven days – at least that is the theory.

At the end of the fermentation period you have decided upon, set aside one-quarter of the mix as the basis for the next starter and process the rest as follows (The portion to be used for the next starter should be mixed with enough warm water to make a smooth, thick batter, covered with a damp cloth and fed at twenty-four hour intervals as before.)

The Bread

INGREDIENTS

> Remaining three portions of starter
> 1 lb (450g) stoneground wholemeal flour
> 1 teaspoon (5g) salt
> Warm water to mix

METHOD

Mix the starter, flour and salt with just enough warm water to produce a rough, dryish dough. It must not be at all sticky. Allow to rest for 10 minutes before adjusting the consistency if necessary.

Turn out the dough and knead for 600 strokes by which time it will become rather elastic. Kneading will be difficult at first because the dough is dry and crumbly, but as kneading progresses it will become more manageable and eventually have a shiny surface and be slightly tacky.

Place in a fairly large ceramic, glass or plastic container, cover, and set into a warmish area to rest for ten hours. The optimum temperature is 65-70°F (19-21°C), much higher and the bread will be inferior.

After ten hours the dough will have risen very little, if at all, but punch or deflate it towards the beginning of the last hour to invigorate the leavening organisms, then knead for a further 100 strokes. It should still be shiny and rather sticky. This marks the end of the cool risings.

Cover and place in a warm place (70°F, 21°C or a little higher) for about four hours or until the dough has expanded and the surface is now dry to the touch and the shine has gone off it. It will not rise to the same extent as ordinary doughs so do not wait for it to double in volume as in other recipes.

Turn out and knead for 100 strokes, allow to rest for 10 minutes, then knead again for a further 50 strokes. Allow to rest for a further 10 minutes before dividing into the required number of portions, mould to shape and either put into pre-warmed greased and floured tins or on to a greased and floured baking sheet.

The loaves must be proved in a very warm (90°F, 32°C), damp atmosphere (as near to 100% humidity as you can arrange) for about four hours. They are ready for the oven when they feel spongy and may even sag a little. The lightness of the final loaf depends to a great extent upon the temperature and humidity at this proving.

Pre-heat the oven to 450°F (230°C, Gas Mark 8) and place a pan containing a pint (550ml) of boiling water on the lower shelf. The oven must be prepared to accept the loaves as soon as they are ready.

Before placing the loaves on the centre shelf of the oven stab the surface in a few places with a warmed skewer to prevent the crust separating. Bake for 15 minutes at 450°F (230°C, Gas Mark 8) then reduce the temperature to 350°F (180°C, Gas Mark 4) for a further 45 minutes.

Test by tapping the base of a loaf with the fingertips, if it sounds hollow it is done. The surface should be a smooth golden brown but this is no guide to the correct amount of cooking, the fingertip test is crucial.

Set the loaves on to a wire rack to cool and do not cut for at least four hours. Because of the omission of fats it tends to dry out rather rapidly and so does not freeze too well.

Note: Several factors affect the time taken for this bread to bake – temperature, water content, quality of the flour, fermentation time, utensils, etc.

This recipe uses all wholemeal flour, but it works just as well with a proportion of strong white flour substituted for some of the wholemeal, but less water will be required in the mixing.

Each time a portion of the starter is re-energized it will strengthen. It follows that bread made with a starter which is several generations old will be quite different to that made from a new starter. As a general rule the younger the starter the milder the flavour, so if a strong sour taste is not to your liking, make a new starter every time.

Dilly Cheese Bread★★

This recipe came originally from the southern states of the USA but similar ones abound all over America. Makes one fairly large round loaf, but two smaller ones can be substituted

if preferred. The bread keeps well and can be frozen, it has a light, open crumb dotted with cheesy bits, and the medium-hard crust is beautifully marked with darker spots.

It rises furiously in the oven, which is why deep tins are needed, and the loaf produced has a rather flat top. It is unsuitable for tray baking.

INGREDIENTS

2 teaspoons (10g) granulated dried yeast
2 teaspoons (10g) sugar
½ pint (280ml) warm water
1 lb (450g) strong white flour, unbleached preferably
1 teaspoon (5g) salt
½ oz (15g) dried dill
4 oz (110g) Cheddar cheese, grated
5 tablespoons (75ml) melted butter
2 eggs, size 3

METHOD

Dissolve the yeast and sugar in the warm water and set aside to activate; it is ready to use when the surface is covered in frothy bubbles.

Sieve the salt and flour together into a large bowl, add the dill and mix thoroughly. Add the grated cheese and mix it into the flour.

Beat the butter and eggs together until blended.

When the yeast liquid is frothy add the butter and egg liquid and whisk to blend. Add the liquid to the flour and beat with a whisk or wooden spoon until all the flour is incorporated into a soft moist batter.

Cover the bowl with a damp towel or polythene film and

put it into a warm place to rise. When it has doubled in volume it is ready for the next operation.

Lightly stir the mixture to deflate it, then pour it into a large well-greased cake tin or souffle dish (about 8 ins diameter by 6 ins deep, 20 × 15cms) or two smaller receptacles. (See notes at end of recipe.)

Cover and put back into a warm place to rise until it has again doubled in volume (usually about 45–60 minutes), then bake on the centre shelf of an oven pre-heated to 350°F (180°C, Gas Mark 4) for 1½ hours. Remove the bread from the tins and bake upside down for the last ten minutes or until the loaf sounds hollow when the base is tapped with the fingertips.

Cool on a wire rack.

VARIATIONS

Some recipes use dill seed instead of the dried foliage detailed above; in those cases use exactly the same quantity. If fresh dill is used you will need double the quantity.

A stronger cheese than Cheddar can be used, but it must be a hard cheese, soft cheeses melt too quickly in the oven and make the crumb doughy.

Note: The water should be a *little* warmer than usual to prevent the butter coagulating as it is blended in with the eggs – 100°F (38°C) is about right.

Line the tin or tins with baking parchment before use as the mixture can adhere to the sides and ruin the loaf. It is essential to use high-sided tins and to fill them not more than half full.

It is not easy to find really high-sided tins, and one solution to prevent the batter flopping over the edges is to line the tins with greased kitchen foil cut 6 ins (15cms) high. You will need at least three layers of foil to support the batter.

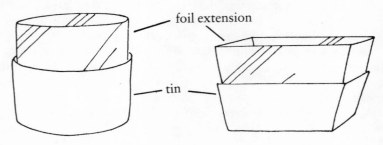

foil extension

tin

Softcrust Vinegar Bread★★

The vinegar in this recipe is barely discernible yet the bread
has an appealingly different flavour. It bears no resemblance
to a sourdough. It keeps well and can be frozen and makes
excellent toast and sandwiches. The recipe makes three small
loaves or fewer larger. The rather slack dough is unsuitable
for tray-baking.

INGREDIENTS

    2 teaspoons (10g) granulated dried yeast
    2 teaspoons (10g) sugar
    1 pint (550ml) warm water
    1 lb (450g) strong white flour, preferably unbleached
    1 lb (450g) stoneground wholemeal flour
    2 teaspoons (10g) salt
    4 oz (110g) kibbled wheat
    2 fl. oz (55ml) olive oil
    1 fl. oz (30ml) malt vinegar

METHOD

Dissolve the sugar and yeast in the warm water, and set aside
to activate. It is ready for use when the surface is covered in
frothy bubbles – usually about 10 minutes.

Sieve the flours and salt together into a large bowl and mix
thoroughly. Add the kibbled wheat and stir into the flour
until it is evenly incorporated.

When the yeast liquid is ready, add the oil and vinegar and
whisk rapidly until a creamy-smooth emulsion is formed,
then pour this into the flour and stir with a wooden spoon
until a rough, even dough results.

Turn out on to a lightly floured surface and knead for 100
strokes by which time the dough will have become smooth
and silky.

Form it into a ball and place in a lightly greased bowl,
cover with a dry cloth overlaid with a damp one, and set to
rise in a warm place until it has doubled in bulk.

Turn out again and knead for a further 100 strokes, then
divide into equal portions, roll each into a ball and elongate

slightly into a torpedo shape and half-fill pre-warmed and greased tins. Cover with a dry cloth and put into a warm, draughtproof place to prove. The loaves are ready for the oven when the dough has risen level with the top of the tins.

Bake on the centre shelf of an oven pre-heated to 450°F (230°C, Gas Mark 8) for 35–40 minutes. Test by tapping the base of a loaf with the fingertips, if it sounds hollow it is done.

Remove from tins and cool on a wire rack.

VARIATIONS

The ratio of white to wholemeal flour can be adjusted to suit personal preference; all white flour will require a little less water, all wholemeal a little more, but the mixture must never become sticky.

Lard or margarine can be substituted for the olive oil but 'low-fat spreads' are unsuitable. The fat must be rubbed into the flours (before the kibbled wheat is added) until the mixture resembles fine breadcrumbs, then continue as described.

Chopped nuts can be used instead of the kibbled wheat, but the nuts should be lightly toasted and cooled before adding to the flour.

Calcutta Naan Bread★★★

This is the traditional bread which often accompanies tandoori and similar Indian foods. Almost every Indian housewife has her own variation of the basic recipe, passed down from generation to generation. Naan bread should be soft and flat with a moist crumb; the outside is normally slightly scorched and it is served still warm from the oven. The recipe makes about six ovals. They do not keep well and are not very good if reheated after freezing but freshly baked they are delicious. Genuine Naan bread is baked in a clay tandoor; modern ovens are an inferior substitute so this recipe has been designed for grilling to yield an acceptable alternative.

INGREDIENTS

¾ lb (340g) self-raising white flour, preferably unbleached
¾ lb (340g) white chapatti flour
2 teaspoons (10g) baking powder (not soda)
1 teaspoon (5g) salt
4 tablespoons (60ml) warm water
¾ pint (420ml) natural yogurt
4 oz (110ml) melted butter ghee
Spices to taste (optional)

METHOD

Sieve the flours, salt and baking powder into a large bowl and mix thoroughly.

Add the water to the yogurt and whisk until a smooth creamy liquid results. Add this to the flour and stir with a wooden spoon.

Turn the dough out on to a lightly floured surface and knead for 40 strokes, return to the bowl and allow to rest in a warm place for 1 hour, then divide into 6 equal portions and form roughly into torpedo shapes.

Using ¼-in (6mm) wooden guides, roll each piece into an oval on a lightly floured surface. You can use thicker guides if you prefer the bread to be more bulky.

Put the portions on a greased baking sheet and brush with the melted ghee.

Grill under maximum heat for three minutes each side (remember to butter the under side when you turn it over), or until beginning to brown.

Serve immediately on warm plates.

VARIATIONS

A variety of spices can be mixed into the dry flour, sesame, caraway and nutmeg are all good. The tops can be sprinkled with chopped nuts, olives, etc.

Note: Ghee (clarified butter) will keep for months once set. Gently melt the butter over a low heat. When fully melted raise the temperature slightly and cook for one hour without burning. Do not stir. Skim off the impurities floating on the surface but do not disturb the bottom. Cool slightly before filtering through muslin. It will solidify as it cools but still be fairly soft.

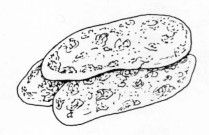

Vienna Bread★★★

Vienna bread is thought to have come to England from Austria in the early 1900s. Certainly by 1920 there were established Viennese bakeries in many areas of London and when I was a child there were at least four such bakeries within walking distance of my home, all producing bread quite different in quality to the normal English bread and nearer in flavour and texture to French bread. My grandmother, who would eat only cottage loaves, regarded it as 'dreadful foreign rubbish', but in general my generation thought it an improvement especially when eaten fresh from the bakery and still warm. It is seldom seen today.

As with French bread, it requires steaming to produce a good crust, especially during the first fifteen minutes in the oven and, as with French bread, it cannot be rushed. Makes three small loaves or two larger.

INGREDIENTS

4 teaspoons (20g) granulated dried yeast
¼ pint (140ml) warm water
Pinch of sugar
2 lb (900g) strong white flour, preferably unbleached
2 teaspoons (10g) salt
1 egg size 3
2 tablespoons (30ml) vegetable oil
1 tablespoon (15ml) pasteurized honey
Extra ¼ pint (140ml) warm water

METHOD

Dissolve the yeast in the ¼ pint warm water with a pinch of sugar and leave to activate. It is ready for use when the surface is covered in frothy bubbles.

Sieve the flour and salt together into a large bowl.

Beat the egg, gradually adding the oil, honey and the extra water. Add the mixture to the yeast liquid and stir well to ensure thorough dispersal.

Make a well in the flour, pour in the liquid and stir with a wooden spoon until it is thoroughly mixed. The dough should be slightly lumpy and rather crumbly; if it is too stiff add a teaspoon (5ml) of extra water.

Turn out the mixture and knead for 200 strokes by which time it will be smooth and silky. If it is at all stiff extra water can be added by wetting the hands during the kneading or lightly spraying with a hand-sprayer.

Return the dough to the bowl, cover with a damp cloth, and place in a warm place (80°F, 27°C max) to rise which will take between one and two hours. The dough is correctly risen when it has doubled in volume.

Turn out on to a lightly floured surface and knead for another 40 strokes before returning the dough to the bowl for its second rise – about 45 to 60 minutes.

Turn it out again on to a lightly floured surface and knead for 20 strokes before dividing into two or three equal portions depending upon the size of loaf required. Gently form into balls and tuck the edges underneath; leave to rest for 10 minutes or so until they regain their suppleness.

Lightly grease a baking tray, wipe off the surplus, then thoroughly dust with flour making certain it is completely coated. Alternatively the sheet can be covered with non-stick baking parchment.

Take each ball of dough and form it into a torpedo shape about three times as long as it is wide, the ends rather pointed and the middles quite plump. Place the loaves side by side on the baking tray and put them into a warm place to prove. They are ready for the oven when they have doubled in size.

The oven should be pre-heated to 475°F (240°C, Gas Mark 9). With a sharp knife make three diagonal slashes across each loaf, then spray over with warm water before quickly placing them on the centre shelf of the oven. Just before closing the oven door spray the inside walls and roof with water, then quickly but gently close the door.

After 5 minutes carefully open the oven and spray the inside and the loaves with water and repeat three times at

5-minute intervals. After the final spraying reduce the oven temperature to 350°F (180°C, Gas Mark 4) and bake for about 30–40 minutes until the loaves are a golden brown.

Vienna bread should not be overcooked or the flavour will be impaired, and it is best eaten while still warm. It can be frozen.

Note: A dish of boiling water placed in the oven 20 minutes before baking commences will help to create the right atmosphere for Vienna bread.

Caution. Steam is dangerous. Exercise great care when opening the oven door to spray the loaves. Ensure your arms are protected and keep your face well away from the rush of steam that escapes as the oven door is opened. *Keep children well away.*

Vienna Rolls★★★

To make Vienna rolls prepare the dough exactly as for Vienna bread but add an extra tablespoon of water to the initial mixture so that a softer, smoother dough is produced, but it must not be sticky. If it is too wet a little extra flour can be added during kneading.

The dough should be set to rise exactly as for bread, and when ready, cut into four equal portions. Gently roll each portion into a ball and set aside for 10 minutes or so to relax; then press it flat to deflate and roll out with a rolling pin until the dough is not more than ¼ in (6mm) thick. If it is rolled out unevenly the finished rolls will be different sizes and the cooking times will vary.

Cut out circular discs using a 3½-in (9cms) cutter (a serrated cutter gives a prettier effect). The ragged fragments of dough remaining can be rekneaded into a ball then rolled out again to provide more discs until it is all used.

Take one disc and spray the surface lightly with warm water or brush over making sure it is completely covered right to the edges, then fold in half keeping the dampened surfaces inside to make a kind of purse. Press both surfaces together and pinch the semi-circular edges all round so that they are very securely attached to each other. Do the same with the rest of the discs then set them out on a baking tray with at least 1½ins (4cms) of space between them with the seams upright.

Lightly coat a baking tray with grease or oil, then thoroughly dust with flour and shake off the surplus. Alternatively use non-stick baking parchment. The batch of rolls can now be placed in a warm, draughtproof place to prove until they have doubled in size.

Pre-heat the oven to 475°F (240°C, Gas Mark 9).

Spray the rolls lightly with warm water then place them on the upper shelf of the oven, spraying the inside of the oven with water before gently closing the door.

At 5-minute intervals open the oven carefully and respray the rolls and the oven walls. Do this twice then reduce the temperature to 350°F (180°C, Gas Mark 4) and bake until the rolls are an even golden brown – do not overcook or the flavour will be impaired; 15–20 minutes baking is usually all that is required but the colour of the crust is the best guide. Cool on a wire rack.

Although best eaten fresh from the oven Vienna rolls can be frozen.

Caution: Great care must be exercised when the oven door is opened to spray the rolls, for steam can cause severe scalding. Ensure that your arms and hands are protected and keep your face well away from the rush of steam that will escape as the oven door is opened. *Children should be kept out of the kitchen.*

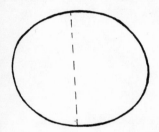 

Confederate Country Bread★

This recipe is supposed to have originated in North Carolina at the time of the American Civil War but, to date, I have found no evidence to support this theory. It is an easily made quick bread requiring no kneading, but producing an open soft crumb and a medium-crisp crust. In the USA it is normally baked in a 9-in (23cm) round cake tin, but rectangular tins will do just as well if that is your preference. The bread keeps well and can be frozen. Makes one round loaf or the equivalent rectangular. The mixture is too loose for tray baking. In California it is often toasted and eaten with guacamole.

INGREDIENTS

2 teaspoons (10g) dried granulated yeast
1 teaspoon (5g) sugar
1 pint (550ml) warm water
1 lb (450g) strong white flour, unbleached if possible
¼ lb (110g) stoneground wholemeal flour
2 teaspoons (10g) salt
1 oz (30g) fresh ground ginger
4 teaspoons (20ml) olive oil

METHOD

Dissolve the sugar and yeast in the warm water, stir briefly and set aside to activate; it is ready for use when the surface is covered in frothy bubbles.

Sieve the flours, ginger and salt together into a large bowl and mix thoroughly.

When the yeast liquid is ready add the olive oil (slightly warmed) and whisk until a smooth emulsion results with no visible globules of oil. Pour the liquid into the flour a little at a time and beat vigorously with a wooden spoon or beater until a smooth, rather loose batter is obtained.

Cover the bowl with a damp cloth and leave to rise in a warm place until it has doubled in volume. When the dough is sufficiently risen, beat it again for several minutes until it is quite smooth.

Line a warmed 9-in (23 cm) round cake tin with baking parchment. Pour the batter into the cake tin and smooth the surface. Set aside in a warm draughtproof place to prove for about 30 minutes or until it has about doubled in volume.

Spray the surface with warm water and bake on the lower shelf of an oven pre-heated to 475°F (240°C, Gas Mark 9) for 10 minutes then reduce the temperature to 400°F (200°C, Gas Mark 6) and bake for another 30 minutes.

If the bread shows signs of browning too quickly, place a piece of baking foil over the top. However, the oven must not be opened for the first 20 minutes of baking or the loaf may collapse.

Test by inserting a warmed skewer or long needle into the centre of the loaf (as you would for a cake) – if it comes out perfectly clean the bread is done; if not, return it to the oven for a few more minutes.

After removing from the oven allow the bread to rest for 10 minutes or so before turning it out and cooling on a wire rack.

VARIATIONS

Traditionally the top is criss-crossed by cuts with a sharp knife or razor blade just before it goes into the oven.

Lancashire Garlic Bread★★

There are several ways of making garlic bread; the more usual these days is to take a French loaf and cut it diagonally at intervals without severing the slices. Garlic butter is then inserted between the cuts, the loaf wrapped in foil and placed in a hot oven for a few minutes to allow the butter to melt into the crumb. But garlic bread was eaten in Britain when French bread was virtually unknown here.

This recipe is said to have been traditional in the northern counties of England in Elizabethan times with slight variations from county to county. No doubt in those times the garlic used would have been the English Wood or Wild Garlic *Allium ursinum* which still grows wild in woodlands and damp places. The garlic used today is the cultivated variety *Allium sativum* which was probably brought to England from central Asia.

Fresh cloves of garlic can be crushed and chopped to add to the dough and this gives the best results. Although garlic powder can be used it is a poor substitute.

This recipe produces a mild garlic flavour; it is easy to add more garlic if too mild. The bread is best eaten warm, thickly spread with butter or margarine. It can be frozen for about two months. Makes three large loaves or five small ones.

INGREDIENTS

> 1¼ pints (700ml) warm water
> 2 teaspoons (10g) granulated dried yeast
> 2 teaspoons (10g) sugar
> 1 lb (450g) stoneground wholemeal flour
> 2 lb (900g) strong white flour, preferably unbleached
> 2 teaspoons (10g) salt
> 2 oz (55g) lard
> 2 oz (60g) chopped garlic

METHOD

Hand-mixing. Dissolve the yeast and sugar in the warm water and leave to activate. It is ready for use when the surface is covered in frothy bubbles.

Sieve the flours and salt together into a large warm bowl and mix thoroughly. Rub the lard into the flour until the mixture resembles fine breadcrumbs.

Mix in the chopped garlic until evenly distributed.

Make a well in the centre of the flour mixture and pour in the yeast liquid. Stir with a wooden spoon until all the ingredients are incorporated to form a stiff, coarse dough – do not add water to slacken it. Turn out on to a lightly floured surface to knead.

Machine-mixing, using a dough hook. Place the yeast, sugar and warm water in a basin, stir briefly to disperse evenly then allow to rest until the surface is covered in frothy bubbles.

Sieve the flours and salt together into the machine bowl and mix thoroughly. Add the lard cut into small pieces and run the machine on the slowest speed until the fat is broken down, then increase the speed and continue running until the mixture resembles fine breadcrumbs. (If using a Kenwood Chef substitute the K-beater for the dough hook to break down the fat).

Mix in the chopped garlic until evenly distributed.

With the machine on the lowest speed gradually add the yeast liquid until all is in the bowl; run for about 3 minutes until a ball of dough adheres to the hook, then increase the speed to about half the maximum and run for a further 2 minutes.

Turn out on to a lightly floured surface for kneading.

From then on the methods are identical

Knead for 300 strokes, then form the dough into a ball and return to the bowl, cover with a damp cloth or lightly greased polythene and set to rise in a warm, draughtproof place.

When it has doubled in volume turn out the dough on to the lightly floured surface and knead for a further 100 strokes before dividing into five small loaves or three larger.

Roll each portion with a rotary action into a torpedo shape and half-fill pre-warmed greased tins. Cover tins with a dry cloth (if a damp cloth is used the dough may adhere to it as it rises and the bread ruined) and put into a warm, draughtproof place to prove which will take about half the time of the first rise.

When the dome of the dough has reached the level of the top of the tin the bread is ready for the oven.

Pre-heat the oven to 450°F (230°C, Gas Mark 8) and bake the loaves on the centre shelf for 15 minutes, then reduce the temperature to 425°F (220°C, Gas Mark 7). After a further 30 minutes take a loaf out of the oven and test by tapping the base with the fingertips; if it sounds hollow it is done.

Loaves baked in tins will normally have a dark top crust and paler, softer sides; if you prefer your loaves crustier all around bake them for the last 5 or 10 minutes upside down out of their tins.

Place the loaves on a wire rack to cool and do not slice for one hour.

VARIATIONS

The ratio of white to wholemeal flour can be adjusted as required.

Block margarine can be used instead of lard but 'low-fat' spreads are not suitable.

Millet Bread★★★

I cannot claim this as my favourite bread, but many people think it marvellous. It keeps well, makes excellent toast, and can be frozen. There is no doubt that it is best made by the long fermentation method, and that is what I have described. For this you will need a very large bowl or, better still, a plastic bucket. The recipe makes five small loaves or fewer larger.

INGREDIENTS

2 teaspoons (10g) dried granulated yeast
2 teaspoons (10g) sugar
1¼ pints (700ml) warm water
2 lb (900g) strong white flour, preferably unbleached
1 lb (450g) stoneground wholemeal flour
2 teaspoons (10g) salt
2 oz (55g) lard
½ oz (15g) dried thyme or fennel
¼ lb (110g) millet seed

METHOD

Dissolve the yeast and sugar in the warm water and leave to activate – it is ready to use when the surface is covered in frothy bubbles.

Sieve the flours and salt together. Rub the lard into the flour until it resembles fine breadcrumbs. Add the thyme or fennel to the flour and mix in.

Stir the yeast liquid into the flour until a rough dough is formed; it might seem dry and crumbly but do not add more water at this stage.

Knead for 200 strokes by which time the dough should be smooth and silky but not at all sticky; if it is sticky knead in more flour.

Carefully oil all the inner surfaces of the large bowl or bucket and put the dough into it. Lightly oil the surface of the dough, cover with a damp cloth and set aside to rise overnight.

Soak the millet seed overnight in cold water, then drain

thoroughly and put aside to dry out a little.

Allowing at least twelve hours rising time, turn the dough out on to a lightly floured surface and knead for a further 200 strokes working the millet into the dough as you knead.

Divide into equal portions and roll each into a ball between the palms. Mould into a torpedo shape and half-fill warm pre-greased tins, cover with a *dry* cloth and set to prove in a warm place.

When doubled in volume or the domes of the loaves are level with the top of the tins, bake on the centre shelf of an oven pre-heated to 400°F (200°C, Gas Mark 6) for about 45 minutes or until the loaves sound hollow when tapped on the base with the fingertips. A firmer crust can be obtained by baking the loaves out of their tins for the last 10 minutes.

Cool the bread on a wire rack.

VARIATIONS

The quantity of millet can be varied to suit individual tastes, as can the thyme or fennel.

The ratio of white to wholemeal flour can be adjusted as required, but the higher the wholemeal content the more water will be needed.

Block margarine can be substituted for the lard but low-fat spreads are not suitable.

Before baking the tops of the loaves can be brushed with milk and sprinkled with millet seeds.

Sage and Onion Bread★★

This recipe has been adapted from an ancient French recipe which was dictated to me by an 80-year-old peasant lady living on a remote farm in the Pyrenees. Language difficulties made an exact transcription almost impossible (impeded rather than assisted by my schoolboy French), so a certain amount of adjustment has been necessary in order to arrive at an extremely appetising result. The bread has a fairly soft crust, toasts and keeps well, can be frozen, and is a delicious complement to soups or cheese. Makes five small loaves or fewer larger.

INGREDIENTS

2 teaspoons (10g) granulated dried yeast
2 teaspoons (10g) sugar
1¼ pints (700ml) warm water
2 lb (900g) strong white flour, preferably unbleached
1 lb (450g) stoneground wholemeal flour
4 oz (110g) potato flour
1 tablespoon (15g) salt
4 oz (110g) lard
1 oz (30g) dried sage
6 oz (170g) raw onion, finely chopped
2 eggs, size 3

METHOD

Dissolve the sugar and yeast in the warm water and set aside to activate. It is ready for use when the surface is covered in frothy bubbles.

Sieve the flours and salt together into a large warmed bowl and mix thoroughly. Rub in the lard until the mixture is the consistency of fine breadcrumbs, then add the sage and mix until it is evenly distributed.

Sauté the onion in a little oil for a few minutes until it is tender but not brown. Remove from the heat, drain and cool before mixing into the flour until it is evenly distributed.

When the yeast liquid is ready, break the eggs into it and beat until a creamy mixture results – using a mechanical beater or liquidizer if possible. Add this liquid to the flour and work with the hands until a rough dough results. Turn out on to a lightly floured surface and knead for 200 strokes.

Form the dough into a ball and place in a large warm bowl. Cover with a dry cloth overlaid with a damp one, and set to rise in a warm place for about an hour or until the dough has doubled in volume.

Turn out and knead for a further 200 strokes then return it to the warm place for the second rise which will take about half the time of the first.

When again doubled in volume, knead gently for 30 strokes then divide into equal portions. Form each portion into a ball, then either gently elongate to a torpedo shape and place in pre-warmed and greased tins, or set on to greased baking trays if round loaves are preferred and leave to prove in a warm, draughtproof place. They are ready for the oven when the dome of the dough has risen level with the rim of the tins, or the trayed loaves have doubled in volume.

Bake on the centre shelf of an oven pre-heated to 400°F (200°C, Gas Mark 6) for 45 minutes, then test by tapping the base of a loaf with the fingertips – if it sounds hollow the bread is done.

Cool the loaves on a wire rack.

VARIATIONS

The ratio of white to wholemeal flour can be adjusted to suit individual tastes.

The quantities of sage and chopped onion can be varied as required. The above formula gives a nicely balanced flavour but it is inevitable that some will prefer more or less of these ingredients.

Block margarine can be substituted for the lard but low-fat spreads are not suitable.

Pineapple sage, a new variety, is excellent used as a poultry stuffing but I have yet to try it in bread, mainly because it is not easy to find. It has a strong pineapple aroma and should be worth an experiment.

Note: Because onions have a high water-content this recipe calls for less water than normal. If the mixture seems dry at first it will get moister as kneading proceeds; do not add more water unless after the second kneading it seems dry and crumbly. If the dough seems too wet and sticky, more flour can be added as you knead.

English Breakfast Rolls★

The standard bread roll is universally popular and certainly not restricted to the U.K.; neither is its consumption limited to breakfast-time. The recipe makes about twenty rolls depending upon size. They keep quite well and can be frozen. These are quite different to the **First Time Rolls**; the crust is softer and the crumb more open. Try them both and decide which you prefer.

INGREDIENTS

1 tablespoon (15g) dried granulated yeast
2 teaspoons (10g) sugar
1¼ pints (700ml) warm water
2 lb (900g) strong white flour, preferably unbleached
2 teaspoons (10g) salt
2 tablespoons (30ml) olive oil
1 egg, size 3
Egg white for glazing

METHOD

Dissolve the yeast and sugar in the warm water and set aside to activate. It is ready for use when the surface is covered in frothy bubbles.

Sieve the flour and salt together into a large bowl and mix thoroughly.

When the yeast mixture is ready, add the olive oil and the egg, and whisk until a smooth emulsion results with no visible globules of oil.

Pour the liquid into the flour and mix with a wooden spoon until all the ingredients are evenly assimilated into a rough dough.

Turn the dough out on to a lightly floured surface, and knead for 200 strokes by which time it will have become smooth and silky. It must not be at all sticky, if necessary knead in extra flour.

Form the dough into a ball and return it to the bowl, cover with a dry cloth overlaid with a damp one, and put it into a warm place to rise at a temperature between 70° and 80°F

(21° and 27°C). This will take about an hour.

When the dough has doubled in volume, knead for a further 20 strokes, then divide it into 20 equal portions (less if you prefer larger rolls, more if smaller).

Roll each piece into a ball using a rotary motion between the palms of the hands.

Place the rolls on a greased baking sheet allowing at least 1 in (2.5cms) between them, cover with a polythene sheet supported so it cannot touch the rolls, and put them into a warm place to prove.

When they have doubled in size brush the tops with lightly beaten egg white before baking them on the centre shelf of an oven pre-heated to 450°F (230°C, Gas Mark 8) for about 20 minutes or until they are a golden brown.

VARIATIONS

Wholemeal flour can be substituted for strong white, or a proportion of each.

If a bap shape is required, make each ball of dough larger, then flatten the rolls with a rolling pin and dust with flour before putting into the oven. They will take a little longer to bake and the crust will be softer.

Crescent Rolls★★

These are the British equivalent of the French croissants. They are at their best served hot from the oven but they will keep for a few days and can be frozen without much loss of character if they are defrosted before being placed in a hot oven for a few minutes. Makes about 12–16 rolls depending upon size.

INGREDIENTS

2 teaspoons (10g) granulated dried yeast
1 teaspoon (5g) sugar
15 fl.oz (450ml) whole milk
1 lb (450g) stoneground wholemeal flour, strong white flour (preferably unbleached), or any mixture of the two
1 teaspoon (5g) salt
1 oz (30g) cooking margarine
1 egg, size 3

METHOD

Scald the milk, cool to blood heat then add the sugar and yeast. Stir briefly to disperse, then set aside to activate; it is ready to use when the surface is covered in frothy bubbles.

Sieve the flour and salt into a large bowl and mix thoroughly. Melt the margarine in a saucepan over a low heat.

When the yeast liquid is ready add the melted margarine and the egg, and whisk vigorously to get an even dispersal or use a liquidizer if you have one.

Add the liquid to the flour and mix with a wooden spoon until a soft dough results; it may be necessary to complete the mixing by hand. Knead for 200 strokes after which the dough should be soft and pliable but not sticky – knead in more flour if it feels at all wet.

Put the dough into a warm bowl, cover with a damp cloth and stand in a warm place to rise for about an hour or until it has doubled in bulk.

Turn out and knead for 100 strokes on a lightly floured surface, divide into two equal portions, form each into a ball and gently flatten with a rolling pin. Then roll each piece out into a circle about ⅛ in (3mm) thick using roller-guides to ensure even thickness.

Carefully score guide lines on each circle of dough radiating outwards from the centre, then with a sharp, lightly greased knife cut out six triangles of dough (or more if you wish for smaller crescents).

Lightly brush each triangle with warm water (they should be just damp, not wet), then roll up each one beginning with the wide base of the triangle and rolling towards the tip.

Place each piece, tip downwards, on a lightly greased baking tray and gently form into a curve. When all the rolls have been assembled on the tray, cover with a dry cloth and put into a warm, draughtproof place to prove. They are ready for the oven when they have doubled in volume.

Bake on the centre shelf of an oven pre-heated to 425°F (220°C, Gas Mark 7) for between 8 and 12 minutes. They are ready when the crust is just beginning to brown.

Set to cool on a wire rack.

Note: Poppy Seeds can be sprinkled over the rolls as a decoration – paint the surface with a mixture of egg white and water just before they go into the oven and the seeds will adhere to the surface.

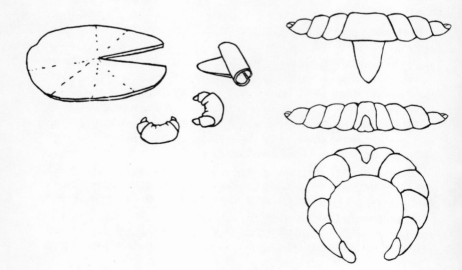

Nutty Wholemeal Bread★★

A wide range of different nuts can be used in this recipe except perhaps peanuts which have a rather overpowering flavour. I use mixed chopped nuts because I can get them from a local delicatessen which has a rapid turnover. Stale chopped nuts can be hosts to moulds which, although invisible, can affect the bread adversely; if in any doubt chop your own and use immediately. The bread makes excellent toast and gives a different character to sandwiches. It keeps well and can be frozen. The recipe makes five small loaves or fewer larger.

INGREDIENTS

1¼ pints (700ml) warm water
4 teaspoons (20g) granulated dried yeast
4 teaspoons (20g) sugar
2 lb (900g) stoneground wholemeal flour
1 lb (450g) strong white flour, preferably unbleached
1 tablespoon (15g) salt
4 oz (110g) lard
¼ lb (110g) fresh chopped mixed nuts

METHOD

Stir the sugar and yeast into the warm water and leave to activate. The mixture is ready for use when the surface is covered in frothy bubbles.

Sift the flours and salt into a large bowl and mix thoroughly. Rub the lard into the flour until it resembles fine breadcrumbs.

Toast the chopped nuts gently under a grill until they are just golden, then set aside to cool before mixing into the flour.

Hand-mixing. When the yeast mixture is ready add it to the flour and mix well with a wooden spoon at first, finishing by hand to get even distribution.

Machine-mixing using a dough hook. Warm the bowl of the mixer and the dough hook. Pour the yeast liquid into the mixer bowl and start the machine at its lowest speed.

Gradually spoon in the flour mixture and continue mixing until all the ingredients are incorporated.

Continue mixing on the slowest speed for 5 minutes or until a ball of dough is attached to the dough hook. If after 5 minutes some dry flour remains in the bottom of the bowl you can add a teaspoon of warm water, but very seldom is more than three teaspoons of extra water necessary. The dough must not be sticky.

When all the dough is attached to the dough hook increase the speed to the maximum and run for 2 minutes.

From then on the methods are identical.

Turn the dough out on to a lightly floured surface and knead for 200 strokes, then form into a ball and place it in a large warm bowl for its first rise, covering it with a dry cloth overlaid with a damp one. Set in a warm place for about an hour or until the dough has doubled in bulk.

Turn out the risen dough on to a lightly floured surface and knead for a further 200 strokes. If it seems at all sticky work a little more flour into the dough as you knead. Then once more form it into a ball and return it to a warm place for its second rise, covering it as before with a dry cloth overlaid with a damp one.

The second rise will take about half the time of the first. The dough is ready when it has again doubled in bulk.

Turn it out on to the lightly floured surface and knead for a further 40 strokes, then allow to rest for 10 minutes.

Divide into equal portions, mould to shape and put into warmed, greased tins, or set on to a greased baking tray and put them into a warm, draughtproof place to prove. Those in tins will be ready for the oven when the dough has risen level with the top of the tins, those to be tray-baked will have doubled in volume.

They should be baked on the centre shelf of an oven pre-heated to 450°F (230°C, Gas Mark 8) for 15 minutes, then reduce the temperature to 400°F (200°C, Gas Mark 6) and bake for a further 30 minutes. Test by tapping the base of a loaf with the fingertips; if it sounds hollow the bread is done.

Place the loaves on a wire rack to cool. The bread can be

eaten about two hours later but is best left overnight.

VARIATIONS

The loaves can be rolled in chopped nuts immediately before moulding or tinning. Paint the surface with warm milk or water before sprinkling with the chopped nuts or rolling the loaves in them; this gives a very pretty effect although the nuts do tend to burn during cooking and get very brittle.

4 fl.oz of olive oil can be substituted for the lard. Add it to the yeast liquid when the yeast is working well, and mix thoroughly (use a liquidizer if possible) before pouring into the flour, but in this case reduce the amount of warm water in the recipe to 1 pint (550ml)

The ratio of white to wholemeal flour can be varied to taste.

The correct amount of water to be incorporated is a matter of feel and experience – the greater the wholemeal content, the more water will be required and *vice versa*.

Harvest Festival Bread★★

Although I first tasted this bread in Sicily, it is fairly common all over the Mediterranean area and appears under a variety of names with slight local variations in the ingredients. It is not difficult to make, and you can vary the vegetables to suit your own taste as long as you keep the proportions roughly as specified – if you overload the dough with vegetables some very strange results can occur. The recipe makes five small loaves or fewer larger. The bread will keep for about a week and can be frozen.

INGREDIENTS

4 teaspoons (20g) granulated dried yeast
2 teaspoons (10g) sugar
1¼ pints (700ml) warm water
2 lb (900g) strong white flour, preferably unbleached
½ lb (225g) stoneground wholemeal flour
4 oz (110g) potato flour
2 teaspoons (10g) salt
Carrots, onions, celery, black olives, red pepper and a few leaves of fresh mint, to a total weight of 6 oz (165g)
4 tablespoons (60ml) olive oil
1 egg, size 3

METHOD

Dissolve the sugar and yeast in the warm water, stir to blend, then set aside to activate. It is ready for use when the surface is covered in frothy bubbles.

Sieve the flours and salt together into a large bowl and mix thoroughly.

Chop all the vegetables roughly into ¼-in (6mm) dice and incorporate them into the flour, making sure they are all separately coated. Finely chop the mint and distribute it evenly throughout the mixture.

When the yeast liquid is ready add the oil and the egg and whisk until a smooth creamy emulsion results, pour this into the flour and mix in.

Turn the dough out on to a lightly floured surface and

knead gently for about 50 strokes. It is not easy to knead a dough with vegetables in it and too much kneading can do more harm than good.

Divide the dough into equal portions, roll each into a ball, then gently elongate to roughly fit the shape of the tin. The tins should be well greased and warm, and not more than about half filled with dough.

Cover with a dry cloth and put into a warm place to rise – this will take between 60 and 90 minutes according to the temperature. The rise is complete when the dome of the loaves has risen level with the top edge of the tins.

Bake on the centre shelf of an oven pre-heated to 400°F (200°C, Gas Mark 6) for about 45 minutes or until the bread sounds hollow when the base of a loaf is tapped with the fingertips.

Cool on a wire rack.

Note: The vegetables must be quite dry when they go into the flour or the water ratio will be affected.

The carrots will still be slightly crunchy after baking; if you prefer them softer blanch them, then dry and cool before adding to the flour.

If the dough seems harsh and dry a little more water can be added during kneading but it must never become sticky.

In my opinion larger loaves have a better texture and yield a more useful size slice. They can be tray-baked in the round but this dough is unsuitable for rolls or fancy shapes.

Irish Potato Soya Bread★★

This recipe comes from the Emerald Isle and is the basis of many Irish home-baked yeast breads. It makes a loaf with a moist, open crumb and attractive flavour which keeps well. Much depends upon the quality of the potatoes used and the variety *Maris Piper* is one of the best for mashing. The only variety I have found to be quite unsuitable is *King Edward*, because it does not easily break down to a floury consistency. This recipe makes five small loaves or fewer larger ones. Hand-mix for the best results.

Although this recipe is popular because it needs less kneading there is really little saving in time because of the extra work involved in preparing the mashed potatoes.

All breads made without fat or oil take longer to rise – don't increase the temperature or the yeast will be killed, and don't increase the yeast content or the bread will taste 'yeasty' and unpleasant.

INGREDIENTS

½ lb (225g) cooked mashed potato (weighed after mashing)
2 tablespoons (30g) sugar
2 teaspoons (10g) granulated dried yeast
½ pint (280ml) warm water
¾ pint (425ml) fresh soya milk
2 lb (900g) strong white flour, preferably unbleached
½ lb (225g) stoneground wholemeal flour
1 tablespoon (15g) salt

METHOD

Inspect the potatoes and discard any that are showing blemishes or damage to the skin where water can penetrate during cooking. Wash them thoroughly and boil until quite soft, drain and leave for a few minutes to cool before carefully removing the skin and cutting out all eyes and blemishes. It is essential that only perfect material is used. Mash thoroughly with a potato masher (a fork is not so efficient and will leave lumps) for several minutes until an even floury consistency is obtained, then weigh out the ½ lb (225g) required for the recipe. If the potatoes are peeled *before* boiling they will absorb water and produce a wet mash which will result in heavy bread.

Dissolve the yeast in the warm water to which one tablespoon (15ml) of the sugar has been added. It is ready for use when the surface is covered in frothy bubbles.

Bring the soya milk to the boil and simmer for one minute, stir in the remaining tablespoon (15ml) of sugar and set aside to cool.

Sieve the flours and salt together into a large bowl and rub in the mashed potato with the hands until it is completely mixed and resembles fine breadcrumbs. It is important to do this thoroughly or the texture of the crumb will be impaired.

Make a well in the centre of the flour and pour in all the liquids, then stir with a wooden spoon to mix, finishing off by hand-mixing until a soft dough is formed. The dough will appear to be slightly tacky but should not be so wet as to adhere to the sides of the bowl.

Turn out on to a lightly floured surface and knead for 100 strokes after which the dough should be soft and smooth. If it shows signs of stickiness add more flour to the surface and work in as kneading progresses; if it is too dry incorporate extra water by lightly spraying over the dough and kneading it in.

When the dough is soft and pliable form it into a ball and return it to the bowl, cover with a damp cloth and set into a warm, draughtproof place for rising which will take between one and two hours depending upon the temperature, 70°F (21°C) is ideal. A slow rise is not detrimental.

When it has doubled in bulk turn the dough out on to a lightly floured surface and knead for 20 strokes. Allow to rest for 10 minutes, then divide into equal portions as required.

Roll each portion into a torpedo shape with a rotary action and place into well-greased tins. Return the tins to a warm, draughtproof place to prove which, at the same temperature, will take about half the time of the first rise. Cover with a damp cloth but support it so that it does not come into direct contact with the dough.

If tray-baked loaves are preferred the general principles are exactly the same except that the torpedo-shaped portions can be moulded into any desired shape before placing on to a well-greased baking tray.

When the dome of the dough has risen level with the top of the tins, or tray-baked loaves have doubled in volume they are ready for the oven.

A better rise will be obtained if the dough does not form a skin before being baked as this tends to restrict the dough's ability to expand. Covering it at all times with a damp cloth is essential, and a light spray with warm water just as the loaves go into the oven will usually last long enough for the spring to be unrestricted.

Loaves in tins can be further assisted by covering with a loose 'tent' formed from kitchen foil, lightly greased on the inside and supported so that contact with the rising dough is prevented. If this covers the loaves for the first 20 minutes or so it will prevent the skin forming long enough for the spring to be completed, after which it should be removed and baking continued as normal.

Bake on the middle shelf of an oven pre-heated to 350°F (180°C, Gas Mark 4) for about 60 minutes, then test by tapping the base of a loaf with the fingertips – if it sounds hollow the bread is done. Cool on a wire rack. Do not cut for at least one hour.

VARIATIONS

The proportion of white to wholemeal flour can be varied but the more wholemeal used the more water will be needed, perhaps an extra tablespoon (15ml).

Golden syrup or pasteurized honey can be substituted for the sugar.

Rice Bread★★

It seems to make little difference which type of rice is used in breadmaking, white or brown, polished or natural, but bear in mind that unpolished brown rice takes longer to cook and absorbs more water. Recipes vary as to the ratio of wheat flour to rice, and you can add more or less as you become more confident; the following yields two small loaves (or one large) with light open crumb and medium crust. It can be frozen but stales rather quickly.

INGREDIENTS

    4 oz (110g) rice (uncooked weight)
    1 teaspoon (5g) granulated dried yeast
    1 teaspoon (5g) sugar
    ½ pint (280ml) warm water
    1¼ lb (560g) strong white flour, preferably unbleached
    2 teaspoons (10g) salt
    2 tablespoons (30ml) olive oil

METHOD

Boil the rice in 12 fl. oz (340ml) slightly salted water in a saucepan of not more than 2 pints (1100ml) capacity. Cover closely and simmer until all the water has been absorbed and small holes have formed all over the surface of the rice. Watch carefully to ensure the rice does not burn on the bottom of the saucepan. If unpolished brown rice is used about 3 fl. oz (80ml) extra water will be needed and a much longer cooking time will be required.

Dissolve the yeast and sugar in the warm water and set aside to activate. It is ready for use when the surface is covered in frothy bubbles.

Sieve the salt and flour together into a large bowl and mix thoroughly. When the rice is cooked and still warm, rub it into the flour as you would fat, making sure it is evenly and thoroughly incorporated.

When the yeast is activated add the oil and whisk briskly to produce a smooth emulsion, pour this into the flour and mix until a soft light dough results.

Knead for 20 strokes, then return the dough to the bowl, cover with a damp cloth and put it into a warm place to rise until it has doubled in volume (usually about two hours).

Turn out and knead gently for another 20 strokes, adding a little more flour if it is unmanageable (it is meant to be very soft and loose), then divide into equal portions (if required) and place into greased, pre-warmed tins. The tins should be about two-thirds full. Cover and set to prove in a warm, draughtproof place.

When the dough has risen just above the top of the tins it is ready for the oven.

Bake on the centre shelf of an oven pre-heated to 450°F (230°C, Gas Mark 8) for 15 minutes, then reduce the temperature to 400°F (200°C, Gas Mark 6) and bake for another 20 minutes. Remove from the tins and continue baking for a further 20 minutes at the same temperature.

Test by tapping the base of a loaf with the fingertips – if it sounds hollow the bread is done. Cool on a wire rack.

For a crisp crust spray the top of the loaves with water just before they go into the oven; if a softer crust is required paint the tops with butter or vegetable oil as they come out of the oven.

VARIATIONS

Up to a quarter of the total quantity of white flour can be substituted with wholemeal without affecting the outcome; more than that will require a little extra water, and the delicate flavour imparted by the rice will disappear.

To get the full rice flavour use all white flour for your first attempt and experiment when you have discovered what real rice bread tastes like.

Note: Very little kneading is required for this dough, just enough to ensure it is thoroughly mixed. If the dough is too dry the crumb will be dense, too wet and it may collapse in the oven.

Farmhouse Wholemeal Bread★

A very good, old-fashioned wholemeal loaf, with a richly flavoured dark crumb and crisp crust. After trying this you will never go back to a 'factory wholemeal'. Makes five small loaves or fewer larger. It keeps well and can be frozen.

INGREDIENTS

> 1 tablespoon (15g) granulated dried yeast
> 1 tablespoon (15g) sugar
> 1½ pints (830ml) warm water
> 3 lbs (1350g) stoneground wholemeal flour
> 1 tablespoon (15g) salt
> 2 oz (55g) lard

METHOD

Hand-mixing. Dissolve the sugar in the warm water, add the yeast and set aside to activate. It is ready for use when the surface is covered in frothy bubbles.

Sieve the flour and salt together into a large bowl. Rub the lard into the flour until it resembles fine breadcrumbs, then make a well in the centre and pour in the yeast liquid.

Using a wooden spoon, gradually incorporate the flour from around the edges until all is included and thoroughly mixed.

Machine Mixing using a doughhook. Put the warm water into the mixing bowl of the machine and add the yeast and sugar. Using the dough hook mix on the slowest speed for 20 seconds then set aside until the surface of the liquid is covered with frothy bubbles.

Meanwhile sieve the salt and flour together and rub in the lard until the mixture resembles fine breadcrumbs. When the yeast liquid is ready, start the machine on the slowest speed and gradually spoon the flour into the bowl.

Continue mixing on the slow speed until a ball of dough adheres to the dough hook, then increase the speed to about half the maximum and run for a full 2 minutes. (If a small quantity of flour persistently refuses to join the ball on the dough hook, a teaspoon (5ml) of extra water can be added but do not make the mixture sticky.)

From then on the methods are identical.

Turn the dough out on to a lightly floured surface and knead for 400 strokes. The dough should feel smooth and damp but not sticky. If it is too dry spray it lightly with warm water; if too sticky knead in a little more flour. As a general rule wholemeal bread needs slightly more moisture than white bread, but the dough must never be sticky.

Form the dough into a ball and return it to the bowl, cover with a damp cloth or greased polythene and set in a warm (75°F, 24°C) place to rise. It will take between one and two hours to double in bulk.

When ready turn out the dough on to a lightly floured surface and re-knead for 100 strokes then divide into equal portions according to the number of loaves required. Roll each into a ball with a rotary action on the table top, slightly elongating it into a torpedo shape before half-filling warmed and greased tins.

Return the tins to a warm place for the proving and cover with a *dry* cloth. The dough is correctly proved when the dome of the loaf is just level with the rim of the tin.

It is not usual to decorate wholemeal loaves but, if desired, slash them with a lightly greased sharp knife or blade making cuts at least ¼ in deep just before baking.

Place the loaves on the centre shelf of an oven pre-heated to 475°F (240°C, Gas Mark 9). After 15 minutes reduce the temperature to 425°F (220°C, Gas Mark 7) and continue baking for a further 30 minutes.

Test by tapping the base of a loaf with the fingertips; if it sounds hollow it is done. Cool on a wire rack.

VARIATIONS

Farmhouse Wholemeal is a coarse-crumbed bread. A finer crumb will result from a finer ground flour but it will not then be a genuine Farmhouse Wholemeal.

Golden syrup or pasteurized honey can be substituted for sugar, block margarine for the lard but low-fat spreads are unsuitable.

If vegetable or olive oil is preferred to the lard whisk 3 tablespoons (45ml) into the activated yeast liquid before pouring it into the flour.

Ham and Clove Spiral Bread★★

This is a good way of using left-over ham or ham scraps. Use only lean meat; fat will disintegrate during baking and leave holes in the crumb. The recipe makes five small loaves or fewer larger. The bread keeps well and can be frozen and it makes excellent unusual toast.

INGREDIENTS

2 teaspoons (10g) granulated dried yeast
2 teaspoons (10g) sugar
1¼ pints (700ml) warm water
1 lb (450g) stoneground wholemeal flour
2 lb (900g) strong white flour, preferably unbleached
2 teaspoons (10g) salt
2 oz (55g) lard
10 oz (280g) cooked lean ham, minced or finely chopped
Ground cloves to taste

METHOD

Dissolve the sugar and yeast in the warm water and set aside to activate; it is ready for use when the surface is covered in frothy bubbles.

Sieve the flours and salt together into a large bowl and mix thoroughly. Rub in the lard until the mixture resembles fine breadcrumbs.

When the yeast liquid is ready pour it into the flour and stir with a wooden spoon until a rough dough results. Turn out the dough on to a lightly floured surface and knead for 200 strokes by which time it will become smooth and silky. Form into a ball and return the dough to the bowl, cover with a dry cloth overlaid with a damp one and leave to rise in a warm place for one or two hours until doubled in bulk.

When it has risen, turn it out on to a lightly floured surface and knead for a further 200 strokes then divide into equal portions and form each into a torpedo shape.

Roll out each piece with a floured rolling pin, using guides of ¼ in (6mm) thickness to ensure the dough will be even. Set the guides slightly narrower apart than the length of the tins to be used – for a tin 5½ ins (14cms) long the gauges should be about 4½ ins (12cms) apart.

You will now have a piece of dough in the form of a long rectangle. Sprinkle it sparingly with ground cloves, then with 2 ozs (55g) of the minced or chopped ham, making sure the dough is evenly covered. Spray over lightly with warm water – just to dampen it, it must not be at all wet – then roll up taking care that the ham does not fall out of the sides as you roll.

You will find that the dough tapers off at the end of the rolling but this does not matter. Each torpedo is now placed into a pre-greased, warm tin, with the taper of the roll underneath so it cannot unroll as it bakes, and put into a warm place to prove for about 40 minutes.

When the dough has risen level with the top of the tins it is ready for the oven.

Bake on the centre shelf of an oven pre-heated to 450°F (230°C, Gas Mark 8) for 15 minutes, then reduce the temperature to 400°F (200°C, Gas Mark 6) and bake for a further 30 minutes or until the base of a loaf sounds hollow when tapped with the fingertips.

Place the loaves on a wire rack to cool.

VARIATIONS

The proportions of white to brown flour can be varied as desired.

The amount of ground cloves can be varied according to personal taste or omitted altogether.

Some cooks push whole cloves into the top crust at random or in set patterns just before the bread goes into the oven. This gives a very pretty effect but they should be removed before the bread is served as whole cloves are unpalatable if eaten.

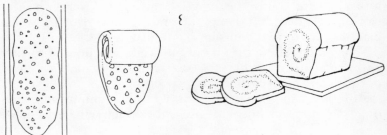

East Anglian Saffron Bread★

Originating near the town of Saffron Walden, this bread is something between a normal loaf and a tea bread. The amount of sugar in the recipe makes it suitable for all normal purposes such as sandwiches and toasting, but by increasing the sugar and perhaps decorating with chopped almonds it becomes a tea bread. Makes two small loaves or one large.

INGREDIENTS

2 teaspoons (10g) granulated dried yeast
2 oz (55g) sugar
1 pint (550ml) milk, scalded and cooled to blood heat
½ teaspoon (2.5g) salt
½ teaspoon (2.5g) ground saffron
1½ lb (700g) strong white flour, preferably unbleached
7 oz (200ml) melted butter
1 egg, size 3

METHOD

Dissolve the yeast and sugar in the warm milk and set aside to activate; it is ready for use when the surface is covered in frothy bubbles. Sift the flour, salt and saffron into a large bowl, mixing thoroughly.

When the yeast liquid is ready add the melted butter and the egg to it and whisk briskly until a smooth emulsion results, then pour this liquid into the flour and mix until a workable dough is obtained.

Cover with a clean towel or polythene and set aside in a warm place to rise. When it has doubled in volume turn the dough out on to a lightly floured surface and knead for 200 strokes by which time it will be smooth and pliable. If it is sticky knead in a little more flour.

Divide into portions and mould roughly to shape before putting each piece into a warm, pre-greased tin. Cover the tins with a dry cloth and put into a warm place to prove.

When the dough has risen level with the top of the tins it is ready for the oven.

Bake on the centre shelf of an oven pre-heated to 450°F

(230°C, Gas Mark 8) for 10 minutes, then reduce the temperature to 400°F (200°C, Gas Mark 6) for a further 40 minutes. Test by tapping the base of a loaf with the fingertips – if it sounds hollow it is done. Cool on a wire rack.

VARIATIONS

The flavour of the bread can be intensified by mixing the saffron with a teaspoon of brandy or rum then adding it to the yeast mixture just before it is poured into the flour.

Oatmeal Bread★

Oatmeal is rich in fat but poor in gluten content so for breadmaking it is usually combined with wheat flour. There are several grades of oatmeal, fine, medium and coarse, and of these, fine and medium are best suited for breadmaking. A small proportion of oatmeal to wholemeal flour gives a pleasant flavour to the bread.

Oatmeal bread is only seldom obtainable from professional bakeries these days although for centuries past it was widely available in the north of the British Isles. It is one of the easiest breads to make and less labour-intensive than most since it requires less kneading to arrive at the desired consistency. It produces an excellent crumb and the delicate flavour makes it a favourite with many people.

Raw oatmeal has a very limited life span before it becomes stale and bitter so make sure your supplies are fresh, and buy in quantities sufficient for one baking at a time.

Makes three small loaves or fewer large.

INGREDIENTS

    1 tablespoon (15g) granulated dried yeast
    1 pint (550ml) warm water
    2 tablespoons (30ml) cream
    ½ lb (225g) medium grade stoneground oatmeal
    1 lb (450g) strong white flour, preferably unbleached
    ½ lb (225g) stoneground wholemeal flour
    1 tablespoon (15g) salt

METHOD

Dissolve the yeast in the warm water and when the surface is covered in frothy bubbles stir in the cream. The omission of sugar in this recipe means that the yeast will take longer to activate.

Mix the flours, oatmeal and salt thoroughly in a large bowl before adding the yeast liquid; continue mixing until all ingredients are thoroughly incorporated and a rather moist dough results; if it is too dry and crumbly extra warm water can be added a spoonful at a time but the dough must not become sticky.

Turn out and knead for 100 strokes, return to the bowl, cover with a damp cloth or polythene and set in a warm place to rise for about two hours or until it has almost doubled in volume.

Then turn the dough out on to a lightly floured surface and knead for about 40 strokes. If it seems too wet add a coating of oatmeal to the working surface and knead until it is absorbed. The dough should feel clammy but not sticky. Form into a ball, cover and return to a warm place to rise for about one hour or until almost doubled in volume.

Again turn the dough out on to a floured surface and knead for a further 40 strokes then divide equally into the number of portions required, and roll each into a ball with a rotary action of the palm of the hand, flatten slightly, then make a series of criss-cross deep cuts over the surface to give a chequered pattern. The bread is now ready to go into a warm place for proving which will take about 30 minutes.

Place the loaves on a lightly greased and floured baking tray and bake on the centre shelf of an oven preheated to 450°F (230°C, Gas Mark 8) for 20 minutes, then reduce the temperature to 425°F (220°C, Gas Mark 7) and continue baking for another 20-30 minutes. Test by tapping the base of a loaf with the fingertips; if it sounds hollow it is done and can be placed upon a wire rack to cool.

Oatmeal breads do not rise as much as those made with wheat flours so the crumb tends to be more dense.

VARIATIONS

Although oatmeal loaves are traditionally round and baked on a baking tray they can be just as easily made in tins but the tins should be filled rather more than half-full because the dough will not rise so much. Tins should be carefully greased then coated with flour before being filled.

A dish of boiling water placed in the bottom of the oven 30 minutes before baking will help in the formation of a crisper crust.

If your oven is large enough a Pyrex basin inverted over each round loaf for the first 20 minutes will give a higher rise and better crust, but the basin must be large enough to allow the dough to rise without touching. Most ordinary earthenware basins are unable to withstand the high temperatures required for baking, and plastic will, of course, melt or distort. A clean clay flowerpot will serve the same purpose but it must be soaked in water for twenty-four hours before use, and the hole in the base partially sealed with a piece of quarry tile or similar material – stones can explode when heated and should not be used.

Farmhouse Cobs★

These little rolls are very popular in the Cotswolds where they are said to have originated, although they are so widespread over the country that it is difficult to confirm or deny the claim. They can be made with white or wholemeal flour or any combination of the two. Although best served hot from the oven, they can be frozen and reheated later. They tend to go stale quickly if not frozen. The recipe will make about 24 small rolls.

INGREDIENTS

4 fl. oz (110ml) warm water
12 fl. oz (340ml) milk, scalded and cooled to blood heat
2 teaspoons (10g) dried granulated yeast
2 teaspoons (10g) sugar
2 lb (900g) strong white flour (preferably unbleached) or a mixture of white and wholemeal
2 teaspoons (10g) salt
4 oz (110g) cooking margarine
2 eggs, size 3

METHOD

Mix the warm water and the scalded milk in a basin and add the yeast and sugar. Stir to disperse, then set aside to activate. It is ready for use when the surface is covered in frothy bubbles.

Sieve the flour and salt together into a large bowl and mix thoroughly. Rub in the margarine until the mixture resembles fine breadcrumbs.

When the yeast mixture is ready, break the eggs into it and

whisk until a smooth creamy liquid results. Pour this liquid into the flour and mix with a wooden spoon until all the ingredients are evenly combined into a rough dough.

Turn the dough out on to a lightly floured surface, and knead for 200 strokes by which time it will have become smooth and silky. It must not be sticky, if necessary knead in extra flour.

Form the dough into a ball and return it to the bowl, cover with a dry cloth overlaid with a damp one, and put it into a warm place to rise at a temperature between 70° and 80°F (21° and 27°C).

When it has doubled in volume, knead for a further 20 strokes, then divide it into 24 equal portions. Roll each piece into a ball between the palms of the hands and with a sharp knife cut a deep cross in the top of each roll (about ½ in (1.25cms)).

Place the rolls on a greased baking sheet allowing at least 1 in (2.5cms) between them, cover with polythene supported so it cannot touch the rolls, and put them into a warm place to prove.

When they have doubled in size bake them on the centre shelf of an oven pre-heated to 400°F (200°C, Gas Mark 6) for about 20 minutes or until they are a golden brown.

If a soft crust is preferred brush the tops with melted butter before putting the rolls into the oven. For a harder crust brush them with water.

VARIATIONS

This is the traditional shape for a Farmhouse Cob with the cuts opening out to form four little peaks; however, you don't have to stick with tradition, you can leave the tops uncut, or make several more cuts. You can even make little cottage loaves by putting a smaller piece of dough on top of a larger base portion and pushing a wooden skewer down through them to give the indentation normal in a cottage loaf. They may need a little longer in the oven than the traditional cobs but in all other respects the same recipe applies.

Novelty Fried Egg Bread★★★

This is a way of impressing your friends, or of entertaining the children at breakfast-time. The recipe makes three loaves which keep and freeze well. You will require a 7 in (18cms) high-sided cake tin and an empty 15 oz (420g) baked bean or similar can for each loaf.

INGREDIENTS

> 4 teaspoons (20g) granulated dried yeast
> 4 teaspoons (20g) sugar
> 1¼ pints (700ml) warm water
> 1 lb (450g) stoneground wholemeal flour
> 2 lb (900g) strong white flour, preferably unbleached
> 4 teaspoons (20g) salt
> 2 oz (55g) lard
> Ground cloves to taste
> 10 oz (280g) cooked lean ham, minced or finely chopped

METHOD

Dissolve the sugar and yeast in the warm water and set aside to activate; it is ready for use when the surface is covered in frothy bubbles.

Sieve the flours, salt and ground cloves together into a large bowl and mix thoroughly. Rub in the lard until the mixture resembles fine breadcrumbs, then stir in the minced ham until it is evenly distributed.

When the yeast liquid is ready pour it into the flour and stir with a wooden spoon until a rough dough results, then continue mixing with the hands until it can be formed into a ball.

Turn the dough out on to a lightly floured surface and knead for 200 strokes by which time it will become smooth and silky. Return it to the bowl, cover with a dry cloth overlaid with a damp one and leave to rise in a warm place for one or two hours until doubled in bulk.

When it is correctly risen, turn it out on to the floured surface and knead for a further 200 strokes then divide into three equal portions and form each into a torpedo shape.

Roll out each piece with the hands until it is extended into a long sausage about 15 ins (38cms) long and as even as possible.

Warm a 7-in (18cms) cake tin not less than 3½ ins (9cms) deep for each loaf, and line it with baking parchment. Take the empty baked bean can (or similar) and wrap it in aluminium foil between the flanges, to compensate for the width of the flanges, then wrap this also in baking parchment. Place the can in the middle of the cake tin and fit the dough sausage around it, dampening the ends and squeezing them together to make a complete ring of dough. With the knuckles gently work the dough until evenly spread around the cake tin which should be about half-filled.

Put each loaf into a warm place to prove. They are ready for the oven when the dough has risen level with the top of the cake tin.

Bake on the centre shelf of an oven pre-heated to 450°F (230°C, Gas Mark 8) for 15 minutes, then reduce the temperature to 400°F (200°C, Gas Mark 6) and bake for a further 20 minutes.

Remove the loaves from the oven and allow to cool for 10 minutes, then turn each loaf out of its tin (the can will easily slide out of the centre) and tap the base with the fingertips – if it sounds hollow the bread is done, if not return it to the oven without the tins for a few more minutes.

Carefully place the loaves on a wire rack to cool; at this stage they are easily damaged.

Do not attempt to cut them until they are at least a day old or they will collapse under the knife. Slice them across with a bread saw, cutting slices about ½ in (12mms) thick to provide bread rings with a hole in the centre of each. An electric carving knife is ideal for this purpose because no pressure is needed.

When ready to serve, dip each ring briefly into warm water (just a quick dip, not a soak) and drop it into the frying pan in which a little fat has already been heated, fry one side until just brown, then turn the bread over and break an egg into the centre hole and cook gently until fried to your liking.

Serve immediately on warm plates.

The upper and lower crusts of each loaf should be served

crust uppermost and the crusty sides should not be fried too long or they can get very hard.

VARIATIONS

The proportions of white to brown flour can be varied as desired, and the amount of ground cloves can be increased or reduced according to personal taste.

Vegetable oil can be substituted for the lard, but in this case it should be whisked into the activated yeast liquid.

The rings can be decorated with mushrooms or tomatoes, or anything else that takes your fancy such as circles of black pudding or sausagemeat. Let your imagination run riot with this recipe: breakfasts will never be the same again.

The rings can be toasted if you wish to avoid frying, and the eggs poached before being thoroughly drained and dropped into the centre hole before serving.

Note: Good quality baking parchment should not need greasing but beware of inferior products. If the bread sticks to the cake tin or the can it will be ruined, and any rough handling when it is turned out of the tin will cause it to collapse.

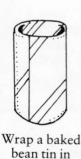

Wrap a baked
bean tin in
foil

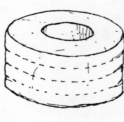

Slices

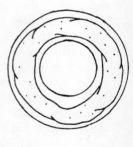

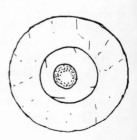

Italian Marbled Tomato Bread★★

This recipe originated in southern Italy in the area to the east of Naples. It makes a soft-crusted loaf with a pretty pink crumb. The flavour is rather too strong for sweet spreads but it is excellent with savoury ones and as a complement to soups. It is also good with fish dishes. The bread toasts well, freezes and has good keeping qualities. The recipe makes five small loaves or fewer larger ones.

INGREDIENTS

¾ pint (420ml) warm water
4 teaspoons (20g) granulated dried yeast
4 teaspoons (20ml) sugar
3 lb (1150g) strong white flour, preferably unbleached
4 oz (110g) potato flour
4 teaspoons (20g) paprika powder
4 teaspoons (20g) salt
3 fl.oz (80ml) olive oil
½ pint (280ml) concentrated tomato juice
About half a tube of concentrated tomato paste

METHOD

Dissolve the sugar and yeast in the warm water and set aside to activate. It is ready for use when the surface is covered in frothy bubbles.

Sift the flours, salt and paprika together into a large bowl.

When the yeast liquid is ready add the olive oil, and whisk until completely emulsified. The best results will be obtained from a liquidizer.

Make a well in the flour and pour in the emulsified liquids together with the tomato juice. Mix with the hands until a coarse, rather slack dough results.

Turn out on to a floured surface and knead for 100 strokes by which time the dough will have become quite smooth and silky. A little more flour can be kneaded in if the dough is very sticky but this is intended to be rather wetter than most doughs; it should be just tacky when being handled. Form it into a ball and put into a warm place for about an hour or until it has doubled in volume.

Turn it out on to a lightly floured surface and pat with the hands or roll out until it is about ½ in thick, then squeeze lines of tomato paste on to the dough, making a trelliswork pattern. Keep the paste away from the edges.

Roll up the dough and knead for about 30 strokes, then divide into portions, mould into shape and place each portion into a pre-warmed and greased tin (or on to a greased baking tray if round loaves are preferred).

Set the loaves into a warm draughtproof place to prove for about half an hour or roughly half the time taken for the first rise. When the dome of the bread has risen level with the top edge of the tins, or the trayed loaves have doubled in volume, they are ready for the oven.

Bake on the centre shelf of an oven pre-heated to 400°F (200°C, Gas Mark 6) for about 45 minutes. Remove one loaf and test by tapping the base with the fingertips; if it sounds hollow the bread is done.

Cool on a wire rack and do not cut for two hours.

VARIATIONS

A finely chopped clove of garlic can be added to the dry flour mixture if you wish.

The quality of commercial tomato juice varies considerably; the best is thick without the addition of chemical thickeners.

Mexican Corn Bread★

This is said to have been discovered by the Spaniards when they invaded Mexico, and brought back to Spain from whence its popularity spread. Even if the legend of its origin is doubtful, this recipe is certainly widespread in Spain and the Balearic Islands, and is occasionally found in the eastern Algarve. It is very easy to make and has a pale yellow dense crumb, very popular with children. The crust may appear to be underdone, showing little or no signs of browning, but it is quite crisp. It makes excellent toast, keeps well and can be frozen. The recipe makes five small loaves or fewer larger.

INGREDIENTS

    4 teaspoons (20g) dried granulated yeast
    4 teaspoons (20g) sugar
    1¼ pints (700ml) warm water
    2 lb (900g) strong white flour, preferably unbleached
    1 lb (450g) maize flour (*not* cornflour)
    4 teaspoons (20g) salt
    2 fl.oz (55ml) olive oil

METHOD

Dissolve the yeast and sugar in the warm water and set aside to activate. It is ready for use when the surface is covered in frothy bubbles.

Sieve the flours and salt together into a large warmed bowl.

When the yeast liquid is ready, add the slightly warmed olive oil and whisk briskly until a smooth emulsion results. Add this mixture to the flours and work with the hands until a rough dough results.

Turn out on to a lightly floured surface and knead for 100 strokes, then place the dough in a warmed bowl, cover with a dry cloth overlaid with a damp one, and leave to rise in a warm place until the dough has doubled in volume.

Again turn out the dough on to a lightly floured surface and knead for a further 100 strokes. Return it to the warm place for a second rise which will take about half as long as the first.

When it has again doubled in volume knead for another 40 strokes, then divide into portions, mould to shape and either put each portion into a well-greased tin or place on a greased baking tray. Tins should be just over half full, and tray-baked loaves should be spaced so they do not touch as they expand. Set in a warm, draughtproof place to prove until the dough has risen level with the top of the tins or the trayed loaves have doubled in size. Pre-heat the oven to 450°F (230°C, Gas Mark 8), and bake on the centre shelf for 15 minutes before reducing the temperature to 350°F (180°C, Gas Mark 4) and cooking for a further 30 minutes.

Test by tapping the base of a loaf with the fingertips – if it sounds hollow it is done.

Cool on a wire rack.

Note: Traditionally this bread is tray-baked with a deep cross cut into the surface of each loaf about five minutes before being put into the oven, in the manner of a Coburg.

The final kneading and moulding must be performed gently and with great care. The dough will be of the consistency of shortcrust pastry and rough handling at this stage can cause it to tear.

Beer Bread★★

Many types of beer can be used in making bread, the darker the beer the deeper coloured the crumb; you will have to experiment to find which best suits your palate. The alcohol evaporates during baking so there is no reason for concern about your family developing into alcoholics! Draught beer is best because it is less effervescent but, whether draught or canned, it should be exposed to the air for at least an hour to go flat. The recipe makes two small loaves or one large.

INGREDIENTS

2 teaspoons (10g) dried granulated yeast
2 teaspoons (10g) sugar
4 fl.oz (225ml) warm water
½ lb (225g) strong white flour, preferably unbleached
½ lb (225g) stoneground wholemeal flour
1 teaspoon (5g) salt
1 tablespoon (15g) dried dill (or double quantity fresh)
3 tablespoons (45ml) vegetable oil
8 fl.oz (225ml) warm beer (same temperature as the water)
Beaten egg to glaze

METHOD

Dissolve the yeast and sugar in the warm water and set aside to activate; it is ready for use when the surface is covered in frothy bubbles.

Sieve the flours and salt together into a large warm bowl and mix thoroughly, then stir in the dill.

When the yeast liquid is ready add the oil and whisk vigorously until a creamy smooth emulsion results. Pour in the warm beer and whisk to mix.

Make a well in the flour, pour in the liquid and stir with a wooden spoon to produce a rough dough.

Turn out on to a lightly floured surface and knead for 200 strokes by which time the dough will be smooth and elastic. Knead in more flour if it is at all sticky.

Put into a warm, lightly greased bowl. Cover with a damp

cloth and set into a warm place to rise for about an hour or until it has doubled in bulk.

Turn out on to a lightly floured surface and knead for a further 100 strokes, then divide into portions.

Half-fill warm, pre-greased tins or set on to a greased baking tray, and return to a warm, draughtproof place for about 30 minutes to prove. They are ready for the oven when the dome of the dough has risen level with the top of the tin, or the trayed loaves have doubled in volume.

To glaze, brush the tops with the beaten egg just before they go into the oven. The loaves can be sprinkled with poppy seeds at this point to give an attractive finish.

Bake on the centre shelf of an oven pre-heated to 375°F (190°C, Gas Mark 5) for about 50 minutes or until the bread sounds hollow when the base is tapped with the fingertips.

Remove from the oven, allow to rest for 5 minutes in the tins or on the tray before placing on a wire rack to cool.

VARIATIONS

Caraway, poppy or dill seeds can be used instead of the dried dill.

The bread can be made entirely of white flour if preferred in which case the crumb will be a lighter colour. All-wholemeal flour coupled with a dark beer or stout will produce a very dark crumb.

Milk Bread★★

Milk breads are more nutritious, lighter and keep better than those made with water. Dough made with milk rises a little higher because the casein stimulates the yeast and strengthens the gluten, thus yielding a softer, more delicate crumb and a golden soft crust.

Semi-skimmed milk can be used but the results will be inferior, and skimmed milk is little better than water for this purpose.

Milk must always be scalded before use or it can inhibit the action of the yeast. Scalding is not boiling – milk is scalded when the temperature has been raised sufficiently to form a skin on the surface. Boiling destroys most of the nutrients in the milk, and the rise is then no better than if water had been used.

The following recipe is based upon using white flour. Wholemeal flour can be used, or a mixture of white and wholemeal, but the delicate flavour of the milk bread will not be so obvious and the traditional white crumb will be lost.

Milk breads must not be overcooked or the keeping qualities will be impaired. The crust should be a golden brown and the sides of the loaf slightly tinted. When taken from the oven the loaves must be handled carefully for the first half-hour or so as they can easily be distorted.

Makes five small loaves or fewer larger.

INGREDIENTS

    1 tablespoon (15g) granulated dried yeast
    1¼ pints (700ml) warm whole milk
    1 tablespoon (15g) sugar
    3 lb (1350g) strong white flour, preferably unbleached
    1 tablespoon (15g) salt
    2 oz (55g) lard

METHOD

Hand-mixing. Scald the milk and cool to about 75°F (24°C); much higher and the yeast will be killed.

Add the yeast and sugar to the warm milk, stir for a few

minutes then leave to activate. It is ready for use when the surface of the liquid is covered in frothy bubbles.

Sieve the flour and salt together into a large bowl, rub the lard thoroughly into the flour until it resembles fine breadcrumbs, then make a well in the centre and pour in the activated yeast liquid.

Mix from the centre with a wooden spoon gradually incorporating the flour from around the edges of the bowl until all is included, then turn out on to a floured surface for kneading.

Machine-mixing using a dough hook. Put the scalded and cooled milk into the bowl of the machine, add the yeast and sugar and mix for 10 seconds on the slow speed. Leave to activate until the surface is covered in frothy bubbles.

Sieve the flour and salt together into a separate bowl and rub in the lard until the mixture resembles fine breadcrumbs.

Start the machine on the lowest speed and gradually spoon the flour mixture into the yeasty milk. Continue mixing until a ball of flour adheres to the dough hook, then increase the speed to about half the maximum and run for 2 minutes. Turn it out on to a floured surface for kneading.

From then on the methods are identical

The dough will seem rough, uneven and somewhat sticky but as kneading progresses it will become smooth and silky. Knead for 400 strokes; the stickiness will disappear and the dough become soft and pliable.

Mould the dough into a ball and return it to the bowl, cover with a damp cloth or polythene film and place in a warm place to rise.

The time taken for the rise will depend mainly upon the temperature although milk doughs can be expected to rise a little faster than those made with water. A low temperature will give a slower rise but a high temperature can kill the yeast. The dough will take about an hour to double in bulk at around 75°F (24°C).

When it has doubled in size turn the dough out on to a lightly floured surface and knead gently for 100 strokes then weigh into equal portions.

Roll each into a ball with a rotary action of the palm of the hand, slightly elongating them before half-filling warmed, greased tins which should be returned to a warm, draughtproof place for proving and again covered but with a dry cloth.

Attention to proving is very important for milk breads; a loaf which is insufficiently risen will be heavy and dense in texture. The dough is correctly proved when the dome of the loaf is just level with the rim of the tin *if the correct amount of dough was used*, and if a dry finger is gently pressed on the surface and the depression fills gradually. Inspect the loaves after 20 minutes proving and, if not ready, at 10-minute intervals thereafter.

Place the loaves on the centre shelf of an oven pre-heated to 475°F (240°C, Gas Mark 9) and bake for 15 minutes before reducing the temperature to 425°F (220°C, Gas Mark 7) and baking for a further 15 minutes. It is quite possible for the loaves to be cooked by now but if, upon examination, they require a little longer re-examine them at 5-minute intervals and move them around on the shelf if your oven heat is uneven.

Because milk breads are softer and less crusty than breads made with water it is not possible to test by tapping the base of the loaf with the fingers to ascertain whether it is cooked. A fair guide is to see when the bread has shrunk away from the sides of the tin, but if when knocked out the loaves seem rather damp they can be given a few more minutes in the oven.

Cool on a wire rack and allow to rest for at least an hour before cutting.

VARIATIONS

Pasteurized honey can be substituted for the sugar, but if it is used keep to a level tablespoon (15ml); an excess of sweetener can inhibit the yeast action.

Lard can be replaced by vegetable oil or block margarine (low-fat substitutes are not suitable). Olive oil is not acceptable; use either corn or sunflower oil whisked into the activated yeast for best results.

Clover-Leaf Rolls★★

These soft rolls are best eaten fresh from the oven, but can be re-heated if necessary. Whether they are pulled apart or sliced is a matter of personal preference but they are delicious with fresh butter or cheese. They keep well and can be frozen but there is no doubt that they are at their best freshly baked; for this reason make in small batches. This recipe makes about four clover-leaf rolls.

INGREDIENTS

1 teaspoon (5g) dried granulated yeast
½ teaspoon (2.5g) sugar
¼ pint (140ml) warm water
1 lb (450g) strong white flour, preferably unbleached
¼ lb (110g) potato flour
½ teaspoon (2.5g) salt
1 tablespoon (15ml) olive oil
Poppy seeds for decoration (optional)

METHOD

Dissolve the sugar and yeast in the warm water and set aside to activate. It is ready for use when the surface is covered in frothy bubbles.

Sift the flour and salt into a large warmed bowl and place in the oven for a few minutes at 200°F (100°C, Gas Mark ¼) to warm the flour. Remove from the oven and mix the flour by hand to eliminate any cold spots.

When the yeast liquid is ready add the olive oil and whisk or liquidize until it is thoroughly emulsified then make a well in the flour and pour in the liquid.

Stir with a wooden spoon initially, then with the hands until a silky smooth dough results.

Turn the dough out and knead gently for 60 strokes. Return it to the warm bowl, cover with a damp cloth, and put it into a warm place to rise until it has doubled in volume (normally about an hour at about 70°F/21°C).

When correctly risen deflate by pressing with the palm of the hands, then weigh out into 2-oz (50g) portions. Take each portion and roll it between the palms until it resembles a ping-pong ball. The balls should feel slightly tacky to the hands but not sticky.

Warm and grease a Yorkshire Pudding tray (or any similar 4-in diameter shallow tin), and set three balls of dough to each tin in the form of a clover-leaf. Put the tray into a warm draughtproof place to prove.

When the rolls have about doubled in bulk place them on the centre shelf of an oven pre-heated to 400°F (200°C, Gas Mark 6) and bake for 20 minutes before testing by tapping the base of a roll with the fingertips; if it sounds hollow the bread is done. Cool on a wire rack.

VARIATIONS

A proportion of wholemeal flour can be used in which case a little more water may be needed.

A mixture of half water and half milk can be used. The milk should be scalded and cooled before use.

The rolls can be sprinkled with poppy seeds before being put into the oven or left plain.

Note: Success with this recipe depends upon all utensils and ingredients being warm.

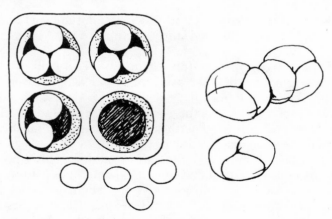

Oatmeal and Walnut Bread**

This gives a light, slightly crunchy slice, probably at its most delicious toasted and spread with butter and marmalade, or to complement a simple traditional Ploughman's Lunch of cheese, some pickled onions and a tankard of beer or cider.

The recipe makes five small loaves or fewer larger. They keep well and can be frozen.

INGREDIENTS

4 teaspoons (20g) granulated dried yeast
4 teaspoons (20g) sugar
1¼ pints (700ml) warm water
3 lb (1350g) strong white flour, preferably unbleached
¼ lb (110g) medium oatmeal
1 tablespoon (15ml) salt
4 oz (110g) lard
¼ lb (110g) chopped walnuts

METHOD

Stir the sugar and yeast into the warm water and leave to activate. The mixture is ready for use when the surface is covered in frothy bubbles.

Sift the flour, oatmeal and salt into a large bowl and mix thoroughly. Rub the lard into the mixture until it resembles fine breadcrumbs.

Toast the chopped walnuts gently under a grill until they are just golden, then set aside to cool. Watch carefully to ensure they do not burn.

Hand-mixing. When the yeast mixture is ready add it to the flour and mix well with a wooden spoon, finishing by hand to get even distribution of the liquid.

The toasted chopped nuts can be added at this point or later as you wish. If added now it is sometimes said to affect the colour of the crumb and give it a slight lavender tint. I have not experienced this and it may be the result of chopping the nuts with a carbon steel blade – I use stainless steel and so far the crumb has been a pale buff colour. If the nuts are added at this point make sure they are well mixed into the dough and evenly distributed.

Machine-mixing, using a dough hook. Warm the bowl of the mixer and the dough hook. Pour the activated yeast liquid into the mixer bowl and start the machine on the lowest speed.

Gradually spoon in the flour mixture, either with or without the chopped nuts (see above) and continue mixing until all the flour is incorporated.

Continue mixing on the slowest speed for 5 minutes or until a ball of dough adheres to the dough hook. If after five minutes some of the flour remains loose in the bottom of the bowl you can add a teaspoon (5ml) of extra water, but very seldom is more than two teaspoons (10ml) required. The dough should feel damp but not sticky.

When all the dough is attached to the dough hook increase the speed to the maximum and run for two full minutes.

From then on the methods are identical.

Turn the dough out on to a lightly floured surface and knead for 200 strokes, then form into a ball and place it in a large warm bowl for its first rise, covering with a damp cloth. Set in a warm place for about an hour or until the dough has doubled in volume.

Turn out the risen dough on to a lightly floured surface and knead for a further 200 strokes. If it seems at all sticky work in a little more flour. Form it into a ball and return it to the bowl and place it in a warm place for its second rise, covering as before.

The second rise will take about half the time of the first. The dough is ready when it has again doubled in volume.

Turn it out on to the lightly floured surface and knead for a further 40 strokes, then allow to rest for 5 minutes (if the nuts have already been added allow a 10-minute rest).

Divide the dough into equal portions.

Now is the time to add the nuts if you are concerned about a lavender-tinted crumb. Spread the toasted chopped nuts evenly over the kneading surface and knead a portion of nuts into each piece of dough before moulding to the required shape or placing into well-greased warm tins.

The loaves must now be put into a warm, draughtproof

place to prove. Those in tins will be ready for the oven when the dough has risen level with the top of the tins, those to be tray-baked will have doubled in volume.

Bake on the centre shelf of an oven pre-heated to 450°F (230°C, Gas Mark 8) for 15 minutes, then reduce the temperature to 400°F (200°C, Gas Mark 6) and bake for a further 30 minutes. Turn out one of the loaves and tap the base with the fingertips; if it sounds hollow the bread is done.

Cool on a wire rack. It can be eaten two hours later but is best left overnight.

VARIATIONS

The loaves can be rolled in chopped nuts immediately before moulding or tinning. Paint the surface with warm milk or water before sprinkling with or rolling them in chopped nuts. This gives a very pretty effect but the nuts tend to burn during cooking and get very brittle. This can be partially overcome by covering each loaf with a tent made of kitchen foil before putting it into the oven, but the foil must never come into contact with the bread. It can be removed during the last 10 minutes of baking.

A proportion of stoneground wholemeal flour can be substituted for the white, but the character of the bread will be altered.

Block margarine can be substituted for the lard but low-fat spreads are not suitable.

Rolled Oat Bread★

This is an alternative to Oatmeal Bread. It does not keep, neither can it be frozen, but eaten whilst still warm from the oven it is delicious when spread with butter, jam or a savoury spread. The recipe makes one medium-sized loaf. There is no kneading, and the dough is unsuitable for tray-baking.

INGREDIENTS

¾ pint (420ml) scalded whole milk
4 oz (110g) rolled oats
1 teaspoon (5g) salt
4 oz (110g) caster sugar
5 teaspoons (25g) fresh baking powder (not soda)
12 oz (335g) stoneground wholemeal flour
1 egg, size 3

METHOD

Pour the hot milk over the rolled oats, stir briefly, and allow to stand until cool.

Sieve the salt, sugar and baking powder into a large bowl then mix in the flour very thoroughly.

Beat the egg and whisk into the cooled oat/milk mixture. When thoroughly incorporated stir into the dry ingredients and mix until smooth and silky.

Place in a well-greased tin and set aside to rest for 10 minutes before baking in the centre of the oven pre-heated to 350°F (180°C, Gas Mark 4) for about 90 minutes.

After 60 minutes test by tapping the base of the loaf with the fingertips – if the bread sounds hollow it is done, if not continue baking, testing every ten minutes.

VARIATIONS

Strong white flour can be used as an alternative to wholemeal but the crumb will tend to be grey and is not so attractive in appearance.

The sugar content can be slightly increased or decreased to suit personal preference; this recipe will produce a relatively sweet bread, very popular with children.

Soya Bean Bread★★★

No other bread contains the same amount of protein or range of minerals and vitamins, but soya protein has an inhibiting effect upon the dough, locking up the gluten and restricting the bread's ability to rise. Because of this bread made with soya beans requires extra preparation and more precise attention to timing if the beans are not to ferment and ruin the bread. That said, well-made soya bread has an unmistakable delicate flavour and a moist crumb which remains fresh for about a week.

The raw beans must be cooked for a long time in a lot of water; if they boil dry they will be useless. Keep the water gently bubbling and test for softness after about six hours but it is more likely they will need longer – eight or nine hours is quite normal. Test by pressing with a fork; if the centre is still hard return to the boil until the whole bean is soft, then drain and mash with a potato masher until quite smooth. Put aside to cool and use as soon as the temperature is down to 70°F (21°C).

Soya beans cannot be cooked overnight for use the next day, nor can they be saved in a refrigerator; they must be used immediately they are cooked or they will begin to ferment and the bread will not rise. The most difficult part of baking with soya is the timing – the whole process must be geared to the requirements of the soya bean.

The soya mash is incorporated into the flour after the first rise, and the art of soya bread-making lies in having the mash ready for use at the exact moment when the first rise is completed – not easy, but unless you are prepared to accept these restrictions the bread will be a failure.

This recipe will make two large loaves or three smaller ones.

INGREDIENTS

 1 tablespoon (15g) granulated dried yeast
 ¼ pint (140ml) warm water
 1 lb (450g) strong white flour, preferably unbleached
 1 lb (450g) stoneground wholemeal flour
 1 tablespoon (15g) salt

3 tablespoons (45ml) pasteurized honey dissolved in ½ pint (280ml) warm water
4 tablespoons (60ml) vegetable cooking oil
5 oz (140g) soya beans pre-cooked and mashed

METHOD

Dissolve the yeast in the warm water and leave to activate until the surface is covered in frothy bubbles. Without sugar the yeast will take longer to activate so allow for this. Sieve the flours and salt together.

Hand-mixing. Pour the activated yeast mixture into the sieved flours and stir from the centre with a wooden spoon, gradually adding the honey liquid and the oil until all is thoroughly incorporated, then turn out on to a lightly floured surface and knead for about 100 strokes to complete the mixing.

Machine-mixing. Using a dough hook. Put the activated yeast liquid into the bowl and, with the machine on the lowest speed, gradually add the flours, mixing for about 5 minutes. Gradually add the honey water followed by the oil, then increase the speed to about half maximum for a further 2 minutes or until a ball of dough adheres to the dough hook. Turn out on to a lightly floured surface and knead for about 100 strokes to complete the mixing.

From then on the methods are identical.

Form the dough into a ball, return it to the bowl, cover with a damp cloth or polythene film and set in a warm, draughtproof place to rise.

When the dough has doubled in volume (about an hour at 70°F, 21°C) turn it out on to a lightly floured surface and gently deflate by flattening with the palms of the hands, spreading at the same time to form a flat pad. Spread the prepared soya mash evenly over the pad and carefully roll up so that all the mash is enclosed in the dough, then knead in the usual way for 300 strokes to produce a smooth and stretchy consistency.

Form into a ball, return it to the bowl in a warm place for a second rise which will take about half the time of the first.

When the dough has again doubled in bulk turn it out on

to a lightly floured surface, deflate gently, then divide into equal portions and knead each for 50 strokes before moulding into rounds.

Cover and allow them to rest for 15 minutes in a warm place, then carefully shape into loaves or set into warmed, greased tins to prove in a warm, draughtproof place. If the dough becomes chilled at this stage the quality of the bread will suffer. A slightly humid atmosphere is best if it can be arranged. (If an airing cupboard is being used a dish of boiling water placed below the bread usually adjusts the humidity sufficiently, or a damp towel positioned nearby will serve the same purpose.)

Soya bread can rise quite rapidly so check after 15 or 20 minutes. When the dough has doubled in bulk or it has risen to the point where it is arched above the lip of the tins it is ready to go into the oven. As a guide, the higher the dough proves the quicker it bakes and the more open the crumb; the lower the prove the longer it will take to bake and the denser the crumb, but beware of overproving which can cause the bread to collapse in the oven.

Pre-heat the oven to 400°F (200°C, Gas Mark 6) and place a dish of boiling water in the bottom. Allow 10 minutes for the steam to be generated, then set the loaves on to the centre shelf and bake for 15 minutes before reducing the temperature to 350°F (180°C, Gas Mark 4) for a further 20 minutes. The time taken for cooking depends upon several factors including the temperature of the mash when it is incorporated into the dough, times taken for the rises and the proving, etc. Check after a total cooking time of 35 minutes, then at 10-minute intervals until it is done – a whole hour is not unusual.

Loaves are cooked when a tap with the fingertips on the base makes a hollow sound. Cool on a wire rack.

VARIATIONS

All wholemeal or all white flour can be used instead of the half-and-half mixture if you wish.

Sugar or golden syrup can be substituted for the honey.

For those who like the flavour, unrefined sesame oil can be substituted for the vegetable oil and the loaves rolled in sesame seeds just before they go into the oven.

Polenta Bread★★

Polenta is the Italian name for the meal ground from maize, sometimes known as cornmeal. There are a great many recipes for preparing this bread, some of them very elaborate and time-consuming, but the following method produces a fairly light, pale-yellow crumb with no more effort than for any other bread. Do not confuse it with corn bread, much favoured by Americans, which in my opinion usually includes so much sugar as to bring it into the category of cake.

The ratio of polenta to white flour can be varied but the following recipe achieves a reasonable balance. Polenta needs the addition of the gluten in white flour to rise – the more polenta used the stodgier will be the bread. The recipe calls for white flour so that the delicate pale-yellow of the crumb adds to its appeal, but wholemeal can be used if preferred. The dough will be rather slack and perhaps a little stickier than normal so it will not be possible to tray bake without the risk of spreading. It will produce five small loaves or fewer larger.

INGREDIENTS

4 teaspoons (20g) granulated dried yeast
4 teaspoons (20g) sugar
1¼ pints (700ml) warm water
2¾ lb (1230g) strong white flour, preferably unbleached
¼ lb (110g) polenta (maize meal)
4 teaspoons (20g) salt
3 oz (85g) lard
1 egg, size 3

METHOD

Hand-mixing. Add the sugar and the yeast to the water and leave to activate until the surface is covered in frothy bubbles. Sift the flour, salt and polenta together into a large bowl and mix thoroughly, then rub in the lard until the mixture resembles fine breadcrumbs.

Beat the egg and whisk into the activated yeast liquid then

make a well in the centre of the flour and pour in the liquid.

Gradually stir in the flour with a wooden spoon until all is incorporated, then continue mixing with the hands until it is evenly moist.

Machine-mixing, using a dough hook. Put the water, sugar and yeast into the machine bowl and mix for 30 seconds on the slowest speed to disperse the ingredients. Leave to activate until the surface is covered in frothy bubbles then add the egg and mix for 1 minute on half speed.

Meanwhile prepare the flour, salt and polenta as for hand-mixing, rubbing in the fat.

Gradually spoon the flour mixture into the liquid with the machine running at its slowest speed until all is in the bowl, and continue mixing until the dough adheres to the dough hook in a ball. Then increase the speed to maximum and run for a full 2 minutes.

From then on the methods are identical.

Turn the dough out on to a lightly floured surface and knead for 100 strokes by which time it will be smooth and silky. Return it to the bowl, cover with a damp cloth or oiled polythene sheet and place in a warm place to rise.

When it has doubled in volume turn out the dough on to a floured surface and knead for a further 100 strokes, then return it to a warm place for the second rise which will take about half as long as the first. When again doubled in volume, turn out and knead again for 50 strokes, then divide into equal portions as required, shape into rough oblongs and half-fill warm, greased tins. Place the tins in a warm, draughtproof place for proving which will take between 15 and 30 minutes depending upon the temperature.

At this stage the bread must be watched carefully; it is ready for the oven when the dome of each loaf rises level with the edge of the tin – if it rises above that point it may collapse when it goes into the oven, or at best a mushroom-shaped loaf will result.

Put the bread on the centre shelf of an oven pre-heated to 400°F (200°C, Gas Mark 6) and bake for about 45 minutes or until the base sounds hollow when tapped with the fingertips. Cool on a wire rack.

VARIATIONS

Really the only permissible variations in the hand-mixing method are to alter the ratio of polenta to flour, or to use wholemeal instead of white flour, but machine-mixing will enable olive oil to be used as a replacement for the fat.

In this case, the lard is omitted and replaced by 3 fl.oz (80ml) of olive oil which is added to the yeast liquid and mixed at top speed for a few seconds until it is thoroughly emulsified, then the flour mixture is added in the normal way.

The use of olive oil tends to yield a slightly denser crumb but otherwise there is little difference in the final product.

Parker House Rolls★★

These are said to have been the invention of the chef at the famous Parker House Hotel in Boston, Massachusetts, but very similar types of bread roll are found in Austria and other regions of Central Europe. Whatever their provenance they are very attractive and quite delicious. The recipe makes about 24 rolls. They can be eaten fresh from the oven or freeze well.

INGREDIENTS

4 fl. oz (110ml) warm water
12 fl. oz (340ml) whole milk, scalded and cooled
2 teaspoons (10g) granulated dried yeast
2 teaspoons (10g) sugar
2 lb (900g) strong white flour, preferably unbleached
2 teaspoons (10g) salt
4 oz (110g) block margarine (not low-fat spread)
2 eggs, size 3
Softened butter for spreading

METHOD

Mix the warm water and the scalded milk in a basin and add the yeast and sugar. Stir to disperse, then set aside to activate. It is ready for use when the surface is covered in frothy bubbles.

Sieve the flour and salt together into a large bowl and mix thoroughly. Rub in the margarine until the mixture resembles fine breadcrumbs.

When the yeast mixture is ready, break the eggs into it and whisk until a smooth creamy liquid results. Pour the liquid into the flour and mix with a wooden spoon until all the ingredients are assimilated into a rough dough.

Turn the dough out on to a lightly floured surface and knead for 200 strokes by which time it will have become smooth and silky. It must not be at all sticky, if necessary knead in extra flour.

Form the dough into a ball and return it to the bowl, cover with a dry cloth overlaid with a damp one, and put it into a warm place to rise at a temperature between 70° and 80°F (21° and 27°C). This will take about an hour.

When the dough has doubled in volume knead it for a further 20 strokes, then roll it out until you have a pad about ¼-in (6mm) thick.

Cut into 4-in (10cm) discs with a floured cutter, and lightly coat the upper surface with the softened butter. Make an indentation with the back of a knife across each disc, slightly off-centre, then fold the small section over the larger and press the edges together to seal rather in the style of a purse.

Place the rolls on a greased baking sheet allowing at least 1 in (2.5cms) between them, cover with polythene supported so it cannot touch the rolls, and put them into a warm place to prove.

When they have doubled in size bake them on the centre shelf of an oven pre-heated to 400°F (200°C, Gas Mark 6) for about 15 minutes or until they are golden brown.

If a soft crust is preferred brush the tops over with melted butter before putting the rolls into the oven. For a harder crust spray them with water.

Traditionally these rolls are always made with white flour but half white and half wholemeal works just as well.

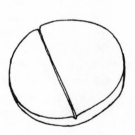 

Porridge Oats Bread★

This may not sound very appetising but is in fact a very pleasing bread with a delicate flavour and excellent moist crumb. It keeps well and can be frozen for about two months. It is not suitable for machine mixing.

Makes five small loaves or fewer larger.

INGREDIENTS

12 oz (340g) raw porridge oats
½ pint (280ml) hot water
1 tablespoon (15g) salt
1 tablespoon (15g) granulated dried yeast
¼ pint (140ml) warm water
3 tablespoons (45ml) pasteurized honey
4 tablespoons (60ml) vegetable oil
2 lb (900g) strong white flour, preferably unbleached

METHOD

Mix the oats with the hot water and bring to the boil. Add the salt and simmer until it thickens, stirring all the time and taking care it does not burn. Cover and leave to cool overnight.

In the morning dissolve the yeast in the warm water and leave to activate. When the surface is covered with frothy bubbles whisk in the honey and vegetable oil.

Sieve the flour into a large bowl, make a well in the centre and pour in the liquid ingredients. Stir from the centre with a wooden spoon until the liquid is thoroughly incorporated into the flour then add the cold porridge and mix in manually.

Porridge oats vary; some will produce a thicker porridge than others, but at this stage the mixture will usually be fairly harsh and dry.

Turn the dough out on to a lightly floured surface and knead for 200 strokes after which it should be becoming more soft and pliable. If there is no sign of improvement add a little water to the dough by dampening the hands and surface and working in the moisture as the kneading progresses. After about 300 strokes the dough should be soft and supple.

If the porridge was very watery and the dough is wet and sticky coat the working surface with flour instead of water and work that into the dough during kneading. Remember that flour absorbs the dampness in the porridge quite slowly so it will probably take all of 200 strokes before the true condition of the dough becomes apparent.

When it is smooth and silky make a ball of the dough, return it to the bowl, cover with a damp cloth or polythene and put it into a warm, draughtproof place to rise which will take between one and two hours according to the temperature (70°F, 21°C is ideal).

When the dough has doubled in volume turn it out on to a lightly floured surface and knead for 20 strokes then return it to the bowl for the second rise in a warm place, covering again with a damp cloth. This rise will take about half as long as the first.

As soon as the dough has again doubled in volume turn it out on to the floured surface and knead for 20 strokes, then divide it into equal portions, mould into the required shapes or half-fill warmed, greased tins and return them to a warm place for proving (about 30 or 40 minutes) at 70°F (21°C). Cover with a dry cloth.

When the dough has risen level with the top of the tins, or the moulded loaf for tray-baking has doubled in volume it is ready for the oven.

Pre-heat the oven to 425°F (220°C, Gas Mark 7), place the loaves on the centre shelf and bake for 15 minutes before reducing the temperature to 375°F (190°C, Gas Mark 5). Bake for a further 30 minutes before testing a loaf by tapping the base with the fingertips; if it sounds hollow it is done, if not give it a further 10 minutes or so.

Loaves on a baking tray usually cook faster than those in tins so it is best to avoid mixing the two. If the top crust of a tinned loaf is cooked but the base is still damp, remove from the tins and replace the loaves upside down in the oven for a few minutes. Cool on a wire rack and do not cut for at least one hour.

VARIATIONS

Molasses can be used instead of honey but this will make the crumb darker and give a slightly stronger flavour. However, molasses has a sulphur-content which can affect some people adversely.

Golden syrup can be substituted for honey.

Wholemeal flour can be used instead of white flour or a half-and-half mixture of both but the character of the crumb will be quite different.

Country Tomato Bread★★

Because it is made with real tomatoes this bread takes longer to make and the flavour and aroma is different to many other tomato recipes. Careful choice of the fruit is important, tomatoes must be firm but not under-ripe, of good colour but not over-ripe. Only perfect fruit should be used, discard any showing signs of greening or having 'woody' cores. Many modern tomato varieties are almost devoid of flavour – *Moneymaker*, for instance – so try to find a non-hybrid if you can. Probably one of the best is *Ailsa Craig*, but you will have to grow it yourself; the trade will not sell it because the fruits are often of irregular shapes and thus difficult to grade.

The bread toasts well, freezes and has good keeping qualities. The recipe makes five small loaves or fewer larger ones.

INGREDIENTS

> 4 teaspoons (20g) sugar
> 4 teaspoons (20g) dried granulated yeast
> 1 pint (550ml) warm water
> 3 lb (1150g) strong white flour, preferably unbleached
> 4 oz (110g) potato flour
> 4 teaspoons (20g) paprika powder
> 4 teaspoons (20g) salt
> 3 fl. oz (80ml) olive oil
> 4 oz (110g) tomatoes, skinned, de-seeded and chopped (weighed after chopping)

METHOD

Dissolve the sugar and yeast in the warm water and set aside to activate. It is ready for use when the surface is covered in frothy bubbles.

Sift the flours, salt and paprika together into a large bowl and mix together very thoroughly.

When the yeast liquid is ready add the olive oil and whisk until it is completely emulsified. Make a well in the flour and pour in the emulsified liquids. Mix with the hands until a coarse, rather dry and crumbly dough results.

Turn out on to a lightly floured surface and knead for 200 strokes by which time the dough will have slackened and become quite smooth and silky. Do not add more water if it still seems rather dry. Form the dough into a ball and return it to the lightly greased bowl, cover with a damp cloth and put into a warm place to rise.

When it has doubled in bulk turn it out on to the floured surface and knead for a further 200 strokes.

Drop the tomatoes into hot water for a few seconds, then cold water, remove and peel. Cut in half and remove the cores and seeds. Coarsely chop the flesh then gently knead it into the dough until it is evenly distributed; this is usually completed in about 20 strokes.

Divide into equal portions, gently mould into shape and place each portion into a warm greased tin (or on to a greased baking tray if round loaves are preferred). Tins must be not more than half-filled.

Set the loaves into a warm, draughtproof place to prove for about half the time taken for the first rise. When the dome of the bread has risen level with the top of the tins, or the trayed loaves have doubled in bulk, they are ready for the oven.

Bake on the centre shelf of an oven pre-heated to 400°F (200°C, Gas Mark 6) for about 45 minutes. Remove one loaf and test by tapping the base with the fingertips; if it sounds hollow the bread is done.

Cool on a wire rack and do not cut for two hours.

VARIATIONS

A finely chopped clove of garlic can be added to the dry flour mixture if you wish.

Note: The water content of tomatoes varies considerably so it may be necessary for extra warm water to be added, but the dough must never become sticky. Keep the chopped tomato as dry as possible by mopping up any surplus liquid with paper towelling.

Devonshire Herb Bread★★

The finest herb bread I have ever tasted was served in a restaurant close to San Diego Airport owned by a Mr Fat. I was, however, unable to get the recipe because it was the chef's night off and my plane left at 7 a.m. the next day.

The following recipe, although not quite as good, is the nearest approximation I have been able to discover. The bread is light and fragrant, toasts well, and is particularly tasty buttered and served with a lightly boiled egg. This recipe uses dried herbs because they are easily obtainable and very convenient but if you prefer fresh herbs it will be necessary to double the quantities listed. Makes five small loaves or fewer larger.

INGREDIENTS

4 teaspoons (20g) granulated dried yeast
4 teaspoons (20g) sugar
1 pint (550ml) warm water
2 tablespoons (30ml) olive oil
2 lb (900g) strong white flour, preferably unbleached
1 lb (450g) stoneground wholemeal flour
3 tablespoons (45g) potato flour
4 teaspoons (20g) salt
2 oz (55g) lard
1 teaspoon (5g) thyme
1 teaspoon (5g) parsley
2 teaspoons (10g) basil
1 teaspoon (5g) oregano
1 teaspoon (5g) marjoram
2 teaspoons (10g) dill
2 teaspoons (10g) garlic, finely chopped (optional)
4 tablespoons (60g) onion, chopped
OR variations of the above to suit individual tastes.

METHOD

Hand-Mixing. Add the yeast and sugar to the warm water, stir for 30 seconds then leave to activate. It is ready to use when the surface is covered in frothy bubbles.

Sauté the onion in the oil until tender but not brown. Set aside to cool.

Sift the flours and salt together into a large warmed bowl and mix thoroughly.

Rub in the lard until the mixture resembles fine breadcrumbs. Add all the herbs and onion and mix thoroughly until evenly distributed within the flour.

Make a well in the centre of the flour and pour in the yeast liquid, then stir with a wooden spoon until all is incorporated into a rough, fairly dry dough.

Turn out on to a lightly floured surface for kneading.

Machine-Mixing: using a dough hook. Put the warm water into the bowl of the machine, add the yeast and sugar, and mix on the slowest speed for 10 seconds. Allow to rest until the surface is covered in frothy bubbles.

Meanwhile, sauté the onion in the oil until tender but not browned. Set aside to cool.

Sift the flours and salt together into another bowl and rub in the lard until the mixture resembles fine breadcrumbs. Add all the herbs and onion and mix thoroughly until evenly distributed throughout the flour.

Start the machine on the slowest speed and gradually spoon in the flour mixture until it is all in the bowl. Continue mixing until a ball of dough adheres to the dough hook, then increase the speed to about half the maximum and run for 3 minutes.

Turn out on to a lightly floured surface for kneading.

From then on the methods are identical

Knead for 300 strokes by which time the dough should have become soft and pliable. If it is still rather harsh and dry a little more water can be added by lightly spraying the dough or by wetting the hands, but avoid making it sticky. A sticky dough will produce an inferior loaf.

Form the dough into a ball and return it to a lightly greased bowl, cover with a damp cloth and set in a warm, draughtproof place to rise. This will take between one and two hours according to the temperature.

When it has doubled in volume, turn out the dough on to the lightly floured surface and knead for a further 100 strokes. Divide into equal portions and roll roughly into torpedo shapes. Half-fill pre-warmed and greased tins, cover with a *dry* cloth and set aside in a warm, draughtproof place to prove. This will take about half the time of the initial rise.

When the dome of the bread has risen level with the top of the tin it is ready for the oven.

The oven should be pre-heated to 450°F (230°C, Gas Mark 8) and the loaves baked on the centre shelf for 15 minutes before reducing the temperature to 425°F (220°C, Gas Mark 7). After a further 15 minutes the oven can be opened and the loaves moved around to compensate for any hot spots. Bake for a further 15 minutes (45 minutes in total) then remove one loaf from its tin and test by tapping the base with the fingertips; if it sounds hollow the bread is done.

Cool on a wire rack and do not cut for at least an hour.

VARIATIONS

Colouring in the form of turmeric can be added if a coloured crumb is preferred. The foregoing recipe yields a pleasantly balanced herb bread so any adjustments should be made sparingly until an acceptable alternative is found.

The ratio of white to wholemeal flour can be varied but the omission of the potato flour will produce a more dense crumb.

Block margarine can be substituted for the lard but low-fat spreads are not suitable.

If the tops of the loaves are to be decorated with poppy or sesame seeds, lightly spray them over with warm water or milk just before they go into the oven, and sprinkle the seeds evenly over the surface.

Wholemeal Soda Bread★★

This loaf is widely popular in Ireland where it is normally baked without butter although it rises better with it. In the past, white flour was only used for very special occasions such as a wedding or christening, but today it is probable that more white than brown is sold. In the whole of Ireland you are unlikely to taste better bread than that baked by Adele Connor at her bakery in Main Street, Schull, County Cork, and her soda bread and sourdoughs are supreme. The following is a variation of her Imelda's Soda Bread. It does not keep well nor can it be frozen but, eaten fresh from the oven or whilst still warm, it is delicious. Makes one large loaf or two small.

INGREDIENTS

    1 lb (450g) stoneground wholemeal flour
    4 oz (110g) strong white flour, preferably unbleached
    4 oz (110g) medium ground oatmeal
    ½ teaspoon (2.5g) salt
    1 teaspoon (5g) baking soda (not baking powder)
    1 teaspoon (5g) cream of tartar
    2 oz (55g) butter (optional)
    1 egg, size 3
    1 pint (550ml) buttermilk

METHOD

Put the wholemeal flour and oatmeal into a large bowl and sieve in the white flour, salt, baking soda and cream of tartar. Mix thoroughly as erratic mixing of the dry ingredients will yield a poor result.

Rub the butter into the flour until it resembles fine breadcrumbs, then add the egg well beaten together with the buttermilk and incorporate into a fairly wet mixture by stirring with a wooden spoon until it is evenly damp and smooth.

The mixture should only just hold its shape when formed into a ball and thrown on to a greased and floured baking tray. Tap the underside of the tray with the knuckles to settle the loaf into a flattish shape rather like a large bap, then cut a deep cross into the top with a sharp knife.

Allow to rest for 5 minutes (any longer and it will spread all over the tray) then bake for 40–45 minutes in a pre-heated oven at 425°F (220°C, Gas Mark 7) or until it sounds hollow when the base is tapped with the fingertips.

VARIATIONS

The butter can be replaced with margarine but low-fat spreads are not suitable.

The ratio of wholemeal to white flour can be varied to suit personal taste and, if buttermilk is unobtainable, natural yogurt will produce a similar loaf.

Milk Soda Bread★★★

This recipe for soda bread uses a mixture of milk and water as a replacement for yogurt or buttermilk. In my opinion it is no better or worse than a yogurt recipe, and makes a very similar loaf. It is not recommended for the beginner. Makes two tray-baked small loaves or one large. As with all soda breads speed is important for good results.

INGREDIENTS

1 lb (450g) strong white flour, preferably unbleached
½ lb (225g) stoneground wholemeal flour
1 teaspoon (5g) baking soda (not baking powder)
1 teaspoon (5g) cream of tartar
1 teaspoon (5g) salt
¼ pint (140ml) whole milk, scalded and cooled
1 teaspoon (5ml) olive oil
¼ pint (140ml) warm water

METHOD

Sieve the white flour, salt, baking soda and cream of tartar together into a large bowl, add the wholemeal flour and mix thoroughly. If not thoroughly blended the bread will rise unevenly, or perhaps not at all.

Mix the milk and water, then add the olive oil and whisk until a smooth emulsion results with no visible globules of oil.

Pour the liquid into the flour mixture and mix with a wooden spoon until a coarse dough is obtained, then turn the dough out on to a firm surface and knead quickly but gently for 40 strokes. The dough should be rather dry but not crumbly; if more water is needed to arrive at the correct consistency add it a teaspoon (5ml) at a time – it must never become sticky.

Form the dough into a ball (or two balls if small loaves are required) and place on to a greased baking tray. Upturn an oven-proof basin over each loaf large enough to allow it to rise without touching the basin, and place on the centre shelf of an oven pre-heated to 475°F (240°C, Gas Mark 9). Bake for 30 minutes, then remove the basin and continue baking for another 10 minutes before testing. The bread is cooked if it sounds hollow when tapped on the base with the fingertips.

Cool on a wire rack, and eat within a few hours if possible. It will be suitable only for the bird-table the next day.

Simple Pumpernickel Bread★★

This bread originated in Central and Eastern Europe but is now very popular in the USA, having been brought there by immigrants from the region who have made the US their home.

There are dozens of different recipes in the USA, many of them incorporating nuts, fruit, chocolate, honey and syrup, but because the sugar content is very high to pander to transatlantic taste I have classed these as cakes and selected a simple bread recipe which anyone can follow. It produces a fairly dark, open crumb and a rather crisp crust. It is ideal toasted, freezes well and makes excellent sandwiches when a day or two old – if thinly sliced when new the crumb tends to disintegrate.

Pumpernickel bread is traditionally made as a round loaf; this recipe makes five small ones or fewer larger. If a paler crumb is preferred see the variations at the end of the recipe.

INGREDIENTS

4 teaspoons (20g) granulated dried yeast
2 oz (55ml) dark molasses
¼ pint (140ml) warm water
1 lb (450g) strong white flour, preferably unbleached
¼ lb (110g) stoneground wholemeal flour
¼ lb (110g) fresh rye flour
4 tablespoons (60g) potato flour
2 tablespoons (30g) salt
1 tablespoon (15g) carob powder
2 oz (55g) lard
1 pint (550ml) plain yogurt (at room temperature)

METHOD

Dissolve the yeast and molasses in the warm water and set aside to activate; it is ready for use when the surface is covered in frothy bubbles.

Sift all the flours together with the salt and carob powder into a large warm bowl and mix thoroughly. Rub in the lard until the mixture resembles fine breadcrumbs.

Whisk the yogurt and activated yeast liquid together. Make a well in the centre of the flour and pour in the liquid. Stir with a wooden spoon until a coarse dough is formed then turn it out on to a lightly floured surface. The dough should be stiff and very difficult to stir but fairly moist.

Knead for 100 strokes, adding more flour if necessary, but the dough should remain a little sticky. Do not over-knead.

Lightly grease the bowl and return the dough to it to rise, covering it with a damp towel or greased polythene film. Set in a warm, draughtproof place until it has doubled in bulk which will take between one and two hours according to the temperature.

Turn out on to a lightly floured surface and knead for a further 50 strokes by which time the dough should be smooth and supple. It will be quite damp but not so sticky that it is impossible to knead – if it is too wet add more flour as you knead.

Divide into equal portions and roll each into a ball. Form into rounds by tucking the edges underneath, and set to prove on a lightly greased and floured baking tray leaving space between each loaf for expansion. When they have almost doubled in bulk the loaves are ready for the oven.

If preferred, the loaves can be glazed at this point by painting the tops with a mixture of beaten egg and water. A sprinkling of sesame or poppy seeds will adhere to the glaze and give an attractive finish if desired.

Bake in an oven pre-heated to 400°F (200°C, Gas Mark 6) for about 45 minutes; test by tapping the base of a loaf with the fingertips, if it sounds hollow it is done.

Cool the bread on a wire rack for at least one hour before cutting or the crumb will collapse. Cut with a bread saw for preference.

VARIATIONS

2 tablespoons (30g) caraway seeds or the same amount of ground nutmeg added to the flours before the liquids are added will give a different flavour.

If a paler crumb is required omit the carob powder and replace the molasses with golden syrup or pasteurized honey. Molasses always has a sulphur-content and this can present a health problem to some people.

Margarine or unsalted butter can be substituted for the lard but low-fat spreads are not suitable.

Slight variations in the ratio of the different flours is permissible but proceed with caution; an excess of rye can completely alter the character of the bread and result in a heavy, dense crumb.

Celery and Onion Bread★★

This is an excellent bread for eating with soup and with cheese, and as the basis for poached egg on toast or scrambled eggs it is unsurpassed. It has a crisp crust and open, moist crumb; it has good keeping qualities and can be frozen. The recipe makes five small loaves or fewer larger.

INGREDIENTS

4 teaspoons (20g) sugar
4 teaspoons (20g) granulated dried yeast
1¼ pints (700ml) warm water
2 lb (900g) strong white flour, preferably unbleached
1 lb (450g) stoneground wholemeal flour
4 oz (110g) potato flour
1 tablespoon (15g) salt
4 oz (110g) lard
1 oz (30g) dried mixed herbs
6 oz (165g) raw onion, finely chopped
6 oz (165g) celery, finely chopped
2 eggs, size 3

METHOD

Dissolve the sugar and yeast in the warm water and set aside to activate. It is ready for use when the surface is covered in frothy bubbles.

Sieve the flours and salt together into a large warmed bowl and mix thoroughly. Rub in the lard until the mixture is the consistency of fine breadcrumbs. Add the herbs and mix until evenly distributed.

Chop the onion and the celery and fry in a little oil for a few minutes until tender but not brown. Remove from the heat, drain and cool before rubbing into the flour until it is evenly distributed.

When the yeast liquid is ready, break the eggs into it and beat until a creamy mixture results – use a mechanical beater or liquidizer if possible. Add this liquid to the flour and work with the hands until a rough dough results. Turn out on to a smooth lightly floured surface and knead for 200 strokes.

Form the dough into a ball and place in a large warm bowl.

Cover with a damp cloth and set to rise in a warm place for about an hour or until it has doubled in volume.

Turn out and knead for a further 200 strokes then return it to the warm place for the second rise which will take about half the time of the first, covered as before with a damp cloth.

When again doubled in volume, turn out the dough and knead gently for 30 strokes then divide into equal portions. Form each into a ball by rolling it on the table with a rotary motion, then either gently elongate to a torpedo shape and place in pre-warmed and greased tins, or set on to a greased baking tray if round loaves are preferred.

The loaves must now be put into a warm, draughtproof place for proving which will take about 30 minutes. They are ready for the oven when the dome of the dough has risen level with the rim of the tins, or the trayed loaves have doubled in volume.

Bake on the centre shelf of an oven pre-heated to 400°F (200°C, Gas Mark 6) for 45 minutes, then remove one loaf and test by tapping the base with the fingertips – if it sounds hollow the bread is done. Cool the loaves on a wire rack.

VARIATIONS

The ratio of white to wholemeal flour can be adjusted to suit individual tastes.

The quantities of herbs, celery and onion can be varied as required. The above formula gives a nicely balanced flavour but it is inevitable that some people will prefer more or less of these ingredients. However, bear in mind that an increase in the celery and onion content will automatically increase the moisture in the dough so it may be necessary to reduce the amount of water called for in the list of ingredients.

If fresh herbs are used double the quantities listed.

Celeriac can be substituted for the celery but it is best finely grated and used raw; it produces a slightly crunchy crumb which goes well with smoked salmon.

Note: Because both onions and celery have a high water-content this recipe calls for less water than normal. If the mixture seems dry at first it will get moister as kneading proceeds; do not add more water unless, after the second kneading, it seems dry and crumbly. If the dough seems to be wet and sticky, more flour can be added as you knead.

Spiral Rolls★

There are two easy ways of making spiral rolls and both are described below. The recipe makes between 12 and 16 rolls according to size.

INGREDIENTS

15 fl.oz (450ml) whole milk
2 teaspoons (10g) granulated dried yeast
2 teaspoons (10g) sugar
1 lb (450g) stoneground wholemeal flour, strong white flour (preferably unbleached) or any mixture of the two
1 teaspoon (5g) salt
1 oz (30g) block margarine
1 egg, size 3

METHOD

Scald the milk, cool to blood heat then add the sugar and yeast. Stir briefly to disperse, then set aside to activate; it is ready to use when the surface is covered in frothy bubbles.

Sieve the flour and salt into a large bowl and mix thoroughly. Melt the margarine in a saucepan or similar vessel over a low heat.

When the yeast liquid is ready add the melted margarine and the egg, and whisk vigorously to get even dispersal; use a liquidizer if you have one.

Add the liquid to the flour and mix with a wooden spoon until a soft dough results. Knead on a lightly floured surface for 200 strokes by which time the dough should be soft and pliable but not sticky – if it is at all wet knead in more flour until the correct consistency is obtained.

Put it into a warm bowl, cover with a damp cloth and stand in a warm place to rise for about 30 minutes or until it has doubled in bulk. Then turn out and knead for 50 strokes on a lightly floured surface.

METHOD 1

Roll out the dough on a lightly floured surface into a

rectangle about ¼-in (6mm) thick and 6 ins to 8 ins (15–20cms) wide. Lightly spray the dough with water so that it is just dampened, then roll up into a long cylinder.

With a sharp, lightly greased knife, cut across the cylinder at approximately 1-in (2.5cms) intervals to produce a succession of spiral rings.

METHOD 2

Divide the dough into 12 or more equal portions. Take each portion and roll it out into a strand 6–8 ins (15–20cms) long. Roll each strand into a tight spiral and paint down the joins with a dampened brush – do not make the dough wet.

Whichever method is used, the rolls are then set out on a greased baking tray allowing space between them for expansion, covered with a dry cloth and set in a warm draughtproof place to rise. They are ready for the oven when they have doubled in volume.

Bake on the centre shelf of an oven pre-heated to 425°F (220°C, Gas Mark 7) for between 8 and 12 minutes. They are ready when the crust is just beginning to brown.

Set to cool on a wire rack.

Note: Smaller rolls will require less time to bake, larger ones will need longer.

Poppy seeds can be sprinkled over the top of the rolls as a decoration – paint the surface with a mixture of egg-white and water just before they go into the oven and the seeds will adhere to the surface.

Method 1   Method 2

Baps★★

Baps originated in Scotland where they were and are eaten as breakfast rolls; now they are widespread in the British Isles and differ from other soft-crust breads only in their shape – usually in the form of a flat pad. Traditionally they can be almost any size or shape although round or oblong baps are most commonly seen today. One occasionally sees glazed baps, but the true Scottish bap is floured with a dented top and is best eaten warm with butter. This recipe makes four fairly small baps or fewer larger ones.

INGREDIENTS

2 teaspoons (10g) granulated dried yeast
1 teaspoon (5g) sugar
¼ pint (140ml) warm water
1 lb (450g) strong white flour, preferably unbleached
2 teaspoons (10g) salt
2 oz (55g) lard
¼ pint (140ml) whole milk, scalded and cooled

METHOD

Dissolve the sugar and yeast in the warm water and set aside to activate. It is ready for use when the surface is covered in frothy bubbles.

Sift the flour and salt into a large warmed bowl and place in the oven for a few minutes at 200°F (100°C, Gas Mark ¼) to warm the flour. Remove from oven and mix the flour by hand to eliminate any cold spots. Rub in the lard until the mixture resembles fine breadcrumbs.

When the yeast liquid is ready add the milk which should be just warm, and whisk until thoroughly mixed, then make a well in the flour and pour in the liquid. Stir with a wooden spoon initially, then with the hands until a silky smooth, rather slack dough results.

Turn the dough out on to a lightly floured surface and knead gently for 60 strokes. Return it to the warm bowl, cover with a damp cloth, and put it into a warm place to rise until it has doubled in volume (normally about an hour at about 70°F (20°C)).

When correctly risen, weigh into four equal portions. Take each portion and roll it into a ball between the floured palms until it resembles a tennis ball.

Warm and grease a Yorkshire pudding tray (or any similar 4-in diameter shallow tin), and set one ball to each tin. Put the tray into a warm draughtproof place to prove.

When the baps have about doubled in bulk paint the tops with warm milk and dust with flour. Make an indent in the centre with a finger to a depth of about ½ in (12mm) and immediately place them on the centre shelf of an oven pre-heated to 400°F (200°C, Gas Mark 6) and bake for 15–20 minutes. Do not overcook or the soft texture will be destroyed – the crust should not be crisp.

Cool on a wire rack.

VARIATIONS

A proportion of wholemeal flour can be used in which case a little more water will be needed.

Block margarine can be substituted for the lard but low-fat spreads are unsuitable.

Note: Success with this recipe depends upon all the utensils and ingredients being warm.

A dough of the correct consistency will flatten out to the correct shape of its own accord, but if it is a little too dry gently flatten the dome of the baps with a floured rolling pin before putting into the oven.

By dispensing with the Yorkshire pudding trays the baps can be made to any size and shape but they must not touch each other or a 'kiss crust' will result.

New England Corn Bread★

This sweet bread was a favourite with the early settlers in the Boston area of New England, and is particularly good toasted and spread with marmalade or honey. It keeps and freezes well. Makes three small loaves or two larger.

INGREDIENTS

12 fl.oz (340ml) warm water
2 teaspoons (10g) granulated dried yeast
6 tablespoons (90ml) molasses or golden syrup
1½ lb (700g) strong white flour, preferably unbleached
½ lb (225g) cornmeal (maize) – *not* cornflour
2 teaspoons (10g) salt
4 oz (110g) butter, warmed until just melted

METHOD

Dissolve the yeast and a little of the molasses in the warm water, stir to disperse and set aside to activate. It is ready for use when the surface is covered in frothy bubbles.

Sieve the flour, salt and cornmeal together into a large bowl.

When the yeast liquid is ready add the rest of the molasses and the melted butter, and whisk briskly until a smooth creamy emulsion results. Pour this into the flour and mix thoroughly to make a stiff dough.

Turn out on to a lightly floured surface and knead for 100 strokes or until all stickiness has disappeared, then form into a ball and place in a lightly oiled bowl, cover with a damp cloth and leave to rise in a warm place until it has doubled in volume.

Turn the dough out on to the floured surface and knead for a further 100 strokes, then divide into equal portions and roll each into a ball. Elongate slightly to form a torpedo shape and place into warm pre-greased tins which must be not more than half filled. Cover and set in a warm place to prove. The loaves are ready for the oven when the dough has risen level with the top of the tins.

Bake on the centre shelf of an oven pre-heated to 375°F

(190°C, Gas Mark 5) for about 45 minutes or until the loaves sound hollow when tapped on the base with the fingertips.

Cool on a wire rack.

Note: The molasses will emulsify better if warmed before mixing with the yeast liquid.

The sulphur in the molasses can adversely affect some people; it can be replaced with golden syrup.

Quick Garlic Rolls★★

INGREDIENTS

15 fl.oz (430ml) whole milk
1 teaspoon (5g) granulated dried yeast
1 teaspoon (5g) sugar
1 lb (450g) stoneground wholemeal flour, strong white flour, or any mixture of the two
1 teaspoon (5g) salt
1 oz (30g) block margarine
1 egg, size 3
6 garlic cloves

METHOD

Scald the milk, cool to blood heat then add the sugar and yeast. Stir briefly to disperse, then set aside to activate; it is ready to use when the surface is covered in frothy bubbles.

Sieve the flour and salt into a large bowl and mix thoroughly.

Melt the margarine over a low heat then allow to cool slightly.

When the yeast liquid is ready add the melted margarine and the egg, and whisk vigorously to get even dispersal; use a liquidizer if you have one.

Add the liquid to the flour and mix with a wooden spoon until a soft dough results; it may be necessary to complete the mixing by hand.

Form the dough into a ball and place in a lightly oiled warm bowl, cover with a damp cloth and stand in a warm place to rise for about 30 minutes or until it has doubled in bulk.

Chop the garlic very finely but do not crush.

Knead the dough for 50 strokes on a lightly floured surface, form into a ball and gently flatten with a rolling pin. Then roll it out evenly using ¼-in (6mm) thick roller-guides.

Using a lightly oiled 2½-in (6cms) cutter (or larger or smaller as required), punch out discs of dough.

Lightly spray each disc with warm water, then sprinkle a

little garlic evenly over the dampened surface before folding in half to form a semi-circular pouch. Pinch the seams together and place on a lightly greased and floured pre-warmed baking tray, allowing at least 1 in (2½cms) between each for expansion.

Cover with a dry cloth and set into a warm, draughtproof place to prove. The rolls are ready for the oven when they have doubled in volume, usually about 30 minutes.

Bake on the centre shelf of an oven pre-heated to 425°F (220°C, Gas Mark 7) for between 8 and 12 minutes or until just beginning to brown. Cool on a wire rack but serve warm. Makes about eight rolls.

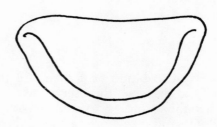

Fantail Rolls★★★

Attention to detail is quite important to obtain attractive, evenly divided fantail rolls, but they create an unusual talking point when they appear on any dining-table. Water content and baking times are critical but must be adjusted to suit your flour and oven temperatures; the recipe can be used only as a guide. Makes about 12 rolls.

INGREDIENTS

4 tablespoons (60ml) milk, scalded and cooled
6 tablespoons (90ml) warm water
1 teaspoon (5g) sugar
1 teaspoon (5g) granulated dried yeast
1 lb (450g) strong white flour, preferably unbleached
½ teaspoon (2.5g) salt
2 oz (60g) softened butter
1 egg, size 3

METHOD

Mix the milk and water, stir in the sugar and yeast and set aside to activate. The mixture is ready for use when the surface is covered in frothy bubbles.

Sieve the flour and salt together into a large bowl and mix thoroughly.

Beat the butter and egg together in a separate bowl until smooth, then add to the yeast liquid and whisk until creamy.

Stir the liquid into the flour and mix thoroughly until a rough dough results. Turn this out on to a lightly floured surface and knead for 100 strokes. The dough should be smooth and pliable but not sticky; if it is too wet knead in more flour.

Put the dough into a large bowl and cover with a damp cloth. Set in a warm place to rise for about an hour or until it has doubled in volume.

Turn out on to a floured surface and knead for a further 100 strokes, then allow to rest for 10 minutes.

Weigh the dough out into 2 equal portions.

Divide each portion into 5 equal pieces and roll each piece

out until it is ¼ in (6mm) thick using roller guides to get it uniform (you can vary the thickness to give more or fewer rolls as required).

Place the five slabs of dough on top of each other and with a sharp knife trim the edges of the stack to give a rectangular block about 2 × 12 ins (5 × 30cm).

Carefully separate the layers and dampen one half of each piece lengthwise (the dampened area will measure approximately 1 × 12 ins (2.5 × 30cms). Then re-assemble the layers making certain that the dampened areas all fall the same way round.

Gently press the stack together then, with a sharp knife (lightly greased) divide it into 2-in (5cms) sections.

The rolls must now be set on to a greased baking tray or into greased tart tins, standing on edge, dampened edges down, and put to prove in a warm place, covered with a dry cloth supported so that it is not in contact with the dough. Proving will take about 30 or 40 minutes; the rolls are ready for the oven when they have almost doubled in volume.

Bake on the centre shelf of an oven pre-heated to 400°F (200°C, Gas Mark 6) for about 20 minutes or until they are just beginning to brown; if they are overcooked the fan will become very brittle.

Cool on a wire rack.

The rolls are best eaten straight from the oven but can be stored for a few days or frozen.

Tea Breads

Caraway Rye Bread★★★

This is a fairly light rye as rye breads go, with a rather more open crumb than most. The traditional torpedo shape is tray-baked, but the bread can be tinned just as successfully. Rye loaves have a tendency to crack if over-kneaded or roughly handled – if this happens slash the tops with a sharp knife in such a way as to disguise the cracks. Makes three fairly large traditional loaves or five small ones in tins. The bread keeps well and can be frozen. The quality will vary according to the type of rye flour used, some have more gluten than others although rye is naturally low in gluten-content. Experiment with different brands until you find one best suited to your own taste.

INGREDIENTS

1 tablespoon (15ml) black treacle or molasses
1¼ pints (700ml) warm water
4 teaspoons (20g) dried granulated yeast
2 lb (900g) stoneground wholemeal flour
1 lb (450g) rye flour
1 tablespoon (15g) salt
2 teaspoons (10g) caraway seeds
1 vitamin-C tablet (25mg) or ½ 50mg tablet
3 tablespoons (45ml) olive oil

For the glaze:
2 teaspoons (10g) cornflour
¼ pint (140ml) boiling water
Sprinkling of caraway seeds

METHOD

Dissolve the treacle in the warm water, then add the yeast. Stir to disperse, then set aside to activate. It is ready for use when the surface is covered in frothy bubbles.

Sieve the flours and salt together into a large bowl, add the caraway seeds and mix thoroughly.

When the yeast liquid is ready crush the vitamin tablet into it, add the olive oil, and whisk vigorously until a smooth emulsion results with no visible oil globules and the vitamin tablet has completely dissolved.

Pour the liquid into the flour and mix thoroughly with a wooden spoon until a rough dough is obtained.

Turn the dough out on to a lightly floured surface and knead gently for 100 strokes, taking care not to tear it. If the dough is dry and crumbly a little extra water can be kneaded in at this stage but it must not be sticky.

Form into a ball and seal inside a large plastic bag which has been well greased all over the inner surface. Put into a warm place until it has doubled in bulk – this can take quite a time but it cannot be rushed.

Turn the dough out and re-knead gently for 20 strokes, then divide into equal portions. Mould into torpedo shapes by tucking the edges underneath, and place on a warm, pre-greased and floured baking tray leaving at least 2 ins (5cms) between each to allow for expansion, or into warm pre-greased tins.

Put the baking tray into a large plastic bag supported so that the dough cannot come into contact with the plastic (or treat the tins similarly), seal the bag and put into a warm place to prove. The loaves are ready for the oven when the dough has almost doubled in volume and springs back when lightly depressed with a dry fingertip.

While the loaves are proving, cream the cornflour in a little cold water, then add the boiling water and stir briskly until a smooth thin paste results. If it does not clear, transfer it to a saucepan and bring to the boil stirring all the time. Set aside to cool before use.

Slash the loaves with three diagonal cuts, then brush them over with the glaze and sprinkle a few caraway seeds on the tops.

Bake immediately on the centre shelf of an oven pre-heated to 425°F (220°C, Gas Mark 7) for 15 minutes, then reduce the temperature to 375°F (190°C, Gas Mark 5) for a further 20 minutes. Open the oven and quickly brush over the loaves with the glaze once more, then bake for another 10 minutes before testing a loaf by tapping the base with the fingertips – if it sounds hollow it is done, if not, give it a few more minutes in the oven.

Cool on a wire rack.

VARIATIONS

Any increase in the ratio of rye flour to wholemeal will adversely affect the rising of the bread; the rye can be reduced if desired so long as it is compensated by an equivalent increase in wholemeal flour.

If molasses is used in the recipe remember that the lighter the colour the sweeter the molasses so you may have to use a little less. The bread is not so good if golden syrup is substituted but some people are allergic to the sulphur in molasses.

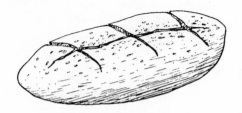

Gleaner's Bread★★

This is adapted from an eighteenth-century recipe from the Lincolnshire Wolds where the children were sent into the cornfields to glean for the grain which had fallen from the sheaves as they were gathered. The children were fed with this bread, some cheese and milk fresh from the cow at intervals during the day – a day which often began at 6 a.m. and ended only when dusk made further work impossible.

We have no means of judging the quality of Gleaner's Bread in days gone by, but this adaptation makes a very tasty tea bread, much appreciated by children and adults alike. It keeps well and can be frozen. Makes two small loaves or one large.

INGREDIENTS

    2 teaspoons (10g) granulated dried yeast
    2 tablespoons (30ml) clear honey, pasteurized
    ¼ pint (140ml) warm water
    1 egg, size 3
    2 tablespoons (30ml) olive oil
    5 tablespoons (75g) kibbled wheat
    2 oz (55g) mixed nuts, chopped
    ½ lb (225g) strong white flour, preferably unbleached
    ½ lb (225g) stoneground wholemeal flour
    1 teaspoon (5g) salt
    4 tablespoons (60g) skimmed milk powder
    5 oz (140g) sultanas and raisins mixed
    1 egg yolk for glaze

METHOD

Put the yeast, the hot water and half the honey in a small bowl and whisk briefly to dissolve. Set aside to activate; it is ready for use when the surface is covered in frothy bubbles.

Whisk the egg, the rest of the honey and the oil together in a large bowl until they are all thoroughly incorporated, then stir in the kibbled wheat and set aside for about 20 minutes.

Spread the chopped nuts on a sheet of foil and lightly grill until they are just showing a tinge of gold; stir from time to time to toast them evenly. Allow to cool before using.

Sift the flours, salt and dried milk together and mix thoroughly, add the fruit and stir it into the flour with a wooden spoon until it is evenly distributed, then mix in the chopped nuts.

When the egg mixture has stood for 20 minutes, pour the activated yeast liquid into it and whisk to produce a smooth creamy emulsion, then pour this into the flour and mix thoroughly until a rather slack dough is formed.

Turn the dough out on to a lightly floured surface and knead for 200 strokes. The dough should be fairly wet so that kneading is just possible – if it is too wet to handle you will have to knead in a little more flour, but this should be kept to the minimum.

Lightly oil the inside of the large bowl and put in the ball of dough, turning it so that it all gets a coating of oil, then cover with a dry cloth (or polythene film) and set aside to rise in a warm place until it has doubled in bulk (usually about two hours at normal room temperature).

Turn out and knead for a further 100 strokes, divide into two equal portions and roll each into a ball. Gradually elongate each ball into a torpedo shape and half-fill warm pre-greased tins.

Place each loaf in its tin in a sealed plastic container (an empty 4-litre ice-cream tub is ideal) and set in a warm place to prove. The bread is ready for the oven when the dome is level with the top edge of the tin.

Beat the egg yolk with a tablespoon of warm water and glaze the tops of the loaves before putting them on the centre shelf of an oven pre-heated to 400°F (200°C, Gas Mark 6). After 30 minutes, test by tapping the base of a loaf with the fingertips – if it sounds hollow it is done, if not, return it to the oven for a few more minutes.

Allow the bread to stand in the tins for 10 minutes, then cool on a wire rack.

VARIATIONS

Golden syrup can be substituted for the honey.

Sunflower seeds can be used instead of the chopped nuts,

and chopped prunes substituted for the raisins.

If one large loaf is preferred it will need longer in the oven.

If you have difficulty finding skimmed milk powder substitute whole liquid milk for the warm water but scald before using.

Mint and Currant Bread★

Although this is a Greek speciality, I first encountered it in Lichfield, Staffs, in the mid-1930s. To be successful, the currants must be plump and juicy, and the mint freshly picked and finely chopped. Dried mint just does not work with this recipe. The proportion of mint used can be varied to suit individual tastes but too much mint can be over-powering. Makes two small loaves or one large. The bread keeps well and can be frozen.

INGREDIENTS

¼ pint (140ml) whole milk, scalded and cooled
¼ pint (140ml) warm water
4 teaspoons (20g) sugar
1 teaspoon (5g) granulated dried yeast
1 oz (30g) fresh mint, chopped
1 lb (450g) strong white flour, preferably unbleached
1 teaspoon (5g) salt
1 oz (30g) block margarine
4 oz (110g) currants
clear honey for glazing

METHOD

Mix the warm milk and water, add the sugar and yeast and set aside to activate; it is ready for use when the surface is covered in frothy bubbles.

Finely chop the freshly picked and washed mint, and set aside to dry. (This is best done earlier in the day; if the mint is at all damp it will not mix properly and tends to 'ball'.) Weigh the mint *before* washing.

Sieve the flours and salt together into a large bowl and rub in the margarine until the mixture resembles fine bread-crumbs, then mix in the currants and chopped mint.

When the yeast liquid is ready, add it to the flour and mix thoroughly until an even, rough dough results.

Turn out the dough on to a lightly floured surface and knead for 100 strokes. Form into a ball and return the dough to the bowl, cover with a dry cloth overlaid with a damp one and stand in a warm place until doubled in bulk. This will usually take about an hour at normal room temperature.

Return the dough to the floured surface and knead for a further 100 strokes, then divide into equal portions and form into torpedo shapes.

Half-fill warm, pre-greased tins, cover with a dry cloth and set aside to prove for about 30 minutes or until the dome of each loaf has risen level with the top of the tin.

Bake on the centre shelf of an oven pre-heated to 450°F (230°C, Gas Mark 8) for 10 minutes, then reduce the temperature to 400°F (200°C, Gas Mark 6) and bake for another 30 minutes or until the loaves sound hollow when tapped on the base with the fingertips.

Cool on a wire rack. Whilst still hot paint the tops with clear honey.

VARIATIONS

Using white flour the mint shows flecks of green in the crumb which is very pretty. You can use a proportion of wholemeal but this effect will then be lost.

Note: Some cooks prefer to add the fruit to the dough *after* the first rise and during the second kneading; this certainly makes the first kneading easier but unless you are very precise the currants will not be distributed evenly throughout the dough.

The mint must be added to the flour *before* the liquids.

Orange and Apricot Bread★★

From sunny Spain comes this recipe for a truly delicious tea bread. The flavour depends to a large extent upon the type and size of orange used; Spanish oranges are very variable in both size and sweetness. (Don't use Seville oranges which are best for marmalade.) I prefer Shemoutis from the Eastern Mediterranean, medium-size (what the fruiterer calls 80s). They must be thoroughly washed in hot water to remove the waxy protective coating before the rind is grated. Makes two small loaves or one large. The bread freezes well but otherwise deteriorates after a few days. It is excellent toasted, or spread with butter and jam topped with clotted cream.

INGREDIENTS

2 teaspoons (10g) sugar
1 teaspoon (5g) granulated dried yeast
¼ pint (140ml) warm water
4 oz (110g) dried apricots
1 lb (450g) strong white flour, preferably unbleached
½ teaspoon (2.5g) salt
1 oz (30g) block margarine
1 medium/large orange
1 egg, size 3
Clear honey for glazing

METHOD

Dissolve the sugar and yeast in the warm water and set aside to activate; it is ready for use when the surface is covered in frothy bubbles. Chop the apricots until the pieces are no bigger than currants.

Sieve the flour and salt together into a large bowl and rub in the margarine until the mixture resembles fine bread-crumbs, then mix in the apricots, evenly distributing them throughout the flour.

Grate the orange peel into the mixture and incorporate. Squeeze the orange and set the juice aside.

When the yeast liquid is ready, beat the egg and add it to the liquid. Whisk until an evenly smooth cream results, then whisk in the orange juice.

Pour the liquid into the flour and mix thoroughly with a wooden spoon to form a rough dough.

Turn the dough out on to a lightly floured surface and knead for 100 strokes. Form into a ball and return the dough to the bowl, cover with a dry cloth overlaid with a damp one and stand for about an hour in a warm place or until doubled in bulk.

Return the dough to the floured surface and knead for a further 100 strokes, then divide it into equal portions and form roughly into torpedo shapes.

Half-fill warm pre-greased tins, cover with a dry cloth and set aside to prove for about 30 minutes or until the dome of each loaf has risen level with the top of the tin.

Bake on the centre shelf of an oven pre-heated to 450°F (230°C, Gas Mark 8) for 10 minutes, then reduce the temperature to 400°F (200°C, Gas Mark 6) and bake for another 30 minutes or until the loaves sound hollow when tapped on the base with the fingertips.

Cool on a wire rack.

Whilst still hot, paint the tops with a brush dipped in clear honey.

VARIATIONS

Sultanas can be substituted for the apricots if preferred. Salt can be omitted, and the sugar replaced by golden syrup.

Note: The amount of water in this recipe may have to be varied to suit the volume of juice in the orange. The dough should be fairly loose but not sticky – if it is too dry after the first kneading a little more water can be worked in (one tablespoon (15ml) is usually ample); if it is too wet knead in more flour.

Currant Bread★

This has been a favourite with children and adults for centuries past and it is still the most popular of all the tea breads sold by bakers. Buy only plump, juicy currants and wash and dry them before use, carefully picking them over for stalks, small stones and any other foreign bodies. This recipe makes two small loaves or one large. The bread keeps and freezes well.

INGREDIENTS

¼ pint (140ml) whole milk, scalded and cooled
¼ pint (140ml) warm water
2 teaspoons (10g) sugar
1 teaspoon (5g) granulated dried yeast
1 lb (450g) strong white flour, preferably unbleached
1 teaspoon (5g) salt
1 oz (30g) cooking margarine
4 oz (110g) currants
Clear honey for glazing

METHOD

Mix the warm milk and water, dissolve the sugar and yeast in it and set aside to activate; it is ready for use when the surface is covered in frothy bubbles.

Sieve the flour and salt together into a large bowl and rub in the margarine until the mixture resembles fine breadcrumbs, then mix in the currants.

When the yeast liquid is ready, pour it into the flour and mix thoroughly until an even, rough dough results.

Turn the dough out on to a lightly floured surface and knead for 100 strokes. Form into a ball and return the dough to the bowl, cover with a dry cloth overlaid with a damp one and stand for about an hour in a warm place or until doubled in bulk.

Return the dough to the floured surface and knead for a further 100 strokes, then divide it into equal portions and form roughly into torpedo shapes. Half-fill warm pre-greased tins, cover with a dry cloth and set aside to prove for about

30 minutes or until the dome of each loaf has risen level with the top of the tin.

Bake on the centre shelf of an oven pre-heated to 450°F (230°C, Gas Mark 8) for 10 minutes, then reduce the temperature to 400°F (200°C, Gas Mark 6) and bake for another 30 minutes or until the loaves sound hollow when tapped on the base with the fingertips.

Cool on a wire rack. Whilst still hot, paint the tops with clear honey.

Note: Some cooks prefer to add the fruit to the dough *after* the first rise and during the second kneading but unless you are very precise the currants will not be distributed evenly throughout the dough.

If you prefer a sweeter crumb knead an extra 2 teaspoons (10g) *caster* sugar into the dough before proving.

Caraway Yogurt Bread★★

This bread can be made either with sheep's or cow's milk yogurt but it must be fresh. It requires very little kneading so long as the dough is allowed a slow rise. More or less caraway seed may be used according to taste. It is particularly good with cheese or toasted and spread with orange marmalade. The recipe makes five small loaves or fewer larger.

INGREDIENTS

¾ pint (420ml) warm water
2 teaspoons (10g) sugar
2 teaspoons (10g) granulated dried yeast
1 lb (450g) strong white flour, preferably unbleached
2 lb (900g) stoneground wholemeal flour
1 teaspoon (5g) salt
1 oz (30g) caraway seed
¾ pint (420ml) plain yogurt at room temperature
4 fl. oz (110ml) olive oil

METHOD

Dissolve the yeast and sugar in the warm water and set aside to activate; it is ready for use when the surface is covered in frothy bubbles. Sieve the flours and salt into a large bowl and add the caraway seed. Mix thoroughly.

When the yeast liquid is ready, add the yogurt and whisk until a smooth creamy liquid results then add the oil and continue whisking until all is thoroughly and smoothly emulsified.

Pour this liquid into the flour and stir with a wooden spoon until a soft pliable dough is formed which is slightly tacky to the touch but not sticky. Turn out on to a lightly floured surface and knead for 40 strokes by which time the dough should be smooth and silky. Form into a ball and, if the liquid content is correct, it should be possible to pass it from hand to hand without it sticking. If it sticks knead in a little more flour.

Lightly oil a large bowl or plastic bucket, and rotate the

ball of dough in it a few times so that the whole surface is covered in a film of oil. Cover with a damp cloth and set into a warm place to rise.

This dough can take all of four hours to double in volume according to the temperature but it must not be hurried.

When fully doubled in volume turn it out on to a lightly floured surface and knead for about 20 strokes then divide into equal portions. Knead each portion for a further 10 strokes and form into a torpedo shape. Place into pre-warmed and greased tins and set into a warm place to prove.

Compared with the initial rising time proving is quite rapid. Inspect the loaves after 45 minutes and then at 10-minute intervals. They are ready for the oven when the dome of each loaf has risen just above the top of the tin – the dough must not overhang the edges or a mushroom-shaped loaf will result.

Bake on the centre shelf of an oven pre-heated to 450°F (230°C, Gas Mark 8) for 40 minutes. If the bread sounds hollow when tapped on the base it is done.

Cool on a wire rack.

VARIATIONS

All white or all wholemeal flour can be used if preferred.

Swiss Cinnamon Bread★★

Popular in Switzerland and parts of Austria, this rather sweet spicy bread is eaten toasted or plain with butter mainly at breakfast or with the mid-morning coffee. Strangely, marmalade is seldom seen on the Continent, but this bread makes wonderful toast spread with it – the Continentals don't know what they are missing! Makes two small loaves or one large. The bread keeps well and can be frozen but is best eaten warm from the oven.

INGREDIENTS

1 teaspoon (5g) granulated dried yeast
2 tablespoons (10g) sugar
4 tablespoons (60ml) warm water
1½ lb (700g) strong white flour, preferably unbleached
1 teaspoon (5g) salt
4 fl. oz (115ml) whole milk
½ lb (225g) butter, unsalted
2 eggs, size 3

for the cinnamon sugar:
4 tablespoons (60g) caster sugar
2 teaspoons (10g) ground cinnamon

METHOD

Dissolve the yeast and sugar in the warm water and set aside to activate. It is ready for use when the surface is covered in frothy bubbles. Sieve the flour and salt together into a large bowl.

Scald the milk and cool to blood heat, gently melt the butter, then combine all with the yeast liquid and whisk until an even creamy mixture results. Beat in the eggs, one at a time, then add the liquid to the flour and beat until a smooth, soft dough results.

Turn out on to a lightly floured surface and knead for 100 strokes or until the dough is smooth and silky.

Form into a ball and return it to the bowl for rising. Paint the surface lightly with vegetable oil or melted butter, and cover the bowl with a dry cloth overlaid with a damp one. Leave to rise for about one and a half hours or until doubled in volume.

Turn out on to the lightly floured surface and knead gently for 40 strokes. Divide into equal portions then roll each portion into a ball and elongate it slightly into a torpedo shape.

Blend the ground cinnamon with the sugar in a teacup so that they are thoroughly mixed, then spread over a large plate, and roll each loaf in the mixture making sure it is evenly covered.

Place each loaf into a warm, pre-greased tin and put into a warm, draughtproof place to prove. The tins should be not more than about half full. When the dough has doubled in bulk and is level with the top of the tin it is ready for the oven.

Bake on the centre shelf of an oven pre-heated to 400°F (200°C, Gas Mark 6) for about 40 minutes or until the base of a loaf sounds hollow when tapped with the fingertips. The top crust should be golden brown.

Cool on a wire rack.

VARIATIONS

This recipe can be adapted for breakfast rolls by dividing the dough before the proving stage into eight or twelve equal portions, and rolling each in the cinnamon sugar before proving. They can either be baked in warm, pre-greased muffin tins or on a greased baking tray. The same temperature will be needed but the baking time will be reduced to about 20 minutes.

Extra sugar can be added to the dough if a sweeter bread is preferred.

Yogurt Soda Bread★★★

There is no doubt that the best soda bread is made with buttermilk but as this is becoming increasingly difficult to obtain the following recipe calls for a mixture of yogurt and water. But if you *can* find buttermilk, use it instead. Makes two small loaves or one large. The bread should be eaten the same day as baked as it deteriorates rapidly and does not freeze well. The texture is quite different to yeasted bread, slightly sweeter and with a more open crumb. Little kneading is required. Soda breads are best tray-baked; tins restrict the sideways expansion and result in a dense crumb.

INGREDIENTS

1 lb (450g) strong white flour, preferably unbleached
¼ lb (110g) stoneground wholemeal flour
2 teaspoons (10g) baking powder (not soda)
1 teaspoon (5g) salt
¼ pint (140ml) natural yogurt
¼ pint (140ml) warm water
1 teaspoon (5ml) warm olive oil

METHOD

Sieve the flours, salt and baking powder together into a large bowl and mix thoroughly.

Whisk the yogurt and water together until a creamy smooth liquid is obtained then add the olive oil and whisk again until it is fully blended.

Add the liquid to the flour and mix thoroughly but quickly, kneading in the bowl only as long as necessary to get an even mixture. The dough should be fairly dry but not crumbly – if necessary add a little more warm water to bring it to the correct consistency.

Divide into two equal portions, form each into a ball and place on a greased baking tray, well spaced to avoid the loaves touching as they expand.

Immediately place on the centre shelf of an oven pre-heated to 450°F (230°C) and bake for about 40 minutes or until the loaves sound hollow when tapped on the base with the fingertips. Cool on a wire rack.

VARIATIONS

As previously stated, ½ pint of buttermilk can be substituted for the yogurt and water.

All white or all wholemeal flour can be substituted but extra liquid may be needed if the wholemeal content is increased.

Bavarian Easter Bread★★

This tea bread originated in Germany but is also popular in Luxembourg and parts of Belgium. It is traditionally baked in a tin and coated with white icing but often the icing is omitted and the top decorated with sliced almonds. The recipe makes one fairly large loaf; it will keep well and can be frozen.

INGREDIENTS

1 teaspoon (5g) granulated dried yeast
2 oz (55g) sugar
4 tablespoons (60ml) whole milk, scalded and cooled
1 egg, size 3
2 oz (55g) melted butter
½ lb (225g) strong bread flour, white or wholemeal
½ teaspoon (2.5g) salt
2 oz (55g) almonds, chopped
1 oz (30g) candied peel, chopped
2 oz (55g) seedless raisins
1 oz (30g) glace cherries, sliced
The grated rind of a lemon

METHOD

Dissolve the yeast and sugar in the warm milk and set aside to activate; it is ready for use when the surface is covered in frothy bubbles.

Beat the egg and add the melted butter.

Sieve the flour and salt together, then gradually add to the egg mixture a spoonful at a time, beating well between each addition.

Stir in the activated yeast liquid and mix thoroughly with the hands until a rough dough results.

Turn out on to a lightly floured surface and knead for 100 strokes, return to the bowl, cover with a damp cloth and set aside to rise.

When it has doubled in volume turn out the dough and knead for a further 100 strokes, then gently spread it out into a rough circle and sprinkle with the almonds, peel, raisins and cherries. Grate the lemon peel over it then roll up into a cylinder before kneading in the usual way for a further 50 strokes.

Place the dough into a warm, greased 2-lb (900g) loaf tin and bake on the centre shelf of an oven pre-heated to 375°F (190°C, Gas Mark 5) for about 35 minutes or until a skewer pushed into the centre comes out clean.

Cool on a wire rack.

VARIATIONS

If the bread is not to be iced, decorate the top with sliced almonds 10 minutes before the end of the baking time.

Barmouth Malt Bread★★

The powerful flavour of malt is one you either detest or love –
some people are almost addicted to malt bread, others will
not have it in the house. There must be dozens of recipes for
malt loaves and this is one popular in mid-Wales where a
local baker gave me the recipe some thirty years ago – it is
said to be a proven aphrodisiac and an infallible aid to
longevity. The malt extract can be either in liquid form or
granulated; I have suggested the liquid product because it is
easier to use and more freely available from chemists and
health food stores. Makes four small loaves or fewer larger.

INGREDIENTS

1 pint (550ml) warm water
3 tablespoons (45ml) pasteurized clear honey
4 teaspoons (20g) granulated dried yeast
1 lb (450g) stoneground wholemeal flour
1 lb (450g) strong white flour, preferably unbleached
2 teaspoons (10g) salt
12 oz (335g) sultanas
4 oz (110g) chopped dates or prunes
1 tablespoon (15ml) cooking margarine melted
2 tablespoons (30ml) black treacle or molasses
4 tablespoons (60ml) liquid malt extract

METHOD

Dissolve 1 tablespoon of the honey in the warm water and
stir in the yeast. Set aside to activate. It is ready for use when
the surface is covered in frothy bubbles.

Sieve the flours and salt together into a large bowl and mix
thoroughly. Some of the larger pieces of the wholemeal flour
will not pass through the sieve; do not waste them, tip them
into the bowl and mix in. Add the fruit and stir thoroughly.

When the yeast liquid is ready add the rest of the honey,
the margarine, the treacle or molasses and the malt extract
and whisk briskly to emulsify. These ingredients will emulsify
more easily if slightly warmed before adding to the yeast
liquid.

Make a well in the centre of the flour and pour in the liquid, stir with a wooden spoon until a rough dough results then turn it out on to a lightly floured surface and knead for 150 strokes.

Form the dough into a ball, place in a lightly oiled bowl, cover with a damp cloth and set into a warm place to rise. When it has doubled in volume – usually between one and two hours – turn it out on to a lightly floured surface and knead for another 50 strokes, then divide into equal portions and mould roughly into torpedo shapes. Place into warm, pre-greased tins that are not more than half filled with dough.

Cover with a polythene sheet arranged so that the rising dough cannot come into contact with it, and put into a warm, draughtproof place to prove. The loaves are ready for the oven when the domes are level with the rim of the tins.

Bake on the centre shelf of an oven pre-heated to 350°F (180°C, Gas Mark 4) for about 40 minutes or until a loaf sounds hollow when tapped on the base with the fingertips.

To prevent the top becoming overcooked and burnt it may be necessary to place a sheet of baking foil over each loaf for the last 15 minutes or so in the oven.

After removing from the oven leave the loaves to rest in their tins for 10 minutes, then de-tin and cool on a wire rack. While still very hot glaze the tops with a solution of honey and hot water – one tablespoon (15ml) honey to the same amount of hot water.

Note: Avoid the boxed dates specially prepared for the Christmas trade as these are often dry and stringy. The best are sold in compressed blocks.

If prunes are used they need to be the best quality, fat and juicy. The finest ones come from Agen in the south of France although the Californian ones are also good.

Some people are allergic to the sulphur in molasses in which case golden syrup can be substituted.

Lemon Nut Bread★

There are many ways of making lemon bread, some extremely complicated and time-consuming; this one is fairly quick and very easy. It is definitely a bread – not a cake, but you can add more sugar if you find it not sweet enough. Makes one medium-sized loaf which keeps well and can be frozen.

INGREDIENTS

¼ pint (140ml) whole milk
2 teaspoons (10g) granulated dried yeast
4 oz (110g) sugar
4 oz (110g) chopped mixed nuts or coarsely chopped walnuts
¾ lb (335g) strong white flour, preferably unbleached
½ teaspoon (2.5g) salt
1 tablespoon (15g) grated lemon peel
1 egg, size 3
1 tablespoon (15ml) olive oil
¼ teaspoon (1ml) almond essence

METHOD

Scald and cool the milk then stir in the yeast and a teaspoon (5g) of the sugar. Set aside to activate; it is ready for use when the surface is covered in frothy bubbles.

Lightly toast the nuts under a grill until they are just beginning to brown – do not burn – and set aside to cool.

Sieve the flour and salt together into a large bowl then add the rest of the sugar and the grated lemon peel. Mix thoroughly. Stir in the cooled nuts.

When the yeast is ready, whisk in the egg and the olive oil and beat until a creamy-smooth emulsion results. Add the almond essence and blend in.

Pour the liquid into the flour mixture and stir with a wooden spoon until a rough dough is produced.

Turn out on to a lightly floured surface and knead for 200 strokes. Form the dough into a ball and place it into a warm bowl to rise. Cover with a damp cloth and put into a warm place for about 60 to 90 minutes or until it has doubled in bulk.

Turn it out of the bowl and knead again for 100 strokes, then form into a ball and elongate slightly to roughly fit the shape of an 8 x 4 x 3 in (20 x 10 x 8cms) tin.

Place the dough into the warm pre-greased tin, cover with a dry cloth and put into a warm draughtproof place to prove which will take about half the time of the first rising.

Bake on the centre shelf of an oven pre-heated to 400°F (200°C, Gas Mark 6) for about 40 minutes or until the loaf sounds hollow when tapped on the base with the fingertips.

Cool on a wire rack; do not cut for at least two hours.

VARIATIONS

The top of the loaf can be glazed when it comes out of the oven. Mix 2 oz (55g) caster sugar with 3 tablespoons (45ml) freshly squeezed lemon juice (warm to dissolve if necessary), then paint the loaf with the glaze *after* the bread has been allowed to cool for 10 minutes.

If you require a stronger lemon flavour in the bread, line the bottom of the bread tin with two leaves of the scented-leaf Pelargonium (Geranium) 'Mabel Gray'; as the bread bakes the lemon aroma will permeate the crumb. Do not use lemon essence.

Leaf of Pelargonium (Geranium) 'Mabel Gray'

Chocolate Loaves★

These are a favourite with children and chocoholics. They are easy to make and keep and freeze well; delicious coated with chocolate or vanilla icing or just eaten plain. Recipe makes two loaves. They will keep for a few days and can be frozen.

INGREDIENTS

4 tablespoons (60ml) warm water
14 fl. oz (400ml) whole milk, scalded and cooled
2 teaspoons (10g) granulated dried yeast
6 oz (160g) caster sugar
4 oz (110g) walnuts, chopped
2 lb (900g) strong white flour, preferably unbleached
1 teaspoon (5g) salt
4 oz (110g) cocoa powder (not 'drinking chocolate')
4 oz (110g) butter
3 eggs, size 3
1 teaspoon (5ml) vanilla essence

METHOD

Mix the water with the warm milk, add the yeast and a teaspoon (5g) of the sugar and stir to disperse. Set aside to activate; it is ready for use when the surface is covered in frothy bubbles.

Toast the chopped nuts under a medium grill until they are just beginning to brown – do not burn – and set aside to cool. Sieve the flour, salt and cocoa together, add the cooled nuts and mix thoroughly.

Cream the butter and the rest of the sugar together in a large bowl, gradually add the beaten eggs and the yeast liquid, whisking continually, then beat in half the flour until a smooth batter results.

Add the vanilla essence and mix thoroughly, then gradually incorporate the rest of the flour to make a soft dough.

Turn out on to a lightly floured surface and knead for 100 strokes.

Form into a ball and place in a lightly oiled bowl, cover

with a dry cloth overlaid with a damp one, and set aside in a warm place to rise for about an hour and a half or until doubled in volume.

Turn out and knead for a further 100 strokes, then divide into equal portions, form each into a ball and place in a warmed and greased 8-in (20cms) round cake tin.

Cover with a dry cloth and put into a warm, draughtproof place to prove until it has doubled in volume – usually about half the time of the first rising.

Bake on the centre shelf of an oven pre-heated to 350°F (180°C, Gas Mark 4) for about 40 minutes or until a skewer inserted into the bread comes out clean.

Cool in the tins for 10 minutes before placing on a wire rack to cool.

Note: The tins must be well greased before use or the bread will be difficult to extract from the tins after baking.

Non-stick tins seldom retain their non-sticking qualities beyond a few bakings so grease them just the same. The black coating tends to result in the crust of the bread adjacent to the metal surface cooking much faster than the crumb resulting in a loaf with burnt sides – glass has a similar effect.

The size of the cake tins is not particularly important; you can use larger tins if more convenient or rectangular ones.

Turkish Yogurt Bread★★

This nourishing bread can be made either with sheep's or cow's milk yogurt. It is said to have originated in the mountainous areas of Turkey where goats were more popular so it seems probable that goat's milk yogurt was normally used. The recipe makes five small loaves or fewer larger.

INGREDIENTS

½ pint (280ml) warm water
2 teaspoons (10g) sugar
2 teaspoons (10g) granulated dried yeast
1 pint (550ml) plain yogurt at room temperature
4 fl. oz (110ml) olive oil
2 lb (900g) strong white flour, preferably unbleached
1 lb (450g) stoneground wholemeal flour
1 teaspoon (5g) salt

METHOD

Dissolve the yeast and sugar in the warm water and set aside to activate; it is ready for use when the surface is covered in frothy bubbles.

When the yeast liquid is ready, add the yogurt and whisk until a smooth creamy liquid results then add the oil and continue whisking until all is thoroughly and smoothly emulsified.

Sieve the flours and salt together into a large bowl and mix thoroughly.

Pour the liquid into the flour and stir with a wooden spoon until a soft pliable dough is formed which is slightly tacky to the touch but not sticky. Turn out on to a lightly floured surface and knead for 40 strokes by which time the dough should be smooth and silky. Form it into a ball and, if the liquid content is correct, it should be possible to pass it from hand to hand without it sticking. If it sticks knead in a little more flour.

Lightly oil a large bowl or plastic bucket, place the ball of dough in it and rotate it a few times so that the whole surface is covered in a film of oil. Cover with a damp cloth and set into a warm place to rise.

The dough can take all of four hours to double in volume according to the temperature but it cannot be hurried. For the first hour or two it will appear to be making no progress but suddenly the yeast awakens and begins to work in earnest. At this stage the dough cannot be over-risen but it should be inspected at hourly intervals to avoid overflowing the receptacle.

When fully doubled in volume turn the dough out on to a lightly floured surface and knead for about 20 strokes then divide into equal portions. Knead each portion for a further 10 strokes and form into a torpedo shape. Place into pre-warmed and greased tins and set into a warm place to prove.

Compared with the initial rising time proving is quite rapid. Inspect the loaves after 45 minutes and then at 10 minute intervals. They are ready for the oven when the dome of each loaf has risen just above the top of the tin.

Bake on the centre shelf of an oven pre-set to 450°F (230°C, Gas Mark 8) for 45 minutes. If the bread sounds hollow when tapped on the base it is done.

Cool on a wire rack.

VARIATIONS

All white or all wholemeal flour can be used if preferred.

An alternative tea bread can be made by using a flavoured yogurt, all white flour, and double the quantity of sugar.

Note: When correctly made this bread has a very high 'spring'. It may be necessary to lower the shelf in some ovens to prevent the top crust burning.

Apple Cinnamon Bread★

Bramley cooking apples are probably the best for this bread but I have used eating apples quite successfully except the French Golden Delicious which I find totally flavourless. The apples should be peeled, cored and thinly sliced before dropping into cold water which contains a little lemon juice or ascorbic acid to prevent discoloration. They must be drained and quickly dried before putting into the bread; if they are wet the bread will be heavy. Makes one square loaf.

INGREDIENTS

2 teaspoons (10g) granulated dried yeast
4 oz (110g) sugar
8 fl. oz (225ml) warm water
2 tablespoons (30g) butter
1 teaspoon (5g) ground cinnamon powder
4 oz (110g) apples, peeled, cored and finely sliced
½ oz (15g) seedless raisins or sultanas
1 egg, size 3
2 tablespoons (30ml) olive oil
9 oz (250g) strong white flour, preferably unbleached
1 teaspoon (5g) salt

METHOD

In a large bowl, dissolve the yeast and 1 oz (30g) of the sugar in the warm water and set aside to activate. It is ready for use when the surface is covered in frothy bubbles.

Melt the butter and pour into a baking tin about 9 x 9 ins (22 x 22cms) making sure the entire base is covered.

Mix the remainder of the sugar with the cinnamon and sprinkle it evenly over the melted butter in the baking tin. Spread the apple slices evenly over the sugar and dot with the raisins or sultanas.

Add the egg and olive oil to the activated yeast liquid and whisk until a creamy-smooth emulsion results.

Sieve the flour and the salt together and mix thoroughly, then gradually add half to the yeast emulsion, whisking continually until a smooth batter is obtained. Continue beating for a full two minutes before adding the rest of the flour and beating until quite smooth.

Drop the mixture over the apples in the tin a little at a time to avoid displacing them, cover with a dry cloth and set aside in a warm place to rise for about an hour until doubled in bulk.

Bake on the centre shelf of an oven pre-heated to 375°F (190°C, Gas Mark 5) for about 35 minutes or until the surface is lightly browned. Test by inserting a skewer into the bread, if it comes out clean it is done, if not, bake for a little longer.

Allow to rest for 10 minutes then place a warm plate over the tin and quickly invert it so that the bread falls out with the cinnamon and apples on top. Cool on a wire rack.

VARIATIONS

The bread can be covered with chopped nuts if desired. The nuts must first be lightly toasted under a grill, cooled, then scattered over the melted butter in the tin *before* the sugar and cinnamon are added.

Grated nutmeg can be substituted for the cinnamon but it must be freshly grated from a whole nutmeg. Ready-ground nutmeg powder has usually lost much of its strength.

Nutty Apricot Bread★

This is a great tea-time favourite whether eaten on its own or spread with butter and apricot jam. It keeps for about a week or can be frozen. Makes one loaf in a tin about 9 x 5 x 3 ins (22 x 13 x 8cms).

INGREDIENTS

8 oz (225g) dried apricots
8 oz (225g) chopped mixed nuts
12 oz (340g) strong white flour, preferably unbleached
½ teaspoon (2.5g) salt
1 tablespoon (15g) baking powder (*not* soda)
2½ oz (70g) block margarine, melted
2 eggs, size 3
4 oz (110g) sugar
8oz (225ml) golden syrup

METHOD

Place the apricots in a bowl and cover with boiling water. Allow to stand for 15 minutes, drain and cool, then cut into ¼ in (6mm) cubes.

Gently toast the nuts under the grill until they are just beginning to turn golden brown, then set aside to cool.

Sieve the flour, salt and baking powder together into a large bowl and mix thoroughly.

In a separate bowl, whisk the melted margarine, the eggs, sugar and syrup until smoothly blended, then stir in the apricots and nuts. Gradually incorporate the flour mixture, stirring until all ingredients are evenly distributed.

Pour into a warm pre-greased tin and bake immediately on the centre shelf of an oven pre-heated to 350°F (180°C, Gas Mark 4) for about 75 minutes or until a skewer inserted into the centre of the loaf comes out clean.

Cool in the tin for ten minutes, then de-tin and continue cooling on a wire rack.

VARIATIONS

The sugar can be reduced or omitted if the bread is too sweet.

Chopped prunes can be substituted for the apricots, or use a mixture of apricots and prunes. The best dried apricots come from California and the plumpest prunes from Agen in south-west France. Both fruits weighed after stoning.

Four-Grain Orange Bread★★

The dark crumb of this tasty bread is laced or dotted with orange peel according to the manner in which you prepare it. The oranges can be grated on a coarse grater or peeled, the pith removed with a sharp knife and the zest finely shredded and cut into 1-in (2.5cm) lengths. The bread keeps well and can be frozen. Recipe makes five small loaves or fewer larger.

INGREDIENTS

1 pint (550ml) warm water
¼ lb (110g) medium oatmeal
4 teaspoons (20g) granulated dried yeast
2 oz (55ml) molasses or golden syrup
1 large or two small oranges
2 lb (900g) strong white flour, preferably unbleached
¼ lb (110g) barley flour
¼ lb (110g) rye flour
1 tablespoon (15g) salt
1 tablespoon (15g) ground ginger (optional)
2 oz (55g) melted butter
4 fl. oz (110ml) whole milk, scalded and cooled

METHOD

Put ½ pint of the warm water into a saucepan, add the oatmeal and bring to the boil. Cook for one minute then remove from the heat and set aside to cool.

Dissolve the yeast with a little of the molasses in the rest of the warm water and set aside to activate; it is ready for use when the surface is covered in frothy bubbles.

Grate or shred the orange peel, squeeze the juice and set aside for later use.

Sieve the flours, salt and ginger together into a large bowl, add the orange peel and mix thoroughly.

When the yeast liquid is ready add the melted butter, the rest of the molasses and the warm milk, and whisk until a smooth, creamy emulsion results. Whisk in the oatmeal liquid, then combine with the orange juice and pour into the flour mixture. Stir with a wooden spoon until a rough dough is obtained.

Turn out and knead on a lightly floured surface for 100 strokes.

Form into a ball and place in a lightly oiled bowl, cover with a dry towel overlaid with a damp one, and set to rise in a warm place for about an hour or until doubled in volume.

Turn out and knead for a further 100 strokes, divide into equal portions and shape to roughly half-fill the tins which must be warm and thoroughly greased. The loaves can be tray-baked if preferred; simply roll each portion into a ball and set out on a greased baking tray allowing at least 3 ins (8cms) between each loaf.

Cover the loaves with a dry cloth and set to prove in a warm draughtproof place for about 35 minutes or until they have doubled in volume or risen level with the top of the tins.

Bake on the centre shelf of an oven pre-heated to 375°F (190°C, Gas Mark 5) for about 40 minutes or until the loaves sound hollow when tapped on the base with the fingertips.

Cool on a wire rack.

VARIATIONS

The loaves can be glazed immediately after being taken from the oven – mix a tablespoon (15ml) pasteurized honey with the same quantity of hot water and brush over the tops of the loaves; a few chopped nuts can be scattered on to the glaze as an added ornament if you wish.

Note: The sulphur-content of molasses can adversely affect some people.

Lincolnshire Fruit Bread★★

This variation of the usual currant loaf is very popular in the Lincolnshire Wolds where it originated and it appears under several names in other parts of the country. It keeps and freezes well, can be toasted, or eaten as plain bread and butter with or without a preserve. It is much less sweet than commercial tea breads, but the sugar content can be increased slightly if preferred. Makes five small loaves or fewer larger.

INGREDIENTS

1 tablespoon (15g) granulated dried yeast
2 oz (55g) sugar
½ pint (280ml) warm water
2 lb (900g) strong white flour, preferably unbleached
¼ lb (110g) stoneground wholemeal flour
2 teaspoons (10g) ground mixed spice
4 tablespoons (60ml) olive oil
1 lb (450g) currants, sultanas and mixed peel (optional)

METHOD

Dissolve the yeast and sugar in the warm water and set aside to activate; it is ready to use when the surface is covered in frothy bubbles.

Sieve the flours and spice together into a large bowl, add the fruit and mix in thoroughly.

When the yeast mixture is ready add the olive oil and whisk rapidly until a creamy-smooth emulsion results, then pour this into the flour and stir with a wooden spoon until a rough dough is obtained.

Turn out on to a lightly floured surface and knead for 100 strokes.

Form the dough into a ball and place into a lightly oiled bowl, cover with a dry cloth overlaid with a damp one and put into a warm place to rise until it has doubled in bulk. The dough should be pliable but not sticky. If it is too dry add a teaspoon (5ml) extra water and knead it into the mixture; if too wet knead in more flour.

Turn out on to the floured surface again and knead for a further 100 strokes, then divide into equal portions, roll each into a ball then elongate slightly to a torpedo shape and half-fill warm pre-greased tins. Cover with a dry cloth and set into a warm place to prove. The loaves are ready for the oven when the dough has risen level with the top edge of the tins.

Bake on the centre shelf of an oven pre-heated to 425°F (220°C, Gas Mark 7) for 30–40 minutes or until a loaf sounds hollow when the base is tapped with the fingertips.

Cool on a wire rack.

Glaze the tops of the loaves as soon as they come out of the oven with a solution of sugar and water – 1 tablespoon (15g) of sugar dissolved in a similar amount of warm water.

VARIATIONS

The wholemeal flour can be dispensed with and white substituted if preferred.

Lard or margarine can be used instead of olive oil but not low-fat spreads. Solid fats must be rubbed into the flour *before* the fruit is added.

Honey and water in the same proportions can be used for the glaze instead of the sugar.

Diet Breads

For those with allergy problems

Wheatless Rye Bread★★★

This is specially formulated for those who are allergic to wheat and wheat products. It makes a loaf with a dark, open crumb and rather rubbery crust. The dough cannot be hurried – it can take several hours to complete the rise. It can be baked in tins or on trays, but tray-baked loaves are liable to split; rye flour is never easy to work with. The bread keeps and freezes well. This bread was fashionable in the early 1950s when several small bakeries were producing rye bread, but its popularity has declined except perhaps among the Jewish and some immigrant communities. It is probably at its best when a day old. Makes 4 small loaves or two large.

INGREDIENTS

1 tablespoon (15g) granulated dried yeast
6 fl. oz (180ml) warm water
4 fl. oz (110ml) molasses
8 fl. oz (225ml) warm tea, freshly brewed
2 fl. oz (55ml) melted butter
½ lb (225g) potatoes (weighed *after* mashing)
3 eggs, size 3, separated
2 lb (900g) rye flour
2 teaspoons (10g) salt
Rice flour

METHOD

Dissolve the yeast in the warm water with a little of the molasses, and set aside to activate. It is ready for use when the surface is covered with frothy bubbles.

In a separate bowl whisk together the warm tea, the rest of the molasses and the melted butter cooled to body temperature. A better mix will be obtained if the molasses is also warmed.

Boil the potatoes in their skins until soft. Cool, peel and mash thoroughly until all lumps disappear and a fluffy consistency is obtained. Weigh out ½ lb (220g) of mashed potatoes into another large bowl, add the yolks of three eggs, and beat to a smooth batter.

Add the tea mixture and beat until smooth, then add the yeast and beat that in also until it is quite smooth. Whip the egg whites until stiff then fold in.

Sieve the rye flour and salt together, mix thoroughly, then gradually combine the flour into the liquid a little at a time, stirring with a wooden spoon until the dough begins to fall away from the sides of the bowl.

Turn the dough out on to a lightly rye-floured surface and knead for 30 strokes. The dough should be fairly stiff but quite damp; if it is too sticky to handle comfortably knead more rye flour into it until the right consistency is obtained. Rye dough must not be over-kneaded or it will tear.

Cover the bowl with a polythene sheet or damp cloth and put aside in a warm place to rise until it has doubled in volume. This can take several hours depending upon the temperature (80°F, 27°C is ideal), but if you have the time leave the dough to rise overnight in a plastic bucket – the bread will be greatly improved.

When it has doubled in volume divide the dough into equal portions and mould into roughly the shape of the tins.

Lightly grease the warmed tins and coat with rice flour to prevent the bread sticking. The tins must not be more than half filled.

Brush the tops of the loaves with melted butter, cover them with a polythene sheet supported so that the bread cannot come into contact with it, and put them into a warm place to prove.

Rye loaves without wheat can take several hours to prove, but if they have been risen overnight the proving time is much shorter. They will rise very little more after they go into the oven, and the 'spring' associated with wheat breads is almost totally absent, so make sure they are fully risen before baking them.

Bake on the centre shelf of an oven pre-heated to 375°F (190°C, Gas Mark 5) for 10 minutes, then reduce the temperature to 350°F (180°C, Gas Mark 4) and bake for another 50 minutes before testing by tapping the base of a loaf with the fingertips – if it sounds hollow it is done.

Cool on a wire rack.

VARIATIONS

The bread can be glazed by painting the tops with egg white lightly beaten in a tablespoon (15ml) of warm water. This is best done towards the end of the baking time.

The salt can be omitted if necessary.

Note: If the potatoes are peeled *before* boiling they will absorb water and yield a wet mash which will result in a heavy dough and an equally heavy crumb. The quality of this bread depends to a large extent upon the potatoes so it may be necessary to experiment with different varieties.

Scottish Hooley Bread★★

This is by far the best of the recipes dispensing with yeast, dairy products and sugar.

Before the eighteenth century the main cereal crop grown in Scotland was oats and this was eaten chiefly in the form of oatcakes made by mixing oatmeal with salt and water and a little mutton fat, and cooked on a griddle.

Wheat flour was a luxury reserved for special occasions and, as the festivities were always planned well in advance, there was ample time for the slow fermentation required because of the absence of yeast, the use of which was unknown in the remote areas of the Highlands.

This recipe was handed down from mother to daughter through the centuries, and came to me via an elderly lady from near Inverness who had received it from her grandmother. The original called for the inclusion of clarified mutton fat but I have substituted olive oil which is more convenient and pleasant to use, and not liable to taint the bread. The quality of the bread depends to a large extent upon the freshness of the flour; try to get flour which is not more than two months old. (See the list of flour mills in Chapter 4.)

This bread cannot be hurried and its keeping qualities are poor. The recipe makes one small loaf which is best eaten within about eight hours of leaving the oven. The crumb is fluffy without crumbling, and the crust is mildly crunchy. The flavour is equal to any yeasted bread.

INGREDIENTS

¼ lb (110g) stoneground wholemeal flour
6 fl.oz (170ml) warm water
½ teaspoon (2.5g) salt
6 oz (165g) stoneground medium oatmeal
2 tablespoons (30ml) olive oil

METHOD

Mix the flour with the water and beat until a smooth batter results. Place into a sealed container such as an empty ice-cream tub, or pudding basin which can be sealed into a plastic bag. Place in an evenly warm atmosphere (such as an airing cupboard) for forty-eight hours or until it shows signs of steady fermentation with bubbles breaking through the surface and has doubled in bulk.

Mix the oatmeal and salt together into a large bowl.

Add the olive oil to the fermented flour and water mixture, and beat well to ensure even distribution, then pour it into the oatmeal and combine all the ingredients by hand.

Turn the dough out on to a floured surface and knead for 100 strokes. At first it will be quite harsh and dry, and difficult to combine all the flour into the ball. Do not add water. Gradually the dough will soften as you proceed with the kneading until eventually it will be smooth and silky. If it is at all sticky knead in a little more flour. Form into a ball and place in a warmed basin. Cover with a damp cloth or polythene film and put in a warm place to rise. Depending upon temperature, (70°F, 21°C is ideal) this can take several hours, seldom less than four, but the dough should almost double in volume before being kneaded again for a further 100 strokes.

Allow to rest for 10 minutes, then form it into a ball by rolling the dough on the floured surface with a rotary motion, tucking the sides underneath to finish.

Traditionally the loaves are tray-baked to produce a rounded pad somewhat similar to a thick bap. If this is your wish remember the dough will spread during cooking so it is best to use a tray or dish with a raised edge. Tinned loaves are easier to manage. Put the dough into a well-greased warm tin or on the tray and put it into a warm place to prove.

The time taken for the dough to prove varies considerably according to the temperature. At about 70°F (21°C) it will take between three and four hours but it is unlikely to develop to anything like the extent of yeasted bread. It is ready for the oven when it has almost doubled in volume. Any attempt to reduce the proving time, by increasing the temperature will result in a fly crust.

Place the bread on the centre shelf of an oven pre-heated to 400°F (200°C, Gas Mark 6) and bake for 40 minutes. Test by tapping the base of the loaf with the fingertips – if it sounds hollow the bread is done. Cool on a wire rack.

Extra Fibre Bread★

This is a very easy bread to make, with an open crumb and crisp crust. It stores and freezes well, and makes excellent toast. This recipe makes three small loaves or fewer large ones.

INGREDIENTS

½ pint (280ml) whole milk, scalded and cooled
¼ pint (140ml) warm water
2 teaspoons (10g) granulated dried yeast
2 teaspoons (10g) sugar
½ lb (225g) strong white flour, preferably unbleached
1 lb (450g) stoneground wholemeal flour
2 oz (55g) bran
2 teaspoons (10g) salt
2 oz (55g) wheatgerm
2 oz (55g) lard
Poppy seeds for decoration

METHOD

Mix the warm milk and water, add the yeast and sugar and leave to activate. It is ready for use when the surface is covered in frothy bubbles.

Sieve the flours, salt, bran and wheatgerm into a large warmed bowl and mix thoroughly. Rub in the lard until the mixture resembles fine breadcrumbs.

Add the yeast liquid to the flour and stir with a wooden spoon, finishing by hand. The result will be a rough, crumbly dough.

Turn it out on to a floured surface and knead for 200 strokes by which time it will have become smooth and even and quite bouncy. If, after kneading, it appears to be too dry a little more water can be added; if it is at all sticky add more flour and knead in.

Form the dough into a ball and return it to the warm bowl. Cover with a dry cloth overlaid with a damp one, and set to rise in a warm place which will take about an hour.

When the dough has doubled in volume, turn it out on to

the floured surface again and knead for a further 200 strokes. Allow it to rest for 10 minutes, then divide it into equal portions.

Take each portion of dough and roll it on the surface with a rotary motion to make a ball, then gently elongate to form a torpedo shape. Place each torpedo into a greased and warmed tin, and put the tins into a warm draughtproof place for proving. The tins must be not more than about half filled with dough.

The loaves are ready for the oven when the domes have risen level with the top rim of the tins. Spray the tops over with tepid salt water and sprinkle with poppy seeds, immediately place them on the centre shelf of an oven pre-heated to 450°F (230°C, Gas Mark 8) and bake for 15 minutes, then reduce the temperature to 400°F (200°C, Gas Mark 6) and bake for another 30 minutes before testing by tapping the base of a loaf with the fingertips – if the bread sounds hollow it is done.

The baked bread should be removed from the tins after resting for 5 minutes, and placed upon a wire rack to cool.

VARIATIONS

All white flour can be used or all wholemeal according to personal preference but in the latter case a little extra water may be needed. The fibre-content will be reduced if all white flour is used.

Olive oil can be substituted for the lard but a softer crust will result. The olive oil must be whisked into the yeast liquid and thoroughly emulsified just before it is added to the flour.

The dough can be made into rolls by weighing out into 3-oz portions, rolling each into a ball and placing on a greased baking tray to prove. They are ready for the oven when doubled in volume and will require only about 20 minutes baking.

Gluten-Free Breads

Gluten-free bread mixes are manufactured and marketed by several companies and obtainable from health food shops and chemists. I have baked one product and found the bread to be close-crumbed, almost a cake texture, and with a rather uninterestingly bland flavour – not the kind of bread anyone would eat from choice.

But for those on a gluten-free diet I am told the taste is soon acquired, and the cost of the mixes will almost certainly repel casual buyers. Many of these products are now available on prescription but even so you would be lucky to produce a small loaf for less than £2.

Gluten-free flours can be obtained for making many items other than bread such as cakes, pastries, quiches, soups, buns, tarts, etc., and some companies have their own bakeries and are prepared to supply ready-baked products.

The following is a full list of suppliers of gluten-free products in the British Isles available at the time of writing. When contacting any of them it is advisable to enclose a large (A4) stamped, addressed envelope.

Everfresh Natural Foods
Gatehouse Close
Aylesbury
Buckinghamshire HP19 3DE

Farley Health Products
Nottingham NG2 3AA

General Designs Ltd
PO Box 38E
Worcester Park
Surrey KT4 7LX

Gluten Free Foods Ltd
8 Queen Anne Street
London W1M 9LD

Jacob's Bakery Ltd
Sutton Busines Park
Earley
Reading
Berkshire RG6 1AZ

JRJ Trading Company
Unit 4, West Burrowfield
Welwyn Garden City
Hertfordshire AL7 4TW

Larkhall Natural Health
225 Putney Bridge Road
London SW15 2PY

Nutricia Dietary Products Ltd
494 Honeypot Lane
Stanmore
Middlesex HA7 1JH

Procea
Alexandra Road
Dublin 1
Eire

Ultrapharm Ltd
PO Box 18
Henley-on-Thames
Oxfordshire RG9 2AW

Scientific Hospital Supplies Ltd
100 Wavertree Boulevard
Wavertree Technology Park
Liverpool L7 9PQ

Gluten-Free Bread★

The following recipe is fairly standard no matter which company's flour you use. It makes one loaf.

INGREDIENTS

2 teaspoons (10g) granulated dried yeast
8 fl.oz (225ml) warm water
1 tablespoon (15ml) olive oil
10¼ oz (290g) gluten-free flour

METHOD

Add the yeast to the warm water and set aside to activate. Because there is no sugar in the recipe it will take longer for the surface to become covered in frothy bubbles but it cannot be used until this condition is reached. When activated, whisk the oil into the yeast liquid until a smooth emulsion obtains.

Put the flour into a bowl, pour in the liquid and beat until a smooth batter results.

Pour the batter into a lightly oiled 1-lb bread tin and bake immediately on the centre shelf of an oven pre-heated to 350°F (180°C, Gas Mark 4) for about an hour.

The bread is cooked if it sounds hollow when tapped on the base with the fingertips.

Allow to rest in the tin for 10 minutes then turn out on to a wire rack to cool. Do not cut until quite cold.

Note: Exact measurements are important.

Most of the manufacturers of gluten-free flours are prepared to supply a variety of recipes using their own products, and coeliacs would do well to send for them.

Ulster Soda Bread★★★

This recipe has been designed specially for those who are allergic to yeast and dairy products. The mixture will not rise as in yeast recipes, and because of the substitution of baking soda for yeast, it must be cooked immediately after mixing with no kneading or proving.

A fairly dense crumb is produced with a rather rubbery texture if undercooked although still edible. It is probably at its best toasted about 4 hours old. It will not keep long and cannot be frozen, so should be made in small batches to be eaten as soon as it has cooled.

This bread must be steamed, not baked, and all the operations are performed at speed if the best results are to be obtained. Make sure the bowl to contain the mixture is oiled and ready to accept the batter before you begin, and that the water in the steamer is boiling.

Use only fresh baking soda and cream of tartar; both deteriorate rapidly in store.

Makes one small loaf.

INGREDIENTS

1 teaspoon (5g) baking soda (not baking powder)
½ teaspoon (2.5g) cream of tartar
3 oz (85g) strong white flour, preferably unbleached
3 oz (85g) stoneground wholemeal flour
½ teaspoon (2.5g) salt
2 fl.oz (55ml) warm olive oil
8 fl.oz (230ml) warm water

METHOD

Put the baking soda and the cream of tartar together into an eggcup or similar small receptacle and thoroughly mix by stirring and shaking.

Sift the flours and salt together with the baking soda/cream of tartar mixture into a large bowl and mix thoroughly.

Mix the olive oil and the water with a whisk or mechanical liquidizer until a smooth emulsion is obtained, then pour the liquid into the flour and beat until a smooth batter results.

Pour the batter into a 2-pint well-oiled basin, cover with foil or greaseproof paper and steam for about four hours or until a skewer inserted into the centre of the loaf comes out clean.

Allow to rest for 10 minutes before turning out on to a wire rack to cool.

Note: Most vegetable oils can be substituted for the olive oil.

All white or all wholemeal flour can be used instead of the mixture, but the latter will require 1 teaspoon (5ml) more water.

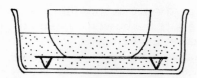

The water level must be maintained below the lip of the basin. The basin must be raised above the base of the saucepan.

Faults

Top Fly-Crust

This is the condition when the top crust separates from the crumb in the baking. There are several possible causes:

1. Proving the dough in a situation where heat is produced above the loaves (such as in some types of cooker's warming compartment) resulting in a dry skin being formed over the top surface of the dough before it goes into the oven.
2. Cooling the baked loaves too rapidly in a very dry atmosphere.
3. Freezing the loaves whilst the centre of the crumb is still slightly warm.
4. Proving at too high a temperature.

Entire Fly-Crust

This is when the entire outer crust of a loaf is detached from the crumb. The crust is brittle and inedible, the crumb rather dry but still usable. It is usually caused by placing warm dough into cold tins. The outer surfaces rise at a slower rate than the mass and become detached in the baking.

Heavy and Dense-Textured Crumb

Usually caused by insufficient rising and proving times. At each stage the dough must be allowed to double in bulk.

A similar result will occur if baked loaves are left to cool in their tins; they should be detinned soon after leaving the oven and cooled on a wire rack.

Very Open-Textured Crumb

The usual result of shortage of fat in the mixture or the dough being over-risen at the proving stage. It can also be caused by proving too rapidly (at too high a temperature).

Large Holes in Crumb

This can be the result of indifferent kneading leaving air pockets in the dough, by poorly distributed fat in the mix, or (rarely) by over-proving an under-kneaded mix.

Dough made from unsieved flour can also occasionally produce a holey crumb but these tend to be smaller and more widely distributed.

Sticky Crumb
This sometimes occurs when a mixture includes raw unpasteurized milk. All milk must be scalded before using for breadmaking.

Dough Does Not Rise
There are several possible reasons for this, some of which are detailed below:
1. Stale yeast: the most frequent cause of failures. If you follow the recipes and ferment the yeast before incorporating it into the flour you will know it is active.
2. Salt added to the yeast has killed it: add the salt to the flour, not the yeast.
3. At some stage the yeast or dough has been subjected to excessive heat (80°F, 70°C is the optimum) and the yeast has been killed.
4. Stale flour: if, after kneading for the recommended number of strokes the dough remains rough and lumpy and shows no signs of becoming silky-smooth, the flour is past its best and the rise will be inhibited. Abandon and start again with fresh flour. The addition of extra yeast will not improve stale flour.

Mushroom-Shaped Slice
Commonly caused by slight over-proving. If the dough is allowed to rise above the edge of the tin it is over-proved; when put into the oven it will expand rapidly and overflow the tin. Tins should not be more than half-filled with dough.

Loaves have a Crisp Crust and Sharp Corners
Bread was made from flour which had been milled at too high a speed and became overheated during grinding. Replace with a different brand.

Top Crust Burnt Before Bread is Cooked
Oven temperature too high or bread placed too high in the oven.

Hard Crusts, Crumb Dry and Harsh

1. Oven temperature too low and baking time extended to compensate.
2. Baked on too low a shelf in the oven.
3. Loaf defrosted in a microwave for a few seconds too long. Defrosting at room temperature is preferable.

Bread Tastes Unpleasantly 'Yeasty'

Too much yeast used, adjust to taste. Each recipe suggests an amount acceptable to most people; using less will extend rising times slightly but will not be detrimental to the bread. Increasing the yeast-content will not improve the rise but will strengthen the flavour.

Dough Rises Well but Collapses in the Oven

Bread was over-proved. Abandon and start again.

Yeast Does Not Ferment

1. Stale yeast: replace with fresh.
2. Yeast granules have become damp in store.
3. Sugar omitted – yeast can be fermented without sugar but it takes much longer.
4. Salt added: yeast killed.
5. Water too hot: yeast killed.

Lop-sided Loaf

Usually the result of baking in an unevenly-heated oven; the yeast is killed on the hottest side whilst the other side is still active and the dough still rising.

Careless moulding can also result in a lop-sided loaf. The final kneading must end with the smooth dome of the dough being on top; if it is turned slightly under the bread will rise unevenly.

Flat-Top Loaf

The dough will not rise to a dome-shape if the mixture is too wet but produces a flat-topped loaf which is usually quite edible but will not spring in the oven and is less appetising in appearance. Reduce the liquid-content by a quarter at the next mixing. In extreme cases the dough will not rise at all and produces a loaf resembling a brick in appearance and texture. No-knead recipes require precise liquid measurement.

Gritty Lumps in the Crumb

This is usually the result of the surface of the dough drying during the rise and the dry skin being kneaded into the dough at the next kneading. It can be prevented by lightly oiling the surface of the dough before putting to rise, or by covering with a damp cloth.

Poor Results with Soda Breads

The problem most frequently encountered with soda breads is a poor rise caused by the use of a stale raising agent. Bicarbonate of soda, cream of tartar and baking soda have a very short shelf life, and precise measurement of ingredients is essential.

4

A List of Small Independent Flour Mills by County

In Shakespeare's time London was quite a small town enclosed in a wall and surrounded by open countryside. Smithfield was actually a field outside the city walls where regular stock markets were held, the beasts being slaughtered on the spot.

For more than fifty years after his death little changed; the fields and meadows all around were dotted with small flour mills, some wind- but mostly water-driven. The historian Thomas Pennant in his *Account of London*, describing the River Fleet (now sadly conduited) remarks that '*Among the pastures and woodlands through which the river wends* (on its way from Hampstead Heath to Blackfriars) *are numerous water-mills whose clack is very pleasing to the ear*'. These mills were necessary to provide flour for the Londoner's daily bread, and were usually sited close to the fields where the cereals were grown.

The city was served by many small bakeries, mostly trading from the ground floor of the premises and having living accommodation above. Such a bakery was that owned by one Farynor, appointed baker to King Charles II. His bakery was situated on the hill between Upper Thames Street and St Paul's Cathedral, close to the great warehouses which lined the bank of the River Thames.

At about 1.30 a.m. on Sunday 2nd September 1666 a fire broke out at his bakery and within hours had spread out of control. So began the Great Fire of London which destroyed over three-quarters of the total area of London as it then was. Thus the history of London – and even of England – is closely linked with the milling and bakery trade.

Until the mid-nineteenth century there were thousands of small flour mills scattered over the British Isles, but the invention of the steel roller mill resulted in the rapid demise of most of them and few survived after the 1914–18 War. Today there has been a revival of interest in ancient mills and milling, and a few have been or are being restored to produce stoneground flour by the process which served our ancestors well in centuries past, using slow-moving abrasive stones driven usually by wind or water power.

A collection of these mills is listed in alphabetical order in the following pages by county to enable them to be easily traced. All produce stoneground wholemeal flour, often from locally grown wheat, with a few exceptions where production is expected to begin or recommence after rebuilding or renovation – you are advised to telephone before visiting to confirm opening times, etc.

Many of the mills manufacture a variety of flours and other grain-based products, and some are prepared to accept mail order if the customer will tolerate the excessive postal charges, but there is no doubt that personal collection is best if it can be arranged. The difference in supermarket wholemeal and that purchased direct from the actual miller has to be experienced to be believed.

Unfortunately I cannot claim the list to be fully comprehensive; of over 200 letters I wrote, this list represents the total of those who replied, with the exception of three or four who very kindly advised me that they are no longer in production.

All the details have been supplied and checked by the mill concerned, and several include details of other attractions either at the mill or in the surrounding location. Many have tea-shops and souvenir shops, and most arrange for mill tours at certain times. A few can even offer bed and breakfast accommodation and sometimes camping facilities.

Every mill is dangerous to some extent, and children must always be under strict control. Dogs are never admitted, and very few offer facilities for the physically handicapped (there are usually several flights of narrow stairs to be negotiated). Most offer free car-parking, and there is usually a small admission charge. Nearly all are owned by enthusiasts and operated by volunteers – their income is derived almost entirely from the sale of flour and the modest admission charges.

If you have knowledge of a working independent mill which is not listed here, whether water or wind-powered, I would be grateful for the information and will endeavour (with the owner's permission) to include it in any future editions of this book.

Bedfordshire

Bromham Watermill
Bromham
near Bedford
Tel. 01234-824330

The Domesday Survey of 1086 mentions two mills in Bromham; presumably one stood on the site of the present mill and belonged to the main manor of Bromham, but little is known of the other except that a lease dated 1719 describes the property as 'all those watermills commonly called Bromham Mills'.

In 1943, after a succession of owners and millers, the mill finally ceased operating by water power but continued as a mill with electric-powered machinery until 1970. Bedfordshire County Council purchased the property in 1973 and it was restored to full working order in 1980. It is situated in a picturesque setting beside the River Great Ouse about 2½ miles to the west of the centre of Bedford, at the foot of Bromham Bridge.

It is open to the public from the beginning of April to the end of October, Wednesday to Friday 10.30 a.m. to 4.30 p.m.; Saturday, Sunday and Bank Holidays 11.30 a.m. to 6 p.m. There is a nominal admission charge and free car-parking. School parties and groups by prior arrangement.

Milling demonstrations producing stoneground wholemeal flour are held on the last Sunday in each month and Bank Holidays during the open season. Regulations prevent the sale of the flour produced at present but it is hoped to be able to sell it in the near future.

The mill building has local crafts and gifts for sale, with an art gallery where the exhibitions change every month, and refreshments are available in the tea-shop. The adjoining water meadow provides the ideal setting for a picnic, and is rich in bird and plant life.

The mill is located at the west end of Bromham Bridge off the A428 Bedford to Northampton road (Bromham bypass). Further details from The Director of Leisure Services, Bedfordshire County Council, County Hall, Bedford MK42 9AP; Tel. 01234-228671.

Ford End Watermill
Ford End Farm
Station Road
Ivinghoe
Leighton Buzzard
Bedfordshire LU7 9EA
Tel. 01582-600391

Although the postal address is Bedfordshire, Ford End Watermill is actually located in Buckinghamshire on the northern outskirts of the village of Ivinghoe which lies about 8 miles south of Leighton Buzzard, 6 miles south-west of Dunstable and 5 miles north-west of Tring. Aylesbury is some 9 miles to the west as the crow flies.

The early history of the mill is still being researched by the

Pitstone Local History Society. The Victoria County History records that 'the water-mill at Ivinghoe was held in the fourteenth century by the Spigurnel and Alberd families' but it is not certain that this refers to Ford End Mill. However, the *Posse Comitatus* of 1798 includes a reference to a water-mill occupied by William Heley, miller, and this ties in with the initials and date 'W.H. 1795' painted on the wall of the stone floor.

During the twentieth century the mill has been part of the farm occupied by the Jellis family. It was in regular use grinding animal feed until 1963, when the wheel boards began to rot and fall off, and it was rapidly falling into a state of disrepair. In November 1964 the Pitstone Local History Society launched an appeal to raise money for the restoration. Half the money needed to get the mill working again was raised, the balance being generously provided by Mr Arthur Jellis.

The millpond, the moat of the farmhouse, is fed by springs which rise from the chalk less than half a mile from the mill and, until recently, the flow was much reduced, but it is now improving. Even so it is only possible to grind for a few hours each day and milling demonstrations are restricted to a few Sundays and Bank Holiday afternoons between 3 and 5 p.m. (Please telephone for details.)

This is the only remaining working water-mill in Buckinghamshire, producing stoneground wholemeal flour from a variety of English wheats. On display in the mill are an iron-age saddle quern and a beehive quern made of Hertfordshire pudding-stone which was found in a Romano-British well on land below Pitstone Hill and dating from the first century AD.

The mill is open to the public every Sunday and Bank Holiday afternoon, 2.30 to 5.30 p.m. from 1 May to 30 September. There is a small admission charge to help in the restoration and maintenance but car-parking is free.

Nearby attractions include the Society's own farm museum with a large amateur collection of rural and agricultural bygones, Pitstone Windmill (NT) – the oldest post mill in the country – and Pitstone Church, now redundant but containing many items of ecclesiastical interest.

Berkshire

Mapledurham Watermill
Mapledurham Estate
Reading
Berkshire RG4 7TR
Tel. 01734-723350

In 1937 I chanced upon Mapledurham Mill during a bicycle tour of the Thames Valley and was immediately fascinated by it even though at that time it was almost derelict and totally neglected. The water-wheel was falling apart, the roof disintegrating and the whole structure covered in ivy. The millpond was choked with weed, and I was convinced that the mill could not survive more than a few years.

There was a mill on this site at the time of the Domesday Survey of 1086 but little is known of it apart from the entry in Domesday Book which states that William de Warene owned it and that it was valued at 20 shillings and ten acres. The present building dates from the fifteenth century and parts of the original structure are still visible although there have been several additions over the centuries. The mill has now been fully restored and visitors will often be able to see flour being produced, using the ancient millstones in the traditional manner. The wooden machinery is powered by an undershot water-wheel, also built of wood.

Mapledurham is the last of the Thames water-mills still operational and producing flour. It is part of the Mapledurham Estate which has been in the Blount family since 1490, and the present house, built in 1588, remains the property and the home of their descendants. The moderate admission charges can include entry to the park, grounds, house and mill, or more limited tours at reduced prices. Flour can be purchased at the mill or from the estate office when the mill is closed.

The mill is open to visitors on Saturdays, Sundays and Bank Holidays from Easter until the last Sunday in September, 1–5 p.m. Groups and school parties at other times by prior arrangement only. The gift shop sells a variety of souvenirs and the tea-shop offers a selection of homemade products, ice cream and beverages.

The tiny village of Mapledurham lies about three miles north-west of Reading as the crow flies, almost halfway between Reading and Pangbourne on the northern side of the River Thames. It is signposted off the A4074 Reading to Oxford road about 2 miles from Caversham Bridge. There is also a river launch which plies between Caversham Bridge and Mapledurham on open days. Telephone 01734-723350 for details.

Buckinghamshire

Lacey Green Windmill
Lacey Green,
Princes Risborough
Buckinghamshire.
Tel. 01844-343560

Lacey Green Windmill is thought to be the oldest surviving smock mill and the third oldest windmill in the British Isles. It was originally built at Chesham, about 10 miles to the east of the present site, and is thought to have been moved to Lacey Green at the orders of the Duke of Buckingham in 1821 when the opportunity was taken to renovate and repair it.

It fell into disuse early in the First World War and soon after was used as a weekend cottage, but little repair work was carried out and time and weather made the structure increasingly unstable. In the mid-1930s money was raised to prevent its total collapse, and during the Second World War the mill served as a watch tower for the Home Guard. Later it was used as a farm store and became so derelict that it seemed past repair.

But in 1971 agreement was reached between the owners and the Historic Works and Buildings Group of the Chiltern Society and the work of restoration put in hand with the object of restoring the mill to its original working order, using as much of the existing timber as possible, and incorporating new materials only when essential.

Restoration was finally completed and the wind turned the sails of Lacey Green Windmill for the first time in nearly seventy years on 23rd April 1983, since when a small granary, dating from the mid-nineteenth century, has been added to the site.

The mill is open to the public from May to September, Sundays and Bank Holiday Mondays from 2.30 to 5.30 p.m. and operational when weather permits. Unfortunately, although fully restored, it cannot be operated regularly enough to produce flour at the moment but it is hoped soon to be in regular production.

There is a small charge for admission and donations towards the upkeep would be appreciated. Parking in Pink Road.

The mill is situated about 2 miles south of Princes Risborough and 6 miles north of High Wycombe, just off the A4010 in the Chiltern Hills between Buckinghamshire and Hertfordshire. Leave the M40 at Junction 4 and head north towards Aylesbury.

For further information contact the Honorary Secretary, Lacey Green Windmill Restoration Committee; Tel. 01844-343560.

Cambridgeshire

Downfield Windmill
Fordham Road
Soham
Ely
Cambridgeshire CB7 5BG
Tel. 01353-720333

The first mill erected on this site was a smock mill about 1726, since when it has had several owners and numerous alterations and renovations. The brick base upon which the original smock stood was raised in the 1860s by jacking up the wooden tower and extending the brick base vertically, but in 1887 the mill was wrecked in a gale and was then rebuilt in its present form, entirely of brick, by the local millwright – Tom Hunt.

It fell into disrepair in 1958 and was not used for several years, but a programme of restoration was commenced between 1975 and 1980, and in April 1980 the mill was finally operational and began producing again.

It is now in full commercial production, supplying a variety of flours to retail outlets as far distant as Cornwall and London, and it is open to the public on Sundays and Bank Holidays from 11 a.m. to 5 p.m.

There is a nominal admission charge and free car-parking. Groups and school parties can be admitted by prior arrangement.

Flours produced and on sale at the mill include organic and non-organic stoneground wholemeal, stoneground white, pastry flours, rye, barley, maize, oatmeal, bran and semolina.

The mill is situated just off the A142 – the Ely to Newmarket road, close to the junction with the A1123, about 5 miles north of Newmarket and 7 miles south-east of Ely.

Houghton Water Mill
Mill House
Mill Street
Houghton
Huntingdon
Cambridgeshire PE17 2AZ
Tel. 01480-301494

For a thousand years there has been a mill on this site at Houghton and now it is one of the few remaining watermills once common on the River Ouse. Set against an attractive background of the river, overhanging trees and grazing pasture, the seventeenth-century timber-constructed mill is a popular subject for artists and photographers.

Much of the machinery has been restored including the speaking tube which allowed millers to shout instructions to each other over the noise of grinding. The ancient timbers, wooden stairs and stone floors show all the fascinating scars of time. A charred beam indicates a past fire, and the floor is worn with the passing of millers' feet.

The mill is a National Trust property and open to the public every Saturday and Sunday afternoon from the end of March to the middle of October. There is a moderate admission charge (free, of course, to NT members). Every Sunday and Bank Holiday Monday the mill produces fine stoneground wholemeal flour, and on milling days the admission charge is slightly increased. All flour is milled from National Trust wheat grown at Wimpole Home Farm and can be purchased at the desk. There is no shop or restaurant on the premises but the village of Houghton is a very attractive place to visit, and there are some lovely riverside walks nearby. From June to the end of September one of the large rooms at the mill is converted to an art gallery.

School visits are welcome, especially during the morning, but must be booked in advance. Teaching packs are available. Contact the custodian for details.

There is car-parking on adjacent private land at £1 per day (70p refunded to NT members visiting the mill). Coach-parking is in the village, 300 yards away.

The mill is situated in Houghton Village, 3 miles south-east of Huntingdon off the A1123 Huntingdon to St. Ives road. It is about 10 miles north of St. Neots and 17 south of Peterborough.

Lode Watermill
Anglesey Abbey
Lode
Cambridgeshire CB5 9EJ
Tel. 01223-811200

The mill is situated at the point where Quy Water meets Bottisham Lode, which gives its name to the village. The lodes are man-made waterways built some time between Roman and medieval times to bring supplies to the villages via the River Cam and to take away their produce. Bottisham Lode is the southernmost in this part of Cambridgeshire, and is smaller and shallower than others in the area. Traffic on the Lode ceased around 1890 with the arrival of the railways.

It is probable that a water-mill stood on the site of Lode Mill at the time of the Domesday Survey of 1086, but the present structure most likely dates from the eighteenth century – it was certainly described in a sale notice of 1793 and at that time the lease was held by one James Harris.

In about 1900 the mill was converted from corn grinding to cement grinding which continued until about 1920 when the Bottisham Lode Cement and Brick Company went out of business and the mill became derelict.

In 1926 Anglesey Abbey was purchased by Huttleston Broughton, later Lord Fairhaven, who created the beautiful gardens around the Abbey. In 1934 he acquired the mill and began restoring it to its corn-milling condition. In 1935–6 the removal of the mining and cement-making equipment was completed and the site was cleared, and in 1978 the Cambridgeshire Wind and Watermill Society offered to restore the mill to full working order. In 1982 it was once again grinding corn for sale to visitors. It is now owned and managed by the National Trust as part of the Anglesey Abbey estate.

The mill is normally included in a visit to Anglesey Abbey encompassing the Abbey itself with its 100-acre gardens, and there is a moderate admission charge (free to NT members).

There is an excellent restaurant, shop and plant centre, and flour from the mill is on sale together with souvenirs and gifts. The mill is normally operational and producing flour on the first Sunday of each month. It is open to the public from the end of March to mid-October Wednesday to Sunday (and Bank Holiday Mondays) 1.30–5.15 p.m. School parties and groups by prior arrangement only. Closed Good Friday.

The village of Lode lies about 6 miles north-east of Cambridge on the edge of the Cambridgeshire Fens, just off the B1102 5 miles south-west of Burwell and 9 miles west of Newmarket.

Sacrewell Water Mill
Sacrewell
Thornhaugh
Peterborough
Cambridgeshire PE8 6HJ
Tel. 01780-782222

As it now stands, Sacrewell Mill dates from the middle of the eighteenth-century – a stone in the north-west corner of the main building bears the date 1755 – but there is evidence to suggest that a mill stood on this site much earlier. There are remains of three substantial Romano-British villas on Sacrewell Farm showing evidence of grain drying and malting. The introduction of the water-mill is attributed to the Romans and it seems highly probable that they would have exploited the very convenient water supply as a source of power for the mill.

The Domesday Book records three mills in the parish of Wittering in 1086 and Sacrewell was probably one of them, so it is fairly certain that the water from the little nameless stream has been harnessed by man for at least 1700 years.

The stream which feeds the mill flows from the west under the A1, whence it travels by raised channel until a dam across the valley forms the millpond. There are two flumes which originally drove two water-wheels, one of which remains in operation. Two pairs of millstones are still workable.

Sacrewell Mill is part of the Sacrewell Farm and Country Centre which includes a maze, farm trails, a tree trail, domestic barn and visitor centre, gift shop, gardens with free-roaming peacocks, restaurant facilities and toilets. There is a reasonable admission charge and free car-parking. School and group visits must be booked in advance.

Full restoration of the mill has recently been completed but at the moment regulations prevent it producing flour for human consumption; it is hoped this facility may be added in the near future. Meanwhile stoneground wholemeal flour is produced on a little electric stone mill and this flour can be purchased at the mill shop in 1 lb bags.

The Mill is situated half a mile to the east of the Great North Road (A1) in the north-east angle of the junction between the A1 and A47, about 5 miles south of Stamford and 8 miles west of Peterborough.

Stevens' Windmill
Mill Lane
Burwell
Cambridgeshire CB5 0HJ
Tel. 01638-741689 or 742847

Stevens' Windmill is the sole survivor of four windmills which once served the village of Burwell. It last worked in 1955 and still retains all its machinery, and remains an outstanding landmark seen from all approaches to the village.

The mill is fully restored but has one set of sails missing; flour is produced and sold but not on a regular basis, and the public are admitted at their own risk by prior arrangement only. There is no charge for admission but donations towards the upkeep would be welcomed.

Adjoining the mill is Burwell Museum, a re-erected eighteenth-century timber-framed barn beside a smithy and wheelwright's shop. The museum is open every Sunday from Easter until the end of September from 2 to 5 p.m.

Burwell is located approximately 15 miles north-east of Cambridge on the B1102 and 4 miles west of Newmarket at its junction with the B1109.

Swaffham Prior Windmill
Mill Hill
Swaffham Prior
Cambridgeshire CB5 0JZ
Tel. 01638-741009

Swaffham Prior Windmill was built about 1860 on the site of an earlier post mill, its two sets of millstones grinding wheat and other grains until 1946.

Swaffham Prior is one of the very few locations in England where two windmills may be seen within a few hundred yards of each other. One, a smock mill has recently been restored as part of a house, the other, a tower mill containing most of its original machinery, has been restored to working order by the present owner Michael Bulleid.

Restoration was completed in 1991, and on 1 June of that year wheat was once more milled here. Since then the mill has operated to meet customers' requirements. It is one of a small number of windmills (remaining from several thousand a century ago) now milling wheat by the use of wind power only – a few others use auxiliary sources of power on occasions.

Flour is ground from organically-grown wheat from Radwinter near Saffron Walden in Essex, and may be purchased from the mill at any reasonable time and is also available from a number of local shops and health food outlets (details upon application).

The public are admitted on the first and third Sundays in each month from April to October, 2–5 p.m., and also on Bank Holiday Sundays and Mondays in those months, otherwise by appointment only. Milling on these dates cannot be guaranteed; it depends upon the strength of the wind and other factors, but the machinery is fascinating anyway.

There is no admission charge but the mill relies upon donations and the sale of flour to meet the heavy cost of maintenance. At the time of writing only stoneground wholemeal flour is produced and although it can be sent by post, the high postal charges do not encourage this.

The Mill is located about 9 miles north-east of Cambridge on the B1102 Cambridge to Mildenhall road and is within a short drive of several tourist attractions including Anglesey Abbey (NT) with Lode Watermill in the grounds; the smock drainage mill at Wicken Fen (NT), and Newmarket with its horse racing connections. Incidentally, Swaffham Prior is in Cambridgeshire, many miles away from Swaffham in Norfolk.

Cornwall

Trewey Mill
Wayside Museum
Zennor
near St. Ives
Cornwall TR26 3DA
Tel. 01736-796945

It is said that Cornwall had as many as 3,000 wind and water-mills centuries ago but they were such an accepted part of rural life that nobody bothered to record them. At the time of the Domesday Survey of 1086 only five mills were listed – Cargoll, Connerton, Launceston, Liskeard and Trevisquite – although many more must have then been in operation to serve such a large area. Several theories have been advanced to cover this omission, but the most likely reason would seem to be the inaccessibility of the locations to the recording agents, bearing in mind the primitive transport available and the distance from the Conqueror's headquarters in London. Very few roads existed in Cornwall before the 1800s, and at the time of Domesday pack animals and sledges were the normal means of moving goods around the county.

To date I have been unable to trace a single working mill anywhere in Cornwall in spite of contacting every possible source of information including the Tourist Boards, libraries, museums and bakeries.

The Wayside Museum does not yet have a working mill among its attractions, but there has been a mill on this site for hundreds of years grinding corn and animal feed for local farmers, and the mill building still exists and is gradually being restored and refurbished. The millwheel has already been rebuilt and much of the original machinery and millstones are in place, and it is hoped before long to begin the production of stoneground wholemeal flour, if not on a commercial basis at least in sufficient quantity to meet the demands of visitors.

Trewey Mill was originally one of four on the river that flows through the Foage Valley down to the sea and Mermaid's Cove. The last working mill in Zennor (the last before the sea) was Eglos Meor Mill which was operated by the Stevens family, one of whom, James Stevens, wrote *A Cornish Farmer's Diary* which covers the period 1877–1912. Eglos Meor Mill was finally swept away by a great flood on 12 November 1894, when a torrent of water some twenty feet high rushed down the valley. Today only the ruins stand below the millpond.

Meanwhile the museum contains a vast collection of agricultural implements from the past including ploughs, tools, harness, etc., domestic items such as primitive washing machines, sewing machines, typewriters, cooking ranges, and a room displayed as a nineteenth-century kitchen, with another as a sitting-room of the period.

The Wayside Museum claims to be the oldest private museum in Cornwall covering every aspect of life in Zennor and district from 3000 BC to the 1930s. The mill is fed by the waters of the Zennor Quoit which rises in the hills behind the village, which is situated beside the B3306 − the coastal road between St Ives and St Just, about 4 miles due north of Penzance.

There is a nominal admission charge, a gift and bookshop and refreshments. The museum is open from Easter to the end of October every day from 10 a.m. to 6 p.m. (plus evenings during high summer). Parties by prior arrangement. Free parking nearby. Occasional craft demonstrations.

Cumbria

Eskdale Watermill
Boot
Eskdale
Holmrook
Cumbria CA19 1TG
Tel. 019467-2335

This is reputed to be one of the oldest working water-mills in England; it is certainly the oldest boasting two massive water-wheels. The first documented evidence of Eskdale Mill dates from 1578 when brothers Henry and Robert Vicars were the tenants at an annual rental of eight shillings (40p).

The mill continued to grind cereals until the early 1920s when a dynamo was installed to provide electricity and some degree of comfort for the last miller, Edward Bibby, who died in 1924. The upper wheel of the mill continued to generate electricity until 1955 when mains power came to the valley.

The structure gradually deteriorated until Cumbria County Council purchased the property in 1972 and initiated a programme of renovation and restoration. Today most of the machinery is in working order and the mill can be seen grinding oats and animal feed; it is scheduled to begin producing wholemeal flour for human consumption in the near future.

The mill can be reached by crossing a seventeenth-century packhorse bridge over Whillan Beck, at the northern end of Boot village. Visitors will be able to see a fascinating exhibition explaining the whole milling process and the workings of the unique wooden machinery, and there are informal tours of the mill conducted by the miller.

The public are admitted from mid-April to the end of September, 11 a.m. to 5 p.m. (closed on Mondays). There is a small admission charge with discounts for OAPs and children, and pre-booked parties are welcome.

Car-parking is in Dalegarth Station car-park, and there is a small shop selling souvenirs and light refreshments, a picnic area and toilet facilities.

The mill is situated on the lower slopes of Scafell in one of the most beautiful areas of the Lake District, about 16 miles west of Ambleside via the famous Hardknott Pass, near the head of one of the most picturesque and dramatic valleys in all Cumbria. A delightful wooded area to the rear of the mill where impressive waterfalls provide a powerful head of water to power the two huge water-wheels is well worth a visit.

Heron Corn Mill
Beetham
Milnthorpe
Cumbria LA7 7AR
Tel. 015395-63363

There is no proof that a mill existed on this site in 1096 but it is thought to be very likely since Ivo de Taillebois gave part of the manor of Haverbrack and certain corn tithes to St Mary's, York, during that year.

Haverbrack (or Heron) Mill seems to have been in continuous operation until 1955 when it was closed by the then proprietors W. & J. Pye who were producers of animal feedstuffs.

In 1973 it was leased to the newly formed Beetham Trust by Henry Cooke Limited, whose paper-mill lies on the opposite bank of the River Bela. Henry Cooke made very generous grants toward the cost of renovation to enable the mill to be re-opened by Princess Alexandra in July 1975.

The old barn beside the mill was refurbished in 1988 to commemorate 500 years of paper-making and now houses the Museum of Paper-making. Occasional demonstrations are mounted each season and visitors are invited to try their hand at the craft during these sessions.

The mill is fully restored and capable of producing a variety of flours but prevented from doing so by the local Environmental Health Department's regulations. However, many cereal products can be purchased in the mill shop including coarse ground wholemeal flour, oat flakes, oatmeal, muesli, pearl barley, etc.

An unusual feature is the Fish Ladder passing through the natural cave below the force which supplies the power for the mill. It can be seen from the side of the mill building.

There is a modest charge for admission with discounts for OAPs and children, and special rates for parties of twenty or more. The mill opens to the public from 1 April until the end of September but is closed every Monday (Bank Holidays excepted). There is no charge for car-parking.

Heron Corn Mill lies at the southern edge of the Lake District National Park and at the head of Morecambe Bay, some 15 miles south of Kendal and a mile south of Milnthorpe on the A6. Apart from the well-known attractions of the Lake District nearby places of interest include Leighton Hall, Levens Hall and Seigher Castle.

Opposite the mill is a garden centre and the local village boasts an excellent pub with a reputation for good food.

Further information can be obtained from the administrator, Henry Cooke Makin, Waterhouse Mills, Beetham, Milnthorpe, Cumbria LA7 7AR.

Little Salkeld Watermill
Little Salkeld
Penrith
Cumbria CA10 1NN
Tel. 01768-881523

It is probable that a mill has existed on this site since the Middle Ages, and that it was built on instructions from the lords of the manor, the Salkelds, an important aristocratic family of the time. In the eighteenth century it was owned by the Atkinson family who were responsible for rebuilding it in its present form – a major investment then as it would be today.

The stone used was quarried locally from a seam of red sandstone close to the weir, the millrace was built (nearly half a mile long), and wooden water-wheels fitted. Local Lazonby Sandstone millstones were installed together with the machinery for producing oatmeal (havermeal in Cumberland). In the nineteenth century a pair of French Burr millstones was installed to enable wheat to be ground, and these are still in daily use at the mill. The wooden water-wheels were replaced by iron ones in 1916.

The mill continued to produce a little animal feed into the early 1970s but in 1974 the Atkinsons sold out to the present owners who have refurbished and restored it to full production, concentrating on using British grain grown to organic standards.

The mill is fed by the Sunnygill Beck, a tributary of the River Eden, rising from the slopes of Cross Fell some 9 miles away and over 3000 feet high. The millrace delivers an average of a million gallons a day from the weir, all of which is returned to the beck, unpolluted, to continue its journey to join the beautiful Eden on its way to Carlisle and the Solway Firth.

This is a commercial mill, one of the few producing an 8-page mail order catalogue, listing a wide range of organic products including flours, cereals, animal feeds, pulses, herbs, teas and coffee. It is open to the public for guided tours on Mondays, Tuesdays and Thursdays at 11 a.m., 12 noon, 2.30 p.m. and 3.30 p.m. There is a small admission charge and free car-parking. The mill shop and tea-room open Monday to Friday 10.30 to 5.00 p.m.

Little Salkeld is situated 6 miles north-east of Penrith and about a mile from Langwathby on the B6412, just a few miles from such renowned beauty spots as Long Meg Stone Circle, Lacey's Caves, Nunnery Walks, Alston and Hadrian's Wall.

The Watermill Flat offers ideal accommodation for those wishing to explore the area. Details on application.

Muncaster Water Mill
Ravenglass
Cumbria CA18 1ST
Tel. 01229-717232

Although the present mill building dates from about 1700 it is known that a mill has occupied the same site since at least 1455 when it is recorded that Thomas Senhouse leased it from Sir John Pennington for £3 a year. It was the manorial mill for the Manor of Muncaster, and the Pennington family still owned the mill when it ceased to function in 1961. At that time it was the last of the local mills producing animal feed for local farmers.

After a few years disuse it was restored under the direction of the Eskdale (Cumbria) Trust and by 1978 was once more producing a range of stoneground products including coarse wholemeal flour, fine wholemeal flour, unbleached white flour, semolina, natural bran, etc. all of which can be purchased in the mill shop.

The mill is located on the A595 Barrow-in-Furness to Workington road, 1 mile north of Muncaster Castle and a mile north-east of Ravenglass. It is also adjacent to and served by the Ravenglass & Eskdale Railway and all trains stop by request at the mill.

There is a nominal entrance fee, free car-parking nearby, a picnic area and a children's pets enclosure. In addition the proprietors offer bed and breakfast facilities at the Mill House. Details on application.

It is difficult to imagine an area with more to offer than the Lake District. The mill is within easy driving distance of many of England's most famous attractions including all the lakes, the Hardknott and Wrynose Passes, mountain ranges and beautiful valleys. It is still a walker's and photographer's paradise.

Derbyshire

Stainsby Watermill
Hardwick Hall
Doe Lea
Chesterfield
Derbyshire S44 5QJ
Tel. 01246-850430

Owned by the National Trust, this mill is still in the process of restoration and at present is only in limited operation.

It is open to the public from 1 April to the end of October, Wednesdays, Thursdays, Saturdays, Sundays and Bank Holidays (except Good Friday) from 12.30–4.30 p.m. and there is a moderate admission charge (free to NT members).

Part of Hardwick Hall Estate, Stainsby Mill was built in 1850 to grind flour for the estate on the site of an earlier mill dating back to 1253. It was though not heavily used as the millstones, dated 1849, still have years of life left in them. The mill stands below a causeway which forms the mill dam. The massive 17 ft high water-wheel which powers the work of the mill is turned by water from the mill-pond behind the dam. The streams which supply this pond come from the Miller's Pond below Hardwick Hall, and the pond at Stainsby.

It is situated about 6 miles west of Mansfield and 9 miles south-east of Chesterfield and is easily reached via the M1, Junction 29.

1½ miles away is Hardwick Hall itself, a late sixteenth-century 'prodigy house' designed by Robert Smythson for Bess of Hardwick, with outstanding contemporary furniture, tapestries, a permanent needlework exhibition, etc. There are walled gardens, attractive courtyards, orchards and a herb garden, restaurant and tea room, toilet facilities, etc.

Devonshire

Crowdy Watermill
Bow Road
Harbertonford
Totnes
Devon TQ9 7HU
Tel. 01803 732340

Crowdy Mill lies in a sunny valley on the banks of the River Harbourne, a tributary of the lovely River Dart, with the ancient historic town of Totnes some 3 miles away to the north. The secluded gardens and old orchard provide a quiet and peaceful retreat, and the woods and fields on all sides are rich in wildlife. The area abounds in attractions such as nature reserves, coastal walks, varied sports facilities and river trips on the River Dart.

Little is known of the history of the mill except that there has been a mill on this site for at least 700 years. It is powered by two 12 ft overshot wheels activated by a leat from the Harbourne river which powers two sets of millstones. An unusual feature is that the two wheels turn in opposite directions. Locally grown organic grain is used wherever possible, and an impressive range of flours is produced on a commercial basis to supply bakers and stores locally and as far away as London.

This is the only mill I know of which runs bread-making classes in conjunction with their main business. These are held every week during the winter months and have proved very popular. The one-day course costs £14 (at the time of writing) and includes lunch, tea, and the loaves you have baked. There are also a variety of bed & breakfast options including two-day winter breaks and self-catering accommodation.

The water-mill is open to the public every day, from 10 a.m. to 5 p.m. (or until dusk in the winter months), and pre-booked school parties and groups are welcome. There is a small admission charge and free car-parking. The Crowdy café is licensed and serves lunch, coffee, cream teas, etc. from Easter until November. The adjoining shop sells bread and cakes made from the mill's own flour, home-made jams, free range eggs, and the full range of the mill's flours.

The Old Corn Mill
Hele Bay
Ilfracombe
Devon EX34 9QY
Tel. 01271-863185

Records prove the existence of a water-mill on this site in 1525 and it is believed one was working here prior to that date. The mill has been completely restored by the present owners and is now in full working order, producing wholemeal flour in fine, medium and coarse grades, granary-type flour, kibbled wheat and wheatflakes.

The horizontal millstones are actually artificial ones and the Fine Grade flour is ground on vertical French Burrs, both being driven by the 18 ft overshot water-wheel which is now only powered by a little stream descending from the Trayne Hills behind the mill, as earlier watercourses have been filled in or diverted. This stream, which appears to be nameless, reaches the sea at Hele Bay – an attractive spot on the north Devon coast.

The mill is open from Easter Sunday until the end of October, Monday to Friday 10 a.m. to 5 p.m.; Sunday 2–5 p.m. (closed Saturdays). There is a nominal admission charge and free car-parking. The small shop sells flour in large or small quantities, souvenirs, booklets, etc. There is also a very early porcelain roller mill on display – believed to be the only complete one in the country.

The Old Corn Mill is on the bus route between Ilfracombe and Combe Martin, with a stop just 100 yards from the mill. It is about 1 mile east of Ilfracombe on the A399, almost opposite the turn for Hele Bay itself, 20 minutes' walk from the centre of Ilfracombe.

There are no facilities at the mill, but it is within 400 yards of the beach at Hele Bay where there are restaurants, shops and toilets.

Ilfracombe claims to be the best centre for exploring the north Devon coastline and Exmoor. It is within easy driving distance of Clovelly, Bideford and Barnstaple to the west, and Combe Martin, Lynton and Lynmouth, Porlock and Minehead to the east.

Otterton Watermill
Otterton
Budleigh Salterton
Devon EX9 7HG
Tel. 01395-68521 or 67041

Situated at the western end of the unspoilt Devon village of Otterton, this is one of only three working water-mills I have been able to discover in the county of Devon.

It is known that a mill existed on this site before the Norman Conquest, powered by the waters of the beautiful River Otter about 2 miles above Budleigh Salterton where it flows into the sea. It was restored in 1977 since when it has been producing stoneground wholemeal and unbleached white flour which can be purchased in the shop. Cakes and bread made from Otterton flour are on sale in the bakery, and the restaurant serves coffee, lunches and cream teas.

There is also a Mill Museum and a variety of studio workshops and craft shops; a permanent exhibition of east Devon lace, a bookshop, and the Otterton Mill Gallery where a varied programme of fine art and craft exhibitions are frequently held.

The mill lies about 4 miles along the coast road between Sidmouth and Budleigh Salterton, about a mile off the A376, halfway between Budleigh Salterton and Newton Poppleford. It is open to the public 10.30 to 5.30 p.m. Easter to the end of October, and 11.30 to 4.30 p.m. during the winter months.

There is a modest admission charge which includes entrance to the mill, gallery and lace exhibition with reductions for children and pre-booked groups. Car-parking is free.

Dorset

Cann Mills
Shaftesbury
Dorset SP7 0BL
Tel. 01747-852475

First recorded in the Domesday Survey of 1086, but it is probable that a mill existed on this site prior to the Norman Conquest, one of five mills operating on a short stretch of the River Sturkel in the distant past.

In 1954 the old seventeenth-century building was burned to the ground and replaced with the present structure which includes a nineteenth-century water-wheel built at Bourton, about 9 miles away. At that time the mill was powered entirely by water, but in 1969 a Portuguese windmill was mounted on top of the mill, making milling possible in most climatic conditions using two entirely independent sets of machinery, one powered by wind, the other by water. About 75% of the mill's output is produced by water power and the remainder by electricity.

The Portuguese windmill attracts artists and photographers since the construction is quite different to the designs of British windmills.

The Stoate family, who had been milling in Watchet since 1832, purchased Cann Mills in 1947 and produced animal feeds until the early seventies when they reverted to flour production. The present owner, Michael Stoate, is the fifth generation of Stoates producing stoneground flour for the bakery and health food trades, supplying outlets mainly in the south and west of the country.

This is a commercial mill and is open to the public during normal business hours only for the purchase of flour including organic flour produced mainly from locally-grown wheat. Minimum quantity 8kg.

The mill is located just off the A350 Shaftesbury to Blandford Forum road, about 1½ miles south of Shaftesbury. The town itself offers many attractions and is an ideal centre for exploring the Blackmoor Vale and Thomas Hardy Country, and is only 16 miles from the cathedral city of Salisbury.

Kingsmill
Kingsmill Road
Marnhull
Dorset

The history of this mill is somewhat sketchy until the research is completed, but it is known that the present building, which dates from the 1820s, occupies the site of a much older mill in an area where the Abbotts of Glastonbury were granted vast tithes by King Edgar in 968. It was certainly in regular production until about 60 years ago.

Restoration of the building commenced in 1993 and originally it was scheduled for reopening in 1994 but much of the exterior work, including the restoration of the weir, has been delayed by long periods of extremely wet weather.

The mill is powered by the River Stour via a wide mill-wheel which produces enough energy to drive three sets of mill-stones. When in full production it was capable of an output of three tons of flour per day but it is unlikely that more than one set of stones will be returned to operation when it reopens.

Limited access will be available to the public during the summer months, and it is hoped that stoneground wholemeal flour will be on sale with a range of other products.

The mill is located beside the River Stour just above Kingsmill bridge at a road linking the B3092 (at Marnhull) and the A357 in the Blackmoor Vale, about 3 miles north of Sturminster Newton and 6 miles south-west of Shaftesbury. Kingsmill Bridge is one of several in Dorset bearing a plate warning that any person causing wilful damage to it will be guilty of felony and, upon conviction, liable to be transported for life.

Further details from Mr P. Lush, 61 Broadmeadow Road, Wyke Regis, Weymouth, Dorset DT4 9BT Tel. 01305-782486.

Sturminster Newton Watermill
Sturminster Newton
Dorset DT10 2DQ
Tel. 01258-473082 or 817258

Sturminster Newton is a small market town in central Dorset located at a bridging point across a sweeping meander in the River Stour. Sturminster, the main settlement, lies on a spur of the northern bank and is linked by a road across the water meadows and over a fifteenth-century bridge to the smaller settlements of Newton and Bridge on the south bank. The seventeenth-century mill and its weir is about 260 yards upstream from the bridge.

Originally Sturminster was a royal estate owned by King Alfred (871–899) and subsequently granted to Glastonbury Abbey by King Edgar in 968. There must have been mills on the River Stour in the vicinity of Sturminster Newton during this Saxon period, and it is these which are recorded in the Domesday Survey of 1086: Glastonbury Abbey had three and there was one other. It is most probable that two of these were the predecessors of the mills at Sturminster Newton and Fiddleford.

It is not known what happened to the mill during the period following the dissolution of the Abbey in the reign of Henry VIII, but by the seventeenth-century it formed part of an estate which was to become known as the Pitt-Rivers Estate.

The mill is now leased to the Sturminster Newton Mill Trust Company Ltd., a trust set up by Mr Anthony Pitt-Rivers in combination with the Dorset County Council, the North Dorset District Council and the Sturminster Parish Council with the object of restoring the mill to full working order. It was producing excellent flour until 1991 when stricter regulations were introduced requiring considerable extra investment. It is hoped to resume production in the not too distant future, but meanwhile flour from other mills, some from locally grown grain, can be purchased at the mill in large or small quantities.

The mill is open to the public on Tuesdays, Thursdays, Saturdays and Sundays 11 a.m. to 6 p.m. from Easter to the end of September, also on market days (Monday) 2 to 4.30 p.m. Special interest groups and school parties at these and other times by appointment. There is a nominal admission charge and free car-parking, toilets, souvenir shop and a pleasant picnic area beside the river.

Sturminster Newton is set in the heart of the Blackmoor Vale which offers many attractions for a short or long stay. The Town Museum occupies the former chapel of the Union Workhouse, and although some exhibits change annually to reflect the very varied rural pursuits, others such as those commemorating the lives of local poets and writers William Barnes and Thomas Hardy are on permanent display.

The town is located at the junction of the A357, A3030 and the B3081, about 8 miles south-west of Shaftesbury, 10 miles east of Sherborne and 8 miles south-east of Blandford Forum.

Dumfries & Galloway

New Abbey Watermill
Corn Mill
New Abbey
Nithsdale
Dumfries & Galloway
Tel. 0131-244-3101 or Tourist Information 01387-53862

This range of buildings, which includes the unusual feature of having the kiln and the miller's house built as one unit, has been described as 'a classic example of the Galloway country mill' and is representative of the numerous water-powered grain mills that have served Scotland since about 1750, although every mill, like every miller and almost every owner, had its own methods of getting the work performed.

A mill probably stood on or near this site in the Middle Ages serving the nearby Cistercian monastery, hence the name 'Monksmill' by which it is still known locally. However, the existing building dates only from the late eighteenth century, and was erected by the Stewart family of Shambellie, heirs to part of the medieval monastic estate. It was altered during the nineteenth century and a third floor added, and continued in commercial use until the Second World War. Maintained afterwards as a precious relic by Mr Charles Stewart of Shambellie, it has more recently been fully restored with painstaking care by Historic Scotland and is now open to the public.

Water to power the mill was conducted from the northern end of Loch Kindar via a mile-long lade to the pond which lies just to the south-west of the mill. This too has been restored to working order, with its sluice mechanism, overflow channel – and ducks!

The mill is located on the west side of the A710 near the centre of

New Abbey, 7 miles south of Dumfries and 6 miles north of Kirkbean on the Solway coast.

It is open to the public from April to September, Monday to Saturday 9.30 a.m. to 6.30 p.m., Sunday 2.00 to 6.30 p.m. From October to March, Monday to Saturday 9.30 a.m. to 4.30 p.m., closed Thursday afternoons and Fridays. Pre-booked groups are able to see the mill actually operating. There is a nominal admission charge and free car-parking nearby. Coach parties by prior arrangement only.

The mill shop sells a variety of flours stoneground at the mill, souvenirs and guide books.

Local attractions include Shambellie House and Sweetheart Abbey, but the area abounds in walks and hill climbs, and the Cumbrian coast can be seen across the Solway Firth most days.

Dyfed

Cenarth Watermill
Cenarth Falls
Newcastle Emlyn
Dyfed SA38 9JL
Tel. 01239-710209

The first mill to be built on this site is believed to be that established in the sixth century to meet the needs of the early Christian monastic community founded by Saint Llawddog.

After the final collapse of Welsh resistance to the English in 1284, Edward I became Lord of the Manor of Cenarth and it was eventually passed down to the first Prince of Wales. Almost every mill in Wales was destroyed during the nine years of conflict beginning in 1400 when Owain Glyndwr began his campaign to free Wales from Anglo-Norman influence, but Cenarth Mill appears to have been spared although a second mill erected not far from the present one suffered. That mill and weir appears in records for 1327 but all that remains of it today is the site at the top of the gorge on the Cardigan side of the river where an old road, now just a broad path, comes down to the water's edge to continue up through the woods opposite.

Cenarth Mill was in regular operation until 1939 when it closed down until the Armistice in 1945. The tenancy was then taken over by Mr J. R. Williams who instituted extensive repairs and improvements, but during the 1960s both the mill and weir began to fall once more into disrepair, and it was neglected until 1983 when the present owners, Mr and Mrs Martin Fowler, purchased it.

It has now been fully restored to working order, and the cow sheds and outbuildings converted to the mill cottage where the owners reside.

The National Coracle Centre is on the same site, and includes examples of coracles from all over the world and a workshop demonstrating the ancient craft of coracle making. Occasional coracle trips on the river can be arranged.

There is a tea-room and gift shop which sells wholemeal flour, organic wholemeal, seed and herb flour, garlic and chive, etc. At present the flours are not actually milled at Cenarth Mill but it is hoped to be able to do so in the near future.

The mill is situated on the A484 between Cardigan and Newcastle Emlyn and is well signposted. There is a nominal entrance fee which includes admission to both the mill and the Coracle Centre; free car and coach-parking.

Open to the public from Easter to October, Sunday to Friday 10.30 a.m. to 5.30 p.m., closed Saturdays. Coach parties can be accommodated at other times by prior arrangement only.

The mill is sited beside the beautiful River Teifi close to the Cenarth Falls and Salmon Leap, a wonderful area for walking and watching the wildlife. The Smithy Museum is a few hundred yards up the road.

Felin Newydd – The Mill at Crugybar
Llanwrda
Dyfed SA19 8UE
Tel. Pumpsaint (015585) 375

Although Felin Newydd translates into English as 'the new mill' this mill is thought to occupy the same site as one built during the Roman occupation although documentary evidence does not survive prior to 1430.

Originally known as 'the mill of Glanyrannell' (it lies beside the pretty River Annell) the name was changed to 'The New Mill' after rebuilding in the second half of the seventeenth century. Pieces of millstone from the demolished mill were built into the walls of the new mill and can be seen to this day.

The present owners, Dr and Mrs Beeson, acquired the mill in 1986 and set about restoring it, and it now produces some of the finest stoneground wholemeal flour you are ever likely to discover. The mill is not used for commercial production, its machinery is too old for continuous use, but it is started up and flour produced during every tour (unforeseen circumstances excepted).

It is situated in one of the most beautiful areas of central Wales, roughly halfway between Llandovery and Lampeter (just off the B4302 where it meets the A482) in the southern foothills of the Cambrian Mountains. On a fine day you can take tea in the mill gardens or stroll around the wildlife pond.

Open from Easter to the end of October; closed every Monday except Bank Holidays. There are conducted tours at about hourly intervals.

Admission to the mill itself is by guided tour only (there is a nominal charge), but there is no charge for admission to the tea-room and craft shop, or to the thirteen acres of gardens and private nature reserve. Parking is free but dogs are not admitted. Daily demonstrations of woodturning, lace bobbin production and patchwork pictures are held, and most weekends a local artist is on site.

Stoneground 100% wholemeal flour can be purchased from the shop or will be sent by post if requested. Although postal charges are excessive they are well worth it to discover the taste of *real* bread.

Felin Yr Aber
Llanwnnen
Lampeter
Dyfed SA48 7JY
Tel. 01570-480956

The Rivermouth Mill is an old late seventeenth – early eighteenth century water-mill set within a traditional seventeen-acre organic farm in the heart of the beautiful Teifi valley at the confluence of the Rivers Grannel and Teifi. This restored mill is once again beginning to produce stoneground flour as it did in centuries past.

The mill leat water supply flows for half a mile through pictures-que countryside abundant in wildlife, while the small organic farm supports sheep, ducks, poultry, a goat and other small animals. There is an exhibition of vintage farm machinery, and handmade pottery is also produced on the premises from time to time.

There is no admission charge but donations towards the cost of restoration are welcomed. Fishing is available at a small charge on a daily basis.

Although at present only animal feed is ground, it is intended to resume the production of flour for human consumption in the near future.

Felin yr Aber is located just off the B4337 half a mile south of Llanwnnen which is on the A475 Lampeter to Newcastle Emlyn road. It is about 12 miles from Aberaeron on the beautiful and unspoilt coast of Cardigan Bay to the west, and about the same distance from the lower slopes of the Cambrian Mountains at Tregaron to the north-east.

The mill is open to the public from Easter until 30 September, 10 a.m. to 6 p.m., and during the winter months by prior arrangement.

Melin Maesdulais Water-Mill
Porthyrhyd
Carmarthen
Dyfed SA32 8BT
Tel. 01267-275472

Established in the seventeenth century as a corn mill, Melin Maesdulais was derelict and devoid of any machinery when the present proprietors acquired it in 1976 and began the lengthy process of restoration. The mill began producing flour again in 1982 and has continued doing so ever since.

A wide range of flours is produced using locally grown grains wherever possible, organic and non-organic, and these can be purchased at the mill during normal business hours.

This is a commercial mill and is not generally open to visitors but school groups and organized parties can be accommodated by prior arrangement, and although there is no gift shop or restaurant, there is a small picnic area which groups are welcome to use.

The mill is situated on the B4310 about 8 miles east of Carmarthen and the same distance west of Ammanford. Further information can be obtained from the proprietors Geoffrey and Phillipa Brace at the above address.

Melin Maesdulais is licensed by the Soil Association for the manufacture of organic flours, and these are distributed throughout Wales and the Marches and obtainable from health food shops, bakeries and similar outlets in the region. Wholesale enquiries telephone 01982-553598/9.

Y Felin
The Mill
St Dogmaels
Cardigan
Dyfed SA43 3DY
Tel. 01239-613999

Y Felin straddles the Afon Degwel in the heart of the picturesque fishing village of St Dogmaels – the village named after the saint who lived hereabouts between AD 450 to 500.

Records show that the mill was in existence in the 1640s but it is probably much older and was originally part of the abbey and worked by the monks in the pre-reformation period.

The mill was operational until 1926 when the owner (Mr Evan Gwynne) died. It gradually fell into disuse in the 1930s although it was briefly opened up during the Second World War for the production of animal feedstuffs and some flour. In 1953 the millpond was filled in with rubble and other rubbish. In 1977 it was purchased by the present owners, Mr and Mrs Michael Hall, who have been restoring it to its former glory, renewing parts of the structure and mechanism, and using, wherever possible, the original materials.

The original millwheel was beyond repair and a substitute was purchased from another Welsh mill which had closed. The oak spokes of the wheel have been re-cut and fitted by Mr Hall. Work in clearing the debris from the millpond commenced in 1981, and the pond was re-flooded for the first time on Easter Saturday of that year.

St Dogmaels is about a mile due west of Cardigan on the B4546. The mill is open from Easter until the end of September, 10.30 a.m. to 5.30 p.m. every day. Between October and Easter it is closed on Sundays and sometimes on Saturdays. There is a nominal admission charge but free car-parking.

The tea-room adjacent to the mill is open Monday to Friday and Sunday afternoons from Easter to October but closed during the winter season. Mill products are on sale including stoneground wholemeal flour, unbleached white flour, bran, semolina, rye flour, granary-type flour, seed and herb wholemeal flour, oatmeal, self-raising flour, etc.

Opposite the millpond are the ruins of St Dogmael's Abbey, a twelfth-century structure whose abbott probably built and owned the original mill.

Glamorgan

Melin Bompren
Welsh Folk Museum
St Fagans
Cardiff
South Glamorgan CF5 6XB
Tel. 01222-569441

The Welsh Folk Museum is housed in the magnificent grounds of an Elizabethan manor house built in 1580 within the curtain wall of St Fagans Castle, surrounded by spacious formal gardens and grounds in which numerous exhibits are displayed and operated.

Melin Bompren is just one of the many attractions. It is a water-powered corn mill built about 1852 and used for the production of animal feed and flour, having two pairs of stones; one pair of French Burr stones for milling wheat into wholemeal flour, and a pair of composite stones for animal feed and oatmeal.

The three-storey mill has a corn-drying kiln beside it where the oats were dried before being ground into oatmeal.

For safety reasons much of the machinery is hidden by a screen, but the wooden-toothed gearing can be viewed through a strategically placed mirror.

The mill is open to the public 10 a.m. to 5 p.m. seven days a week except during the winter months (November–March) when it is closed on Sundays. There is a moderate admission charge with discounts for OAPs and children. Free car-parking.

Stoneground wholemeal flour produced at the mill is on sale in the museum bookshop, and fresh bread is baked daily in the kiln oven of Derwen Bakery at St Fagans and can be purchased by visitors.

Access (avoiding Cardiff City) is via the M4 Junction 33 taking the A4232 for about 2 miles when the museum will be signposted.

Hampshire and Isle of Wight

Alderholt Water Mill
Sandleheath Road
Alderholt
Fordingbridge
Hampshire SP6 1PU
Tel. 01425-653130

The mill stands on a tributary of the Hampshire Avon, between Alderholt and Sandleheath on the outskirts of Fordingbridge. The stream forms the boundary between Hampshire and Dorset, and is called the River Allen above the bridge and Ashford Water below. The mill was last in commercial use grinding corn during the Second World War.

Records show that there was a mill on this site in the 1330s but it is quite likely that one existed here long before records were kept. For many centuries it was known as Padner Mill and the first known miller was a William de Padenor whose ancestors may well have come to England from France during or shortly after the Norman Conquest.

The wheel, which is at the back of the mill, replaced one formerly inside the building. It was made by Munden of Ringwood and dates from about 1840. Considerable renovation and maintenance has taken place over the years; the old footbridge over the mill stream has been replaced and a new grid fitted in front of the hatch by the wheel to prevent debris damaging the paddles.

In February 1987, renovations completed, a trial grinding took place and the first flour was produced using the restored machinery. It is significant that all the funding for the renovation has been obtained by opening the mill to the public and with the help of local craftsmen and artists who display and sell their work in the building.

The mill lies about 2 miles west of Fordingbridge. Take the B3078 towards Damerham, turn left in Sandleheath and follow tourist signs to the mill. It is roughly 12 miles from Salisbury and 15 from Bournemouth.

It is open to the public from Easter until the end of September, and from mid-November until Christmas. Tuesday, Wednesday, Thursday, Friday and Sunday 2–6 p.m.; Saturday and Bank Holidays 10 a.m.–6 p.m. Parties by appointment only.

There is no charge for admission but donations toward the upkeep would be appreciated. Coach parties and large groups are charged a nominal entrance fee when special opening hours are requested.

Stoneground wholemeal flour produced from locally grown wheat is on sale, quality crafts, confectionery, ices, etc., and there is an extensive programme of exhibitions held at the mill throughout the year.

The area around is a tourist's paradise; Fordingbridge is on the edge of the New Forest; Dorset Heavy Horse Centre is only 5 miles to the west; Rockbourne Roman Villa less than a mile from Sandleheath; Cranborne Manor and Gardens, and Breamore House both within a 5-mile radius of the mill. For those wishing to explore the area more thoroughly the proprietors, Mr and Mrs Pye, offer bed and breakfast facilities.

Calbourne Watermill & Museum of Rural Life
Calbourne
Isle of Wight PO30 4JN
Tel. 01983-531227

This mill, or one on the same site, is mentioned in the Domesday Book and has been occupied by the same family since 1878. It is unusual in being one of the first mills to convert from stone grinding to rolling, and the installation of a steam engine in 1894 meant that the mill could still be operated even at times when the water supply was low.

The Domesday Book records the existence of thirty-four water-mills on the island but few could have worked full time with such a poor supply of water over the island as a whole. Calbourne Mill was used mainly for grinding locally grown oats, barley and wheat, and had its own bakery supplying local needs. Today it is one of only two surviving mills.

The millrace is fed by a spring rising in the grounds of Westover Park and wanders through picturesque Winkle Street towards the mill. The stream, known originally as the 'Caul'bourne, keeps the millpond at a constant depth of about three feet except during drought periods. After passing over the millwheel the water flows beneath the mill through a conduit to the sea – in past years it operated three more mills below Calbourne.

The mill is situated on the main B3401 Newport to Freshwater road and is open from Easter to the end of October, 10 a.m. to 6 p.m. daily. There is a restaurant, bakery and shop, where Calbourne Wholemeal Flour can be purchased, and a large picnic area in beautiful grounds beside the millpond. There is no charge for car-parking, and the moderate admission fee covers the mill and the extensive Museum of Rural Life.

Eling Tide Mill
Eling Toll Bridge
Totton
Southampton
Hampshire SO4 4HF
Tel. 01703-869575

This mill is quite unique. It is believed to be the only working tide mill *in the world* regularly producing wholemeal flour as it did centuries ago. The earliest record of a mill at Eling is 1086 but the present building dates from the eighteenth century.

Tide mills are usually built on causeways which cross inlets off tidal estuaries. The causeway forms both a bridge and a dam, and the tide rises to fill the estuary behind the causeway. When the tide falls, water is held back by sluice gates and released through a millrace to operate the machinery. About five hours' milling time is available each tide making ten hours' milling a day. Although working hours can be inconvenient at times, tide power is predictable and absolutely reliable.

Eling is a 'double mill' with two sets of wheels side by side in the middle of the mill, each with its own machinery. One set of machinery has been restored to its nineteenth-century working condition and the other retained as a static display.

Obviously the mill is unable to operate at high tide and details of demonstration times can be obtained by telephoning the mill.

It is located about 4 miles west of Southampton just off the A35 to Lyndhurst and is open to visitors from 10 a.m. to 4 p.m. throughout the year except Mondays and Tuesdays. There is a shop selling stoneground wholemeal flour, rural crafts and a very interesting book of the history of Eling Tide Mill.

There is a nominal admission charge with special rates for OAPs and children and car-parking is free. There are interesting walks through Eling village to the Saxon church and Goatee Foreshore overlooking Southampton Water and the area abounds in places to visit including Exbury Gardens and Lepe Country Park, and is only a few miles from the beautiful New Forest.

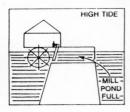 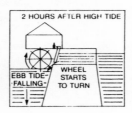 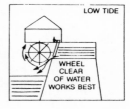

 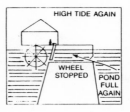

Hertfordshire

Mill Green Mill
Mill Green
Hatfield
Hertfordshire AL9 5PD
Tel. 01707-271362

The mill and the miller's house beside it are part of the Welwyn Hatfield Museum Service situated at the junction of the A1000 and

A414 between Hatfield and Welwyn Garden City.

The water-mill has been restored to full working order after a chequered history dating back before the Domesday Survey. Milling takes place on Sundays 2.30–4.30 p.m., and on Tuesdays and Wednesdays 10.30 a.m. to 12.30 p.m. or 1.30–3.30 p.m. for pre-booked parties. Milling hours are subject to weather conditions and demand for flour.

The Mill House and the water-mill have stood in the hamlet of Mill Green for centuries. The mill was originally built to grind the corn grown by local farmers, and the adjoining house was the home of successive millers and their families. Today the mill is licensed by the Soil Association for the production of organic, stoneground wholemeal flour which is on sale at the mill. The Mill Green Loaf, made with Mill Green flour, is available from a local baker (Simmons).

There is no charge for admission or car-parking but donations towards the upkeep are always welcome.

Kent

Crabble Corn Mill
Lower Road
River
Dover
Kent CT17 0UY
Tel. 01304-823292

The earliest known written evidence for the existence of a mill at Crabble dates from 1227 when Henry III gave the Abbey of St Radigund 'the site of the mill called Crabbehole' from which it received a rent of twenty shillings (£1) a year.

A fire insurance policy of 1788 shows that at that time the mill consisted of a two-storey wooden structure situated on the promontory of land between the weir and the River Dour. It was powered by a breastshot wheel capable of driving two pairs of millstones probably well able to cope with local needs.

But the arrival of a large number of troops in the area during the Napoleonic Wars created an increased demand for flour, and a series of large commercial mills was built along the river, encouraged and aided by the Victualling Department. These were known as the Napoleonic Mills and helped to support the community during the vigorous French blockade of the channel ports.

At Crabble, the new mill was erected alongside the existing

'Charles II' mill to a design markedly different from the older mills. It was first lit by candle and afterwards by gas at a time when gas-lighting was in its infancy. It was a highly efficient flour factory and prospered until the troops dispersed after the defeat of Napoleon at Waterloo and trade slumped. Most of the mills went out of business and Crabble was mortgaged early in the 1820s and finally sold when the owner went bankrupt in 1842.

The new owner, Wilsher Mannering, was a true Victorian entrepreneur who, together with his brother John, virtually cornered the market by acquiring Stembrook Mill in 1836, Town Mill in 1842, Crabble Mill in 1843 and Lower Buckland Mill in 1865. The family remained in business as Dover millers for over a century.

Crabble Mill closed for business in 1893 and was then used for storage, the machinery being retained and the structure of the building well maintained. The Mannerings continued to carry out essential repairs until their business folded in 1957.

By 1972 the building had become so unsafe that there were plans afoot to demolish it and redevelop the site for housing, but a local philanthropist, Mr Fred Cleary, bought the mill, restored it to working order and transferred it on a ninety-nine year lease to Dover District Council. Unfortunately by 1983 the mill was once more in danger of collapse and a charitable trust was formed with a view to saving it from destruction after the Council applied for permission to demolish. It was finally acquired by the Crabble Corn Mill Trust who have completely restored it to full working order, and it can now be seen grinding wholemeal flour.

The mill is open to the public from May to the end of September on Saturdays, Sundays, Wednesdays, Thursdays and Fridays, including Bank Holidays, 11 a.m. to 5 p.m., also on Sundays 11 a.m. to 5 p.m. during March, April, October and November, and during the Easter Bank Holiday weekend (Friday–Monday). It is open every day during the month of August. There is a modest admission charge and free car-parking. Groups and school parties are welcome by prior arrangement.

The Lakeside cafe provides refreshments baked from Crabble flour as well as lunches and cream teas, and the shop sells wholemeal stoneground flour, books and souvenirs.

Crabble Corn Mill is set in the heart of the picturesque village of River which straddles the River Dour just 2 miles north-east of Dover where it joins the sea. Within easy walking distance of the Mill are the lovely grounds of Kearsney Abbey, Russel Gardens and Bushy Ruff – all along the valley of the River Dour with its lakes and wildlife.

Cranbrook Union Windmill

Cranbrook Windmill Association
c/o Mrs P. Fryer
Little Baker's Cross
Cranbrook
Kent TN17 3AG
Tel. 01580-712256 or 712984

Cranbrook Union Windmill was built in 1814 by the local millwright James Humphrey for the miller Henry Dobell. The windmill stands on a three-storey base which, it is said, makes it the tallest smock mill in England.

Henry Dobell was declared bankrupt in 1819 and a Union of Creditors took over the business, hence the name Union Mill. In 1832 they sold it to the Russell family, millers from East Sussex who continued to work the mill until 1958. In that year John Russell, the last miller, died whilst it was being repaired and restored to its nineteenth-century condition.

Later the County Council acquired the windmill and are now responsible for its upkeep, and in 1982 a group of Cranbrook residents founded the Cranbrook Windmill Association and opened it to the public. Voluntary labour and donations enabled much of the machinery to be restored to working order, and now wholemeal flour is once more produced by wind power although in limited quantities.

Two sets of millstones have been restored to full working order but only one is regularly used to grind flour, the other is exposed so that visitors can examine the stones in situ. Whenever possible the windmill is worked and, wind permitting, flour is ground during opening hours so that visitors can witness grinding by wind power exactly as it was done centuries ago.

The windmill is open from April to September on Saturdays and Bank Holiday Mondays, and also on Sundays in mid-July and August, from 2.30–5 p.m. Special arrangements can be made for groups and school parties booked in advance.

Admission is free but donations towards the cost of upkeep and further restoration work are invited. No car-parking is available at the mill but there is free parking nearby in the town. The mill shop sells wholemeal flour, gifts and souvenirs.

The little Kentish town of Cranbrook lies less than half a mile off the A229 Hastings to Maidstone road, less than a mile south-west of Sissinghurst and 3 miles north of Hawkhurst.

Herne Windmill
Mill Lane
Herne
Herne Bay
Kent CT6 7DR
Tel. 01227-361326 or 374539

The present Herne Mill is the latest in a long line of mills that have occupied this site since about 1400.

When this mill was built in 1789 the miller was Job Lawrance, and it remained in the Lawrance family until 1879 when Thomas Wootton purchased it. The use of wind power to operate the machinery was finally abandoned in 1952 when electric milling equipment was installed.

Although much of the machinery is still as it was in the 1950s, work still continues restoring and refurbishing, and many of those exhibits which are in working order are demonstrated as weather conditions permit.

Lack of water makes it impossible to mill flour for human consumption at present, but small quantities of oats are milled for sale as pet food. Eventually it is hoped the mill will be fully operational producing wholemeal flour in compliance with the hygiene regulations.

There is a nominal admission charge but since the mill relies mainly upon the public for income to advance the restoration, donations are welcome. It is open from April to the end of September, Sundays and Bank Holidays 2–5 p.m. From mid-July to the end of August it is also open on Thursdays and Saturdays 2–5 p.m. Children are not admitted without an adult. Parties and school groups by prior arrangement only.

The mill shop sells souvenirs, etc., and the local Girl Guides provide teas on some Sundays. Unrestricted street car-parking.

The mill is situated in the village of Herne, about a mile south of Herne Bay, just off the A299 London-Margate road, about 8 miles from Canterbury and 28 from Margate.

Sandwich White Mill
White Mill Folk Museum
The Causeway
Ash Road
Sandwich
Kent CT13 9JB
Tel. 01304-612076

White Mill was built about 1760 and it is known that the miller in the early 1800s was T.J. Bushell. After a succession of owners it was purchased about 1861 by Alfred and Thomas Stanley and it remained in the Stanley family until 1957 when Victor Stanley moved to the Corn Stores nearer the town.

Milling by wind power ceased in 1926 when one of the sails fell off, and the mill fell into disrepair. The work of restoration began in 1960 funded jointly by Sandwich Town Council, the Society for the Preservation of Ancient Buildings and Kent County Council, and was completed in 1981. In 1983 the White Mill Folk Museum was formed with the object of restoring the other buildings on the site, and opening the mill and museum to the public.

White Mill is unusual in retaining most of its vernacular buildings intact including the miller's house, mill office, cart lodge, cow shed, stable and part of the granary barn. There is a museum of domestic and farming exhibits, and much of the original wooden machinery can be seen working in the mill.

The mill and museum is open to the public from Easter until the end of September, Sundays and Bank Holidays 2.30–5.30 p.m. During December and January, Sundays only 10.30 a.m. to 12 noon. Access at other times by appointment. Groups and school parties welcome by prior arrangement.

There is a small admission charge. Car-parking is free. Stoneground wholemeal flour is on sale in the shop together with souvenirs, postcards, etc.

The white smock mill is situated on the A257 Sandwich to Canterbury road about ½ mile west of Sandwich and 10 miles east of Canterbury.

Sarre Windmill
Canterbury Road
Sarre
Kent CT7 0JU
Tel. 01843-47573

This typical Kentish smock mill was built in 1820 to grind for the surrounding farming fraternity. In 1854 the height was increased by approximately nine feet by jacking up the wooden tower structure, and the supporting brickwork raised. In 1861 a steam engine was installed for auxiliary power, and in 1907 this was replaced by a gas engine with its own gas-producer plant.

The mill ceased working by wind power in the early 1920s and the sails were removed and sold, and in 1940, 120 years after being installed, the millstones ground for the last time. In an advanced state of decay the cap was removed in 1958 and the tower boarded up and left to the mercy of the elements.

The semi-derelict mill tower was purchased by the Hobbs family in 1985 and a programme of reconstruction put in hand. The work was completed in 1991 and the new sails turned for the first time in June that year.

Sarre Mill is now one of the few remaining commercially worked windmills in England, and produces a wide range of stoneground products including wholemeal and white flour, rye and malt products, porridge oats and cereals, all of which are available at the mill shop.

The mill is open to the public throughout the year (except Christmas and Boxing Day) 10 a.m. to 5 p.m. Admission to the mill area is free but there is a nominal charge for viewing the interior of the windmill. There is a tea-room serving bread, rolls and cakes made from the mill's own flour in the mill bakery, a craft shop, and displays of vintage machinery and 'bygones'. Children can mingle with the farmyard animals.

Sarre Village lies at the junction of the A29 Canterbury to Margate road and the A253 Ramsgate to Canterbury road. The mill stands on high ground to the north-east of the village and the entrance is off the A253. It is often referred to as Eight Mile Mill, this being the approximate distance from Margate, Ramsgate, Canterbury and Sandwich.

Leicestershire

Claybrooke Watermill
Frolesworth Lane
Claybrooke Magna
Lutterworth
Leicestershire LE17 5DB
Tel. 01455-202443

The present mill dates back to about 1760 but, according to a local historian, there has been a water-mill on this site for over a thousand years. It is driven by water from a tributary of the River Soar and, although enclosed in the triangle of motorways formed by the M1, M6 and M69, and relatively close to large industrial towns such as Coventry, Nuneaton and Leicester, it is nonetheless situated in a pleasant, rural area.

This is essentially a commercial mill producing a large range of organic and non-organic flours including two unique flour mixes – Nuthatch and Fieldfare. The mill shop is open from 8.30 a.m. to 5.30 p.m. weekdays and 8.30 a.m. to 12.30 p.m. Saturdays (closed Sundays).

The mill products can be purchased by visitors during the above business hours in large and small quantities, and there is also a mail-order service. Calling customers have access to a self-guided tour of the mill. Organized parties by prior arrangement only.

Lincolnshire

Ellis's Windmill
Mill Road
Lincoln
Lincolnshire LN1 3BL
Tel. 01522-523870

There was a mill in Uphill, Lincoln in 1241, and there are records of the owners and occupiers of Ellis's Mill dating back to 1650. Frank Ellis was the last miller to work commercially.

The brick tower was built in 1798, and the mill was in production until the Second World War when the machinery was removed. Later a disastrous fire gutted the building and it became derelict.

In 1977 the Lincoln Civic Trust began the work of restoration, using machinery from mills at Sturton-by-Stow and Toynton All Saints; new sails and some of the other woodwork was manufactured and fitted by Thompsons, the Alford millwrights. The work was completed and the mill once more began grinding corn on 26 April 1981 – the worst April day for seventy-five years with heavy snowfalls.

The mill is owned by the Lincoln Civic Trust and is open to the public on Saturdays and Sundays from 2–6 p.m. (or dusk) every weekend from May to September, and second and fourth complete weekends October to April.

Stoneground wholemeal flour is milled and sold every working weekend, subject to weather conditions.

There is a small admission charge with reductions for children. School parties and groups by prior arrangement only. Private visits and illustrated talks can be arranged by telephoning in advance. Free car-parking.

The City of Lincoln has a great deal to offer in the way of tourist attractions including the magnificent Cathedral dating back to 1072; the Lawn – a large complex with concert halls, a sizeable hothouse, small aquarium, extensive gardens and flower beds, etc.; the Museum of Lincolnshire Life and Lincoln Castle. The city itself has many ancient buildings, Roman walls and gateway, a medieval Guildhall, and the National Cycle Museum.

The mill is located near the Cathedral and very close to the Museum of Lincolnshire Life in Burton Road.

Heckington Windmill
Heckington
Sleaford
Lincolnshire

This remarkable mill is England's only surviving eight-sailed windmill and is preserved in full working order.

The first windmill to be built with more than four sails was designed by John Smeaton in 1758 and erected at Leeds. The idea of multi-sailed mills was not widely adopted except in Lincolnshire which, in the nineteenth century, had at least eleven with five sails and eighteen with six sails. Only seven mills were ever built with eight sails, three of which were in Lincolnshire at Market Rasen, Skirbeck (transferred to Heckington in 1892) and Holbeach.

In its heyday the sails were powerful enough to drive five sets of stones producing over five tons of flour per working day, and they are still capable of working two pairs of stones when there is very little wind.

After local government reorganization in 1974 the mill passed into the ownership of Lincolnshire County Council and they now maintain it together with the windmills at Alford and Burgh le Marsh. Over the past few years a major restoration programme has been undertaken and the mill returned to full working order. It ran for the first time in forty years in 1985 and was officially re-opened by HRH The Duke of Gloucester in 1986.

The Lincolnshire village of Heckington, with its superb fourteenth-century church, is situated between Sleaford and Boston on the A17 which now bypasses it to the north. The mill stands to the south of the village on the B1394 next to the railway station.

The Pearoom Craft and Heritage Centre is beside the station, with a café which is open at weekends. Car-parking is in the station yard – the mill yard is private property and used by heavy lorries. There is a modest admission charge with reductions for children, and special rates for groups. Photographers need to get permission from the yard office.

The mill is operational, conditions permitting, Saturdays, Sundays and Bank Holiday afternoons from Easter to the end of September; Sundays only from October to Easter.

The Windmill Shop is in the Pearoom Craft Centre and in June to August is open from 10 a.m. to 5 p.m. Monday to Saturday, midday to 5 p.m. Sunday. During September to May the shop closes on Mondays but it is open on Bank Holidays 12 noon to 5 p.m. The shop sells stoneground wholemeal flour produced at the mill and bread made from Heckington flour in addition to books, souvenirs, etc.

Further details from George Pacey, Chairman, Friends of Heckington Mill, 188 Main Road, Quadring, Spalding, Lincs. PE11 4PT. Tel. 01775-821171.

Maud Foster Windmill
Boston
Lincolnshire PE21 9EG
Tel. 01205-352188

Maud Foster was an Elizabethan lady who consented to a drain being excavated across part of her land – the Maud Foster Drain beside which the windmill stands.

This fine example of an English tower mill was built in 1819 for the brothers Thomas and Isaac Reckitt who carried on business as millers, corn factors and bakers until, after a succession of poor harvests, the business failed in 1833, the mill was sold and the partnership dissolved.

Isaac Reckitt went to Nottingham and set up as a corn factor once more, but with little success. Subsequently he moved to Hull and went into the starch business which was much more profitable. His company eventually became Reckitt & Sons (the manufacturers of the famous 'Reckitt's Blue' without which no self-respecting washerwoman could perform) now Reckitt & Colman Ltd.

From 1948 when Ostlers, the last millers to own the property until 1987, sold it, the structure of the mill gradually deteriorated as a succession of owners put it to different uses for which it had never been intended. Mr Basil Reckitt, great-grandson of Isaac, came to the rescue and arranged for the two Reckitt Family Charitable Trusts to finance essential repairs in 1953.

By 1987 it had again fallen into disrepair, and the Waterfield family, the present owners, began an extensive programme of repairs and reconstruction with the aid of funds from English Heritage, Boston Borough Council and the Reckitt Family Trusts. The work was finally completed in 1988 and it was fitting that Basil Reckitt was able to perform the official re-opening ceremony on 22nd July.

At 78 feet Maud Foster is the tallest working mill in Britain, and at 37 ft 8 ins the sails are the longest working ones. It can be seen milling on most days when the wind is favourable, and visitors are always welcome on Wednesdays and Sunday afternoons or by prior arrangement.

This is a working mill – not a museum – and produces a wide range of stoneground flours, oatmeal, semolina, muesli, bran, etc., all of which can be purchased at the mill shop. There is a nominal admission charge and free car-parking. It is situated about five minutes walk from the centre of Boston on the bank of the Maud Foster Drain which meets the River Witham about 1 mile away.

Boston is a very attractive town itself and is only some 15 miles north of Spalding, the centre of the English tulip industry. In medieval times it was the most important port in England after London and is still well used although the size of ships is limited by the capacity of the River Witham.

Mount Pleasant Windmill
Kirton-in-Lindsey
Gainsborough
Lincolnshire DN21 4NH
Tel. 01652-640177

This is a traditional four-sailed, brick tower mill built in 1875 on the Lincoln Cliff overlooking Kirton-in-Lindsey with extensive views over the Trent Valley and the Lincolnshire Wolds.

It was built for Rupert Snell. The Snell family lived in the millhouse (now Oxford Lodge), and the mill was operated by Rupert and his son Charles until 1936 when it was purchased by Fred and Harry Banks. During the '50s and '60s the Banks Brothers ran a fleet of lorries and built two large warehouses on the site of the present proprietors' house and barn. The Bankses ceased trading and retired in 1973, and the mill lay idle until 1987 when it was purchased by the present owners.

Considerable renovation was necessary to restore the ravages of time and neglect; a new cap and sails were fitted using as many of the original parts as could be reclaimed, and the interior underwent complete refurbishment.

The windmill re-opened in 1991, and is now producing a range of stoneground wholemeal and white flours from organically grown wheat, including self-raising and 'Maltstone' – a malted breadmaking flour with added wholegrains. None of the products are bleached or adulterated in any way, and all are obtainable from the mill shop.

The mill tea-shop serves a selection of home-made cakes, scones and bread – all made from the mill's own organic flour. There is a nominal admission charge but parking is free to both cars and coaches. The mill is open to the public all year round on Saturdays, Sundays and Bank Holidays (except Christmas) 10 a.m. to 5 p.m.

During August it is also open during the week.

Visits by groups or school parties are welcome by prior arrangement, and conducted tours can usually be arranged. It is regretted that although the mill is in regular operation, milling on any particular day depends upon weather conditions and cannot be guaranteed.

Norfolk

Letheringsett Watermill
Riverside Road
Letheringsett
Holt
Norfolk NR25 7YD
Tel. 01263-713153

The little River Glaven joins the North Sea at Cley-next-the-Sea, some 4 miles north of Letheringsett, after powering this attractive working water-mill which was built in 1802 on the site of an earlier mill dating back beyond the Domesday Survey of 1086. It was restored to full production in 1982 and is said to be the only water-mill still producing flour in Norfolk from locally grown wheat.

It is open to the public throughout the year (except during the Christmas holiday period) every day 9 a.m. to 5 p.m. except Monday. Saturday 9 a.m. to 1 p.m. (Closed every day between 1 and 2 p.m.) Bank Holiday Sundays and Monday 2–4.30 p.m.

There is a nominal admission charge when the mill is not working, slightly higher on demonstration days. Car-parking is free. Flour can be purchased from the mill shop.

The area abounds in attractions including several seaside resorts, and the nearby little market town of Holt is considered by many to be among the most picturesque in the county. The horse bus service between Holt town centre and the Railway Station adds to the enjoyment. It is called *The Holt Flyer* but the children are unlikely to need crash helmets.

The Mill is located almost at the junction of the B1156 with the A148, the Fakenham to Cromer road.

Northumberland

Heatherslaw Corn Mill
Ford Forge
Cornhill-on-Tweed
Northumberland TD12 4TJ
Tel. 01890-820338

The mill was built some time before the thirteenth century and the earliest records show it as a double water-mill, the property of the landowner but leased to a miller-tenant.

The present buildings and equipment date back to the last reconstruction in the middle of the nineteenth century. One mill has been restored to full working order and the other remains as it was when it closed down after the Second World War. The massive water-wheel is powered by water from the River Till which rises in the Cheviot Hills some 15 miles to the south.

It is open to the public from Easter until the end of October from 10 a.m. to 6 p.m. daily. Groups and school parties by prior arrangement with the mill manager. There is a small admission charge with concessions for children and OAPs – car-parking is free.

A large range of cereal products are sold on the premises including muesli, oats, barley and rye flour, as well as Heatherslaw stoneground wholemeal flour. The flour is used by the biscuit bakery on site and the Granary Café which specializes in home baking and also in the famous Tweed Bannocks.

The mill is situated between the villages of Ford and Etal, about 8 miles south-east of Cornhill-on-Tweed and 12 miles south-west of Berwick-upon-Tweed, about a mile from the junction of A697 with B6354.

The surrounding area abounds with places of interest including Lady Waterford Hall, Ford Fountain Crafts, Errol Hut Smithy, Heatherslaw Light Railway, Flodden Field site of the Battle of 1513, Etal Castle and the glorious walking country of the Cheviot range.

Nottinghamshire

North Leverton Windmill
North Leverton
East Retford
Nottinghamshire
Tel. 01427-880662

The old village windmill at North Leverton is the last full-time working mill in the county of Nottingham. Although first built in 1813 and renovated and repaired several times since, the present-day structure looks very much the same as when it was originally constructed.

It was built by and for a group of farmers in the parishes of Fenton, North Leverton, Habblesthorpe and Sturton-le-Steeple who formed a subscription company which lasted until 1956 when it was replaced by a limited company. By the original agreement the mill was to grind corn not only for members of the company, but also for other farmers and 'industrious poor persons', at a fee decided upon by the five appointed directors.

It is open daily to the public from 2–5 p.m. except Tuesdays and Saturdays, but groups can be admitted at any time by prior appointment. Wholemeal flour is milled regularly and on sale in the souvenir shop, and there is a small tea-shop on site.

There is no charge for admission but voluntary donations toward the upkeep are welcomed.

Visits by school or other groups must be booked in advance by contacting Mr K. Barlow, West View, Sturton Road, North Leverton, Retford, Notts. DN22 0AB (tel. 01427-880573) to whom *any* enquiries should be directed.

Oxfordshire

Venn Watermill
Garford
Abingdon
Oxfordshire OX13 5PA
Tel. 01367-718888

This is thought to be the site of the mill at Garford that featured in the Domesday Book of 1086, although 1326 is the first reference to Venn Mill by that name that has been found to date. A house, corn water-mill and stable were combined in a single thatched building on the present site which was insured for £200 by the Sun Insurance Company in 1788, but in 1808 the mill was advertised in the Reading Mercury as 'all that new built Water Corn Mill'.

The building with its machinery is essentially as it was built in about 1800 although there have been several replacements at various times including the water-wheel, half of the pitwheel, the brick wall at the southern end, and other details. The structure of the mill is very functional but it shows an interesting variety of building materials. The loft, constructed of elm, is the finest feature with its central walkway and the corn bins on either side.

The mill ceased working during the early part of World War II although it had been used only to grind animal feed for many years prior to that. Subsequently it housed chickens, and was later turned into a carpenter's workshop, this last phase lasting until the beginning of 1979, so that much of the furniture and ancillary machines and tools were lost. However, considering the uses to which it was put over such a long period and its proximity to a main road, it is surprising that it survived at all.

Restoration work commenced in 1979 with the aid of grants from Oxfordshire County Council and the Vale of White Horse District Council. It is now in working order and producing stoneground wholemeal flour from locally grown wheat which can be purchased at the mill. It is planned to extend the product range in the near future as conditions and regulations permit.

The mill is open to the public from April to the end of October on the second Sunday in the month; 10 a.m. to 5 p.m., and at other times by prior arrangement. There is a nominal admission charge; car-parking is free.

Venn Mill is located about 9 miles south-west of Oxford on the A338, 5 miles north of Wantage on the Childrey Brook – a tributary of the Thames. The ancient Thameside town of Abingdon is a few minutes drive away as are Sutton Courtenay Abbey, Milton Manor and Priory Cottages at Steventon.

Perthshire

Blair Atholl Watermill
John Ridley Projects Ltd
The Mill
Blair Atholl
Pitlochry
Perthshire PH18 5SH
Tel. 01796-481321 or 483317

The mill lies at the junction of the Rivers Tilt and Garry, 7 miles north of Pitlochry on the A9 Perth to Inverness road. The earliest record of the mill is the charter appointing the miller William Burghe in the year 1613 but it is almost certain that a mill existed on or near the site before.

Early in the eighteenth century two prisoners were tried at Logierait for breaking into the mill and stealing two bowls of meal (a bowl in local old measure was about 140 lbs). They were banished from the area for life on pain of being whipped through the streets of the township every week if they ever returned.

Remote country mills began to go out of business with the development of transport which conveyed grain to large town mills and ports. Then, during World War I, an Act was passed requiring the production of white flour only which most country mills could not process. The Act was necessary so that the bran was removed from the flour in order to feed the army's horses in France.

Blair Atholl mill survived until 1929 and until the 1960s it was used as a coal and cattle cake store. In 1975 it was acquired by the present owners, renovated, and put back into production in 1977.

In 1978 the mill stable was converted into a bakery, and the lower granary into a tea-room which is open on the same days and at the same times as the mill.

The mill is open to the public from April to October 10 a.m. to 5.30 p.m. weekdays, 12 noon to 5.30 p.m. Sundays. Viewing of the machinery is dependent upon the milling programme.

Stoneground wholemeal flour is on sale, and the on-site bakery produces bread, etc. made from the mill's own grinding, plus three grades of oatmeal, muesli and groats. Except for a percentage of Canadian hard wheat mixed into the bread flour, all grains are grown in Aberdeenshire, Angus or Perthshire.

There is a nominal admission charge and free car-parking, but coaches are requested to give prior notice of intended visits.

Blair Atholl lies at the centre of several places of interest including Blair Atholl Castle, one of the finest in Scotland (¾-mile); Heritage Museum (½-mile); the famous Killiekrankie Pass (3 miles); and the magnificent Glen Garry begins at the Falls of Bruar, about 4 miles to the north.

Powys

Bacheldre Watermill
Churchstoke
Montgomery
Powys SY15 6TE
Tel. 01588-620489

Bacheldre Watermill was built in 1747 and was fully operational until 1960 when William Crowther, the last miller, retired.

It was acquired by the present owners in 1986 when in need of considerable restoration and refurbishment although much of the original machinery was intact. New wooden teeth were made and fitted to many of the gears, a cast-iron axle installed to replace the old wooden one, and forty new buckets fitted to the water-wheel. The original stones needed dressing but were otherwise in good condition.

Milling began again in March 1987, and the mill now produces a range of stoneground flours for distribution to shops and bakeries in Shropshire, Staffordshire and throughout Wales.

Being a commercial enterprise, the mill is not generally open to visitors, but the public are admitted on Sundays 2–5.30 p.m. from Easter to the end of September, when the mill can be seen working.

There are no restaurant or other facilities, and no shop although flour can be purchased at the mill in large or small quantities. There is a nominal admission charge and free car-parking.

The mill is situated 2½ miles west of Churchstoke and 9 miles east of Newtown on the A489, close to some of the most beautiful Welsh Border country and within easy reach of renowned places of interest including Montgomery, Bishop's Castle, Offa's Dyke and Clun Forest.

Felin Crewi
Penegoes
Machynlleth
Powys SY20 8NH
Tel. 01654-703113

The water-mill is located 2 miles east of Machynlleth just off the

A489 at Penegoes. It is open to the public every day from Easter to the end of September 10.30 a.m. to 5 p.m., and during the winter months every Wednesday.

It has a fascinating history from about 1565 when it was probably one of several such water-mills serving the surrounding countryside, and seems to have been in almost continuous operation until 1940 when milling ceased and the buildings occupied by a local builder. The millwheel was sold for scrap for 10s. (50p).

In 1984 it was purchased by Mr and Mrs Partridge and after considerable restoration and renovation once more began milling in 1985. This is one of only four remaining privately-owned commercial water-mills in Wales, supplying several grades of flour to bakers and wholesalers throughout Wales and the Midlands. The full range of products includes 100% wholemeal flour, 100% wholemeal self-raising flour, strong unbleached white flour, strong unbleached self-raising flour, natural wheatbran and wheatgerm, Old Mill muesli and rolled oats. There is a café (closed on Mondays except during school holidays) and a well-stocked gift shop, a free car-park, and the admission charge is nominal.

But there is much more to Felin Crewi than this. The nature trail goes past the mill pond with its ducks and waterfowl to the weir, and although the River Crewi is not large, it has more salmon and sea trout per cubic yard than any other Welsh river – in the autumn the salmon can be seen leaping the weirs to get to the spawning grounds upriver.

The board walk then takes one through the meadow to see the variety of flora and fauna which abound, and this is accessible to wheelchairs and the disabled. The bird hide is ideally placed for viewing the dippers darting up and down the river and a variety of other water and wildfowl species. The walk continues through areas of broad leaved trees and a wild flower meadow passing a few mountain sheep, two donkeys, goats and geese.

Machynlleth itself is a pleasant little market town where, thirty years ago, the sheep would come down from the hills and wander along the main street in search of food scraps – perhaps they still do. Then, there were two hotels, and most Friday evenings the local Male Voice Choir practised in the public bar of the Wynnstay Arms. The area abounds in glorious walks beside tumbling streams where one can watch the fish in the clear waters and mountain climbing (there is a way up Cader Idris to Lyn Cau which passes more than a dozen waterfalls). From Penegoes itself there is a path up into the hills to Parsons Leap, a deep cleft in the hillside over which the local parson was said to jump each Sunday in order to preach to the villagers on the far side. When old age finally caught up with him he paid for a footbridge to be constructed which is still there today.

Shropshire

Daniel's Mill
Eardington
Bridgnorth
Shropshire WV16 5JL
Tel. 01746-762753

Daniel's Mill has stood on this site for many centuries, its name altering slightly over the years. Originally Donynges Mill, it changed to Dunnings Mill in the seventeenth century, was listed in the 1841 census as Dunnell's Mill, and by 1880 had become Daniel's Mill.

Until the mid-nineteenth century another small mill existed below the dam of the top pool; this was built around 1600 and had a 14 ft wooden wheel. It was known locally as 'the mill in the hole' and was also referred to as Clover Mill. All that now remains of this building is the back wall and the wheel pit.

The present water-mill worked until 1957 grinding all kinds of grain for animal feed, but ceased operation on the death of the miller, the present owner's father. It has been carefully restored using original materials wherever possible, and to all appearances is virtually unaltered since its heyday in the eighteenth century.

The unusually large water-wheel is 38 feet in diameter and was installed around 1855 to fully utilize the power of the water from the Potseething Spring which rises higher up the valley and whose flow is low but constant.

Visitors are welcome at weekends only 2–6 p.m. from Easter to the end of September; Bank Holiday Mondays 11 a.m. to 6 p.m. Organized parties and schools are welcome by prior arrangement throughout the year. There is a modest admission charge with concessions for children and OAPs. Free car and coach-parking.

Light refreshments are available in the old kitchen of the house, and stoneground wholemeal flour is on sale in large and small quantities.

Eardington lies about a mile south of Bridgnorth on the B4555 and the mill is close to the Severn Valley Railway at the point where it crosses the viaduct over the valley. Photographers glory in getting a shot of a steam train passing the mill as the massive water-wheel is in motion.

Somerset

Burcott Watermill
Burcott
Wells
Somerset BA5 1NJ
Tel. 01749-673118

The present building is nearly 200 years old, but there has been a mill on this site since the thirteenth century and possibly much earlier. It is powered by the waters of the River Axe which flows out of the nearby Wookey Hole Caves and eventually reaches the sea in Bridgwater Bay. It is known that the leat was dug in the early 1200s by order of the then Bishop of Bath and Wells to drive six mills, four of which have disappeared and one converted to a house, leaving Burcott Mill as the sole survivor.

A major refurbishment was commenced in 1977 and much of the remaining machinery replaced resulting in a quieter, almost vibration-free operation, with mill-wheels capable of microscopic adjustment. The 100% wholemeal flour is ground to a degree of fineness which surprises many people.

The mill is open to the public from July to September, Wednesday, Thursday and Friday from 2 p.m.–5.30 p.m.; weekends from 11 a.m. to 5.30 p.m. During the winter months it is open Saturday and Sunday from 2–4.30 p.m. Groups and school parties at other times by prior appointment only.

The modest admission charge includes free car-parking, and there are seven craft workshops with a variety of gifts and souvenirs on sale. 100% wholemeal flour is available in large or small quantities. The proprietors also run the old miller's house on a bed and breakfast basis – please telephone for details.

The mill is situated on the B3139 Wells to Weston-super-Mare road, about 2 miles north-west of Wells. It is an ideal centre for exploring many places of interest including Cheddar Gorge and Caves, Wookey Hole, Glastonbury, and the Somerset Levels and Wetlands.

Dunster Watermill
Mill Lane
Dunster
Somerset TA24 6SW
Tel. 01643-821759

The Domesday Book records two mills on the Mohun Estate at

Dunster in 1086, but the upper one has long since disappeared. Although there are records of the lower mill from medieval times, it began to take on its present appearance about 1779 when it was almost completely rebuilt.

The present mill dates from about that time and certainly some of the stone walls are original. Like all mills, however, they are subject to vibration, and much has been repaired, altered or replaced over the years.

In 1977 the mill was silent, derelict, the roof partly open to the sky and the floors collapsing and at the mercy of the weather. It was the property of the National Trust who purchased it together with the Dunster Castle Estate in 1976, but were unable to finance repairs to the mill after their considerable outlay on the castle itself.

The Trust granted a twenty-year lease to Arthur and Laura Capps with the agreement that they repaired the mill at their own expense, with the assistance of such grants as were available. Work commenced in 1979 and a year later the mill was open to the public and one pair of mill-stones was actually making flour.

Dunster Watermill is still National Trust property and part of the Dunster Castle Estate but is now operated independently by Paul and Marcia Marriott.

There is a moderate admission charge, and access to the mill can be gained from the village via Church Street and Mill Lane, or, for visitors to the castle grounds (separate charge) the pathway through the gardens down to the river walk is an extremely pleasant stroll to the mill.

It is open to the public from April to October daily (except Saturday); open every day during July and August. There is no parking or vehicular access in Mill Lane but there is a nearby car-park in Park Street or the castle car-park ten minutes walk away or the main car-park at Dunster Steep.

The mill shop sells stoneground wholemeal flour, muesli and other home-made products, and there is a tea-room beside the pretty River Avill.

The village of Dunster with its ancient Yarn Market is a favourite with tourists, artists and photographers, and is in one of the most beautiful areas of Somerset and North Devon. The seaside town of Minehead is a few minutes away by car and is the terminus of one of the most successful steam railways in the country. A little further west lies the thatched village of Selworthy, and a few miles further on Porlock with its famous hill and weir. Inland is the vast expanse of Exmoor surmounted by Dunkery Beacon.

Dunster Castle (NT) was the fortified home of the Luttrell family for 600 years and dates back to the thirteenth century. There is a terraced garden of rare shrubs and a 28-acre park. The castle is sited on a steep hill overlooking the village on one side and the mill on the other. Parking is at the foot of the hill but cars may set down disabled passengers at the castle before proceeding down to the car-park.

Monksmill
Combe Sydenham Country Park
Monksilver
Taunton
Somerset TA4 4JG
Tel. 01984-56284

and

The National Museum of Baking
Tel. 01984-56181

Incorporated in the numerous attractions of the Combe Sydenham Country Park, the working water-mill, which pre-dates the Domesday Survey, is now fully restored and producing wholemeal flour most days of the week. It was used by the monks living on the site in the thirteenth and fourteenth centuries and then by millers until it became derelict around 1890, following the introduction of steel roller mills to Britain.

The mill lies in a spectacular combe of the Brendon Hills part of which are covered by the 500-acre Combe Sydenham Estate which includes the Elizabethan House and Gardens, Deer Park, country walks and trails, picnic and children's play area. The estate is over half-way through a forty-year restoration programme and completion of the mill has been among the first priorities. It is now one of the finest examples of a small working water-mill, and the flour produced is baked into bread and other bakery products in the estate's own bakery on site. The bakery has recently developed its own brand of biscuit which it is marketing under its 'Monksbite' trade name.

Monksmill wholemeal flour is among the most finely ground flour I have yet seen and the palest in colour. I am told this is achieved by very fine adjustment of the millstones coupled with extremely slow grinding. It is produced from locally grown wheat. The resultant crumb is only slightly darker than an unbleached white flour.

The National Museum of Baking is now part of the Combe Sydenham Country Park complex, having transferred from the Bristol area in 1993. It, too, is in the process of being reorganized and progressively enlarged so visitors are likely to see a steady expansion of exhibits and features for several years to come. Eventually there will be lecture theatres, seminar rooms, audio-visual displays and demonstrations including cake decoration and special instruction sessions for parties of school-children.

In addition there will be displays of raw materials, packaging, bakery equipment, vehicles, photographs, shop fittings, etc. both ancient and modern. Combined with the other attractions of the estate, you will now be able to follow the bakery industry's progress from the very beginning up to the present day, and watch the breadmaking process from the grain of wheat to the final loaf.

The estate is clearly signposted off the B3188 about midway between Watchet and Wiveliscombe, about 12 miles south of Minehead and the same north-west of Taunton.

The modest admission charge includes free car-parking and entry to all of the attractions. There is a small restaurant and a shop offering a range of local products including wholemeal bread direct from the estate bakery, trout from the lake and venison from the estate.

Combe Sydenham Country Park is open one week before Easter until the end of October, Sunday to Friday 10 a.m. to 5 p.m. Closed Saturdays, although estate produce can be purchased from the shop until noon.

There are concessions for school parties and groups by prior arrangement throughout the year, and there is an extensive educational programme covering historical and environmentally 'green' projects.

Suffolk

Bardwell Windmill
Bardwell
Bury St. Edmunds
Suffolk IP31 1AD
Tel. 01359-52094

This is basically a commercial mill and bakery but visitors are not discouraged although they must appreciate that the main purpose of the mill is functional.

The mill was operated by wind power until the 1987 gales destroyed the sails and fantail, since when flour has been ground by electrically-driven stones. It is hoped that it can eventually be restored to full working order by wind power.

An impressive range of flours are produced including organic and non-organic stoneground wholemeal, white, Crunchy Malt and Seedy Cob, and the bakery supplies speciality breads made from the mill's own flours. Visitors requiring flour are advised to telephone first to ensure the product they require is in stock.

Bardwell is 8 miles north-west of Bury St Edmunds and about the same distance south-east of Thetford, about a mile from the junction of the A1088 with A143.

Sussex

Bartley Mill
Bells Yew Green
Frant
East Sussex TN3 8BH
Tel. 01892-890372 or 890820

It is known that a water-mill stood on this site in the thirteenth century but the present building dates from the early 1880s and has been restored to full working order after a long period of dereliction and neglect. It is now milling organic wheat for the first time since the early 1900s in a variety of different qualities and grades.

Although this is a commercial mill, the public are admitted all the year round, and encouraged to watch the traditional milling processes. There is a small admission charge with discounts for children and OAPs; car-parking is free. Coach parties by prior arrangement only.

There is a small museum and farm shop where stoneground organic products, gifts and souvenirs can be purchased, and a tea-room. Trout and coarse fishing is available in the millpond and Winn Stream (details from the shop).

Bartley Mill is situated in the beautiful valley of the Winn Stream, 3 miles south of Tunbridge Wells just off the B2169, 5 miles east of Lamberhurst. There are numerous places of interest in the vicinity including Bayham Abbey, Nap Wood and Royal Tunbridge Wells itself.

Bateman's Park Water-Mill
Bateman's
Burwash
Etchingham
East Sussex TN19 7DS
Tel. 01435-882302

> See you our little mill that clacks
>   So busy by the brook?
> She has ground her corn and paid her tax
>   Ever since Domesday Book.

In December 1902, a few months after purchasing Bateman's and Park Mill, Rudyard Kipling wrote, 'I hold an old house and a mill (water) that dates from 1196'. Five years later he wrote the verse which appears above which suggests an even earlier date for the mill. His authority for these dates is not known, but we do know that two water-mills were built in Burwash in 1246–8 by royal command. The present building dates from about 1750, when it was operated by John Skinner, and was last worked in 1902 by the Richardson brothers.

Rudyard Kipling removed the water-wheel and installed the water turbine which drove a generator and provided Bateman's with electricity for twenty-five years.

This is the mill which figures so prominently in Kipling's Sussex stories – *Puck of Pook's Hill, Rewards and Fairies,* and *Below the Mill Dam.* At present the millpond is fed by two springs, one on the slopes of Pook's Hill and the other beside Nether Forge. The little window under the eaves which looks over the millpond is Duck Window.

Restoration of the water-mill was completed in 1975 after seventy years of disuse during which time it had gradually become derelict. The ground floor had disappeared, the roof was leaking and close to collapse, some of the brickwork was rotten, and the studding and cladding of the walls needed replacement. Woodworm and beetle had attacked the machinery and the framework, and it is doubtful whether the millstones would have held their position for another year before the timbers supporting them fractured. The site was overgrown and the waterways choked with weed and debris.

Seven years of voluntary labour assisted by the Royal Engineers resulted in the mill coming once more into production in 1975, and now locally grown grain is milled regularly on Saturday afternoons and the wholemeal flour is sold at the mill.

Park Mill is part of the National Trust Bateman's Estate covering some 300 acres of which about six acres are open to the public including the extensive gardens through which runs the lovely River Dudwell. Bateman's House, famous as the residence of Rudyard Kipling from 1902 to 1939 was built in 1634 and is interesting in its own right, and the garage still houses Kipling's 1928 Rolls Royce.

The house, mill and garden are open to the public from Easter until the end of October 11 a.m. to 5.30 p.m. daily except Thursdays and Fridays (open Good Friday). During the open season the mill grinds corn every Saturday at 2 p.m. There is a moderate admission charge (free to NT members) and no charge for car-parking. Groups and parties by prior arrangement only.

The tea-room serves refreshments and the Oast House Shop adjoining the house sells National Trust goods, local crafts and books including Kipling's work. Flour ground at the mill is used to make cakes, etc. which are on sale in the tea-room.

Bateman's is situated about ½ mile south of Burwash on the A265, about 8 miles east of Heathfield and 5 miles west of Hurst Green. It is within easy reach of the coastal towns of Eastbourne, Bexhill and Hastings, the South Downs and the Weald of Kent.

High Salvington Windmill
Furze Road
High Salvington
Worthing
East Sussex
Tel: 01903-260218

Less than 4 miles north-west of Worthing, between the A27 and the A24 stands this impressive black post mill which was built between 1700 and 1720. It ceased working in 1897 and was open to the public from 1907 until the early '70s. Restoration to full working order was commenced in 1976 by a team of volunteers. It became fully operational and the first flour was produced in 1991 since when milling has continued spasmodically subject to the strength of the wind.

The mill is open to visitors on the first and third Sundays from April to September from 2.30 to 5.00 p.m., the sweeps being rotated when the wind permits. It is also open on National Mills Day which usually falls on the second Sunday in May each year.

There is a souvenir stall which also sells flour ground at the mill and refreshments; a nominal admission charge (children free), and unrestricted street parking.

Enquiries to Mr Potts, 19 Woodland Avenue, High Salvington, BN13 3AF. Tel. 01903-260218.

Lurgashall Watermill
Weald & Downland Open Air Museum
Singleton
Chichester
West Sussex PO18 0EU
Tel. 01243-811348

Lurgashall is thought to be one of the 157 water-mills in Sussex listed by the Domesday Survey, but the present building probably dates from the seventeenth century and it seems to have been rebuilt and modified many times in its history.

At one time the mill was equipped with two water-wheels working in tandem, each wheel driving its own independent set of machinery, millstones, etc., but, by the time production ceased in the 1930s, only the tailwheel was in use.

The Leconfield Estate donated the mill to the museum in 1973, but the restoration was not completed until 1980. The water to power the mill comes from two ponds, but since the natural water supply is inadequate, a powerful water pump has been installed to recirculate the water after it leaves the wheel.

The mill is just one of several historic buildings which have been rescued from destruction and rebuilt on a beautiful 40-acre site on the South Downs. The stoneground wholemeal flour produced at the mill can be purchased at the Museum Shop in large and small quantities. The modest admission charge covers all the exhibits, and there are reductions for OAPs, and children. Parties and school groups by prior arrangement.

There is no charge for car or coach-parking, and light refreshments are served in a timber-framed medieval hall.

The museum is open from March to October daily from 11 a.m. to 6 p.m. November to February – Wednesdays, Saturdays and Sundays only from 11 a.m. to 4 p.m.; but during the period 26 December to 2 January daily from 11 a.m. to 4 p.m. Last admission one hour before closing.

The Weald & Downland Open Air Museum is situated beside the A286 Chichester to Midhurst road, about 6 miles north of Chichester. It is within a few minutes drive of several places of interest including Goodwood House and West Dean Garden Museum.

Michelham Priory Watermill
Michelham Priory
Upper Dicker
Hailsham
East Sussex BN27 3QS
Tel. 01323-844244

The water-mill is set in the beautiful grounds of Michelham Priory which extends now to twenty-five acres of gardens and woodland including the moat and stewpond which is fed by the Cuckmere River.

The earliest record of a water-mill at Michelham Priory is an agreement dated 1434 made between the Prior and the Abbot of Battle, for the priory to make an annual payment of four shillings for the use of water for the mill, but it is probable that a mill existed here at an earlier date. There is a legend that Thomas à Becket fell into the millrace at Michelham whilst out hunting with his friend Gilbert de L'Agile, Lord of Pevensey, whose grandson founded the priory much later in 1229.

By 1478 the mill was reported to be in a ruinous state, and at the dissolution of the priory in 1537 the profits from the mill were recorded at 53s.3d (£2.66).

The mill has been rebuilt several times, much of the materials being reused. The main three-bay, timber-framed section dates from the fifteenth century; other features, including the brickwork and weatherboarding, were added about 1800. An iron water-wheel was installed in 1896 but this, together with other machinery, was removed about 1924. For a time a turbine and generator were installed to provide electricity for the house, but after 1928 the building was used only as a farm store.

After 1971 new machinery and a water-wheel were installed, and the mill restored to working order by the efforts of the Friends of Michelham Priory assisted by volunteers. The sack-hoist mechanism is the only early feature that remains, but it now produces wholemeal flour from local wheat, and this can be purchased at the mill.

The price of entrance to the mill is included in the house and grounds admission ticket as is the physic garden, the picture gallery, the forge and wheelwright's museum and the rope museum. The old cattle stalls in the farmyard have been converted into a bakery and restaurant.

Michelham Priory is owned and managed by the Sussex Archaeological Society from whom further details can be obtained. Opening times are: daily from 25 March to end of October 11 a.m. to 5.30 p.m.; Sundays only during early March and November

11 a.m. to 4 p.m. Car-parking is free. No dogs allowed. Picnic area and children's playground.

The Priory is located about 2 miles west of Hailsham and 4 miles north of Polegate, off the A22 and A27.

Warwickshire

Wellesbourne Watermill
Mill Farm
Kineton Road
Wellesbourne
Warwickshire CV35 9HG
Tel. 01789-470237

The first mill on this site was built in Anglo-Saxon times. The Domesday Survey provides the first recorded evidence of the mill's existence when it was leased by Saxi from the Earl of Warwick. It was one of three mills on a short stretch of the River Dene (a tributary of the Warwickshire Avon) and served the small town of Walton.

The millpond is filled by restricting the flow of the river with three oak sluice gates and a dam. The level of the millpond can be adjusted by opening and closing the sluice gates and by changing the number of dropboards positioned at the top of the dam. The natural flow of the River Dene is over the dam and down a spillway.

On one of the walls are facsimiles of the mill's mention in Domesday Book, leases of the mill to Gervais da Penna from the Earls of Warwick in the twelfth and thirteenth centuries, and a 1733 enclosure map which establishes the existence of a windmill in the field overlooking the water-mill. The succession of millers leased both mills from the Mordaunt family who owned the Walton Estate which still owns the site and was responsible for restoring the mill to full working order. The water-wheel last turned before the Second World War and photographs show the general dereliction of the mill in 1988 when restoration commenced.

In the meadow outside lies the original 1834 oak wheel-shaft beside an English Peak stone quarried in Derbyshire. In earlier times such stones were in general use but have now been replaced by harder French Burr stones which produce a finer grade of flour. The eel trap in the meadow is thought to have originally been slotted behind the sluice gates.

Several grades of flour are produced including wholemeal, plain white, bran, semolina, etc. – all stoneground and from organic grain. The tea-room sells cakes, rolls, pastries and scones made from Wellesbourne flour, and the various flours are sold in large or small quantities.

The mill is situated in a rural setting 6 miles east of Stratford-upon-Avon and 8 miles south of Warwick on the B4086. It is about 6 miles from Junction 15 of the M40.

It is open from Easter until the end of September, Thursday to Sunday 10.30 a.m. to 4.30 p.m. From October until Easter Sunday afternoons only 1-4.30 p.m. Bank Holidays (except Christmas period) 10.30 a.m. to 4.30 p.m. It is closed during December and January. There is a small admission charge with discounts for OAPs and children. Car-parking is free. Group visits and school parties are welcome by prior arrangement.

Worcestershire

Avoncroft Windmill
Avoncroft Museum of Buildings
Stoke Heath
Bromsgrove
Worcestershire B60 4JR
Tel. 01527-31886 or 31363.

The windmill is one of the features of the Avoncroft Museum of Buildings and was brought to the museum from Tanworth-in-Arden, about 12 miles from Bromsgrove, in 1969.

Reference is made to a mill in Tanworth during the early twelfth century and a map of 1560 shows a mill standing at Botley Farm just outside the village. By the mid-nineteenth century the windmill had been moved to Danzey Green Farm where it worked in conjunction with a water-mill.

During the nineteenth-century restoration the post mill was enclosed in a brick roundhouse, a Midlands feature which stabilized the trestle and post, provided storage space, and allowed longer sails to be fitted.

In 1874 one of the sail whips was torn off in a storm and, by this time, competition from mechanized mills made repairs uneconomic. After standing derelict for nearly a hundred years the mill was dismantled by volunteers and conveyed to Avoncroft where a programme of restoration was put in hand. Milling began again in 1976 and it is now one of the few windmills in the British Isles working regularly and producing stoneground wholemeal flour which can be purchased at the mill. It is thought to be the earliest post mill operating in this country.

The modest admission charge covers all the exhibits at the museum on a site of several acres. Parties at reduced rates by prior arrangement.

Opening times: March and November 11 a.m. to 4.30 p.m., closed Mondays and Fridays. April, May, September and October 11 a.m. to 5 p.m., closed Mondays. June, July and August 11 a.m. to 5.30 p.m. every day. Open Bank Holidays during the above periods.

The museum is located 2 miles south of Bromsgrove off the A38 Bromsgrove by-pass (400 yards north of its junction with the B4091), 3 miles north of M5 Junction 5, and 3½ miles south of M42 Junction 1.

Among other places of interest in the vicinity are Webb's Garden Centre at Wychbold, near Droitwich; Jinney Ring Craft Centre, and Hanbury Hall – both at Hanbury near Bromsgrove; and Forge Mill Museum, Needle Mill Lane, Riverside, Redditch – a water-driven needle mill.

Yorkshire

Crakehall Watermill
Little Crakehall
Bedale
North Yorkshire DL8 1HU
Tel. 01677-423240

They have been milling at Crakehall for over 900 years. The present mill is on the site of one mentioned in the Domesday Survey of 1086, and although nothing remains of the Domesday mill, the present building is still very old, dating from the seventeenth century with machinery from the eighteenth and nineteenth centuries.

It belonged to the Neville family of Middleham Castle in the Middle Ages and became Crown property in the fifteenth century. It was sold by James I in 1624.

The mill passed through many hands and was finally closed in 1927 or thereabouts, and by 1977 was derelict and in need of extensive renovation before it could be restored to working condition. In 1980 Crakehall Mil ground corn again for the first time in over fifty years.

Powered by the water from Crakehall Beck, it produces stoneground wholemeal flour from a mixture of Canadian and English grains and this strong fine to medium flour was used in the

ITV programme *Farmhouse Kitchen* for their breadmaking edition.

The mill is open to the public from Easter until the end of September every day except Mondays and Fridays (open Bank Holidays) 10 a.m. to 5 p.m. There is a nominal admission charge and free car-parking. However, it is not operational every day, so if you wish to see flour actually being produced telephone first to confirm milling times.

The tea-room is open every weekend during the season, selling home-made cakes and scones made from Crakehall flour. Stoneground wholemeal flour is on sale throughout the year. There is also a holiday cottage which can be rented.

The mill is situated beside the bridge over Crakehall Beck on the A684 Bedale to Leyburn road, 3 miles west of Leeming Bar on the A1 and 10 miles south of Scotch Corner.

This area is now known as 'Herriot Country' since the TV series *All Creatures Great and Small* made it famous. It includes Mount Grace Priory at Northallerton, Shandy Hall at Coxwold, Bedale Museum, Thorpe Perrow Arboretum at Snape near Bedale and The Museum of Badges and Battledress at Crakehall.

Skidby Windmill
Skidby
Cottingham
Humberside HU16 5TE
Tel. 01482-840150

The ancient Danish village of Skidby has the only complete working example of an East Riding windmill in existence, and from its dominating position there are far-reaching views of the Wolds countryside.

A mill existed on or close to this site in 1388, and in 1626 a petition to the Lord of the Manor complained of the copyholder's action in pulling down 'the mills' – thus indicating that there were perhaps two mills in the village at that time. In 1821 the lower part of the present tower was erected, probably the first forty feet, and we know that the miller in 1823 was William Watson.

The mill passed through several hands, and in 1855 the Ordnance Survey map shows that it was free-standing, the range of buildings now attached not in existence.

About 1860 the nearby Cottingham Low Mill was demolished, and it is suggested that some of the materials released were used to heighten the tower of Skidby Mill to enable the attached buildings to be built as would be necessary to raise the tower to permit the sails to clear buildings.

In spite of constant repairs and alterations, commercial production ceased in 1966 and the mill was presented to Beverley Rural District Council by Mr Eric Thompson of J. G. & B. Thompson with the expressed wish that the unique structure be preserved for future generations.

Beverley Borough Council became the owners of Skidby Mill in 1974 and have since restored it to full working order. Stoneground wholemeal flour is produced from Yorkshire-grown milling wheat and is available at the mill shop. The Mill House restaurant adjacent to the mill serves refreshments.

The mill is open to the public from Easter to October, Tuesday to Saturday 10 a.m. to 4 p.m., Sundays 1.30–4.30 p.m.; from November to Easter, Monday to Friday 10 a.m. to 4 p.m. (excluding Christmas holidays). Subject to weather conditions, milling takes place on about sixteen Sundays during the year – please telephone for details as below.

There is a nominal admission charge, and car-parking is free. Parties and school groups are welcome if booked in advance. Telephone 01482-883919.

The village of Skidby lies just off the A164 some 4 miles south of Beverley and about 7 north-west of Kingston-upon-Hull. Junction 38 of the M62 is about 7 miles west of the village.

Worsbrough Water Mill
Worsbrough Bridge
Barnsley
South Yorkshire S70 5IJ
Tel. 01226-774527

A Worsbrough Mill was recorded in the Domesday Survey of 1086 but the present building, a water-powered corn mill, was probably constructed about 1625. In 1843 a steam-driven corn mill with two sets of millstones was added to the northern end to cope with the increased demand.

Worsbrough Mill produced only wholemeal flour, and with the coming of the new roller mills, became obsolete when mass-produced, cheap, white flour flooded the market. In 1922 the steam engine was scrapped. The water-mill continued crushing barley, oats, peas and beans for animal feed, but by the 1960s the machinery was barely safe to work and much of the building was almost derelict.

The mill has been restored to full working order and is now an industrial museum. A rare 1911 Hornsby hot bulb oil engine has replaced the steam engine and drives the once steam-powered machinery.

The main power for the mill is provided by a cast-iron water-wheel which is fed from the millpond. The pond is filled from an 800-yard channel called a goit or head race which carries water diverted from Rockley Dike, one of two feeder streams for Worsbrough reservoir. After turning the wheel the water flows into the River Dove.

The mill is set in a 200-acre country park which also includes an open working farm, Wigfield Farm, with a farm trail, animals, including some rare breeds and children's favourites, beehives and a collection of old farm machinery.

Worsbrough Country Park and Mill Museum is situated on the A61 a little over 2 miles south of Barnsley and a similar distance north of Junction 36 on the M1.

The mill is open all year (except Christmas) Wednesday to Sunday 10 a.m. to 5 p.m. (4 p.m. October to March). Wigfield Farm is open every day (including Bank Holidays but excluding the Christmas period). The country park is always open from dawn to dusk. There is no admission charge but donations are welcomed. Groups must be booked in advance.

The souvenir shop at the Mill Museum sells a range of products including stoneground flour produced at the mill.

A number of special events take place throughout the year, usually on Bank Holidays. These include folk dancing, shire horse shows, shearing, bread baking demonstrations, etc.

There is access for the disabled to most of the site and disabled visitors are most welcome. Unfortunately, though, the interior of the mill is unsuitable because of the narrow staircases and uneven floors.

Glossary

A selection of terms used in the baking industry.

Absorption rate   the varying capacities of flours to absorb water.

Bashing   making a hole in the top of a cottage loaf with the thumb.

Bay   indentation or well in flour to hold liquid.

Biscuit flour   flour which is better suited to biscuit or cake production than bread.

Bleached flour   flour treated with a range of chemicals to whiten and age it. Unbleached flour is unsuitable for intensive mechanized bread production.

Blend   combine or mix in.

Bran   outer husk of the grain containing phytic acid. It is a rich source of dietary fibre.

Bread flour   flour with a high gluten content.

Cake flour   made from low protein wheat with a much lower gluten content. Unsuitable for bread production.

Calcium carbonate (chalk)   added by law to all white flour.

Caramelization   heating sugar above its melting point to produce crystallized granules.

Clear   mix until flour and liquid are thoroughly combined in the dough.

Cracked   grains that have been split by pressure into large pieces, usually halves or almost whole grains.

Cream   to beat one or more ingredients until soft and creamy.

Crumb   the soft interior of the loaf contained within the crust.

Crust   the exterior surface of a loaf of bread after baking.

Divider   machine for cutting up dough.

Egg-wash   mixture of egg and water or egg and milk used as a glaze.

Emulsion   a fine mixture of two liquids which would not normally mix such as oil and water.

Extraction   the percentage of flour remaining after 100% wholemeal is sifted. Best quality white flour is about 65% extraction; 35% of the grain removed in the form of bran, wheatgerm, etc.

Ferment   to allow yeast to activate and develop.

French stick wire   long baking tray for French batons.

Gluten   protein produced during the kneading of flour with water, giving the dough elasticity and the ability to sustain a high rise.

Hard wheat   wheat containing a high proportion of protein.

Grown mainly in Canada, USA and the Ukraine.

Improvers   additives used to reduce the time taken to produce bread for the benefit of the manufacturers.

Kibbled   grains that have been crushed into large fragments but smaller than those 'cracked'.

Knead   manipulating dough to produce good gluten formation and elasticity.

Knock back   re-kneading after the first rising.

Leaven   a collection of naturally occurring yeasts used to aerate dough, which perform in a similar way to commercial yeasts and other artificial rising agents. An essential ingredient of genuine sourdough breads.

Meal   coarsely ground grain is termed meal, finely ground, flour. Wholemeal should by law be the whole of the cleaned grain after grinding with nothing added and nothing removed.

Mix to a crumb   rub in fat until the mixture resembles fine breadcrumbs.

Mixer   a machine capable of mixing, usually fitted with a dough hook.

Mould   to form the dough into the required shape.

Organic   there is no legal definition of the term but it is generally taken to mean 'grown without being treated with artificial fertilisers or sprays'.

Peel   long-handled wooden implement for loading and unloading bakers' ovens.

Pin   rolling pin, or the action of applying the pin to a ball of dough.

Pin out   spread the dough out on a flat surface by using a rolling pin.

Prove   the last rise before the bread goes into the oven. Some books refer to every rise as a 'proving' but this is incorrect.

Prover   a machine used in the baking industry in which bread is set to prove.

Reduction   the term used by millers to describe the grinding of grain into flour.

Rest   standing time during which the dough is allowed to recover before being reworked.

Roller milling   a method of reducing whole grains to flour by crushing between steel rollers instead of slowly grinding between stones. High-speed roller milling can heat up the flour and result in an inferior product.

Rope   a microorganism of the genus *Bacillus* which can survive the baking process and produce a mould which will convert the crumb into long sticky strands or 'ropes'.

Quick mix dough   dough that must be made rapidly, soda breads for instance.

Scale off weigh out dough into separate portions.

Short fermentation or *Small fermentation* rapid fermentation.

Slack a soft spreading dough which is usually unsuitable for tray-baking.

Slash to score or cut the surface of the dough before it goes into the oven.

Sole of oven oven floor.

Sourdough bread made without commercial yeast.

Steam injection injecting steam into the oven during baking.

Stoneground flour which has been ground slowly between abrasive stones; considered by many to be superior to roller-milled flour both in flavour and nutritional value.

Tray or *Tray up* to set the loaves out onto trays ready for the oven – a term more often used when making rolls.

Unbleached flour a creamy-white flour containing a small proportion of the natural bran and wheatgerm, the actual amounts depending upon the screening process to which it has been subjected. All 'white' flour has been chemically bleached unless labelled 'unbleached'.

Bibliography

Acton, Eliza, *The English Bread Book* (Longmans Green, London 1857)

American Baker (Miller Publishing Co., Minneapolis 1914–60)

American Journal of Clinical Nutrition No 24

Baking Today (Maclaren Publishers, London 1980–83)

Batten, M.I., *English Windmills* (Architectural Press, 1930)

Bender, A.E., *Dictionary of Nutrition and Food Technology* 4th ed. (Newnes-Butterworth)

Bernard, R.W., *The Chemical Contamination of Bread* (Health Research, California 1976)

Bingham, Sheila, *Dictionary of Nutrition* (Barrie and Jenkins 1977)

Bread: An Assessment of the Bread Industry in Britain (Technology Assessment Consumerism Centre, Intermediate Publishing Ltd., Kettering 1974)

Birch, G.G. & Green, L.F., *Food Chemistry* (London 1976–83)

Burkitt, Denis, *Don't Forget the Fibre in Your Diet* (Martin Dunitz, 1979)

Conning, D.M., Leigh, L. and Ricketts, B.D., *Food Fit to Eat* (British Nutrition Foundation, London, 1988)

David, Elizabeth, *English Bread and Yeast Cookery* (Allen Lane, Penguin Books Ltd. 1977)

Fance, W.J. & Wragg, B.H., *Up-to-date Breadmaking* (Maclaren & Sons 1968)

Gribben, H., *Vienna and Other Fancy Breads* (Maclaren & Sons, London, 1901)

Jago, W & W.C., *The Technology of Breadmaking* (The Northern Publishing Co., Liverpool 1911)

Kent-Jones & Amos, *Modern Cereal Chemistry* 6th ed. (Food Trade Press, London 1968)

Kirkland, John, *The Modern Baker, Confectioner and Caterer* (Gresham Publishing Co., London 1907)

Mayhew, Henry, *London Labour* and *The London Poor* (London 1851)

Masterson, J.J., *Construction and Conversion of Treadmills for the Grinding of Corn in H.M. Prisons* (Baldwin Bros., c 1780)

Ministry of Agriculture, Fisheries and Food:
   Manual of Nutrition (HMSO, London 1970)
   Bread and Flour Regulations (HMSO, London 1984)
   The Food (Revision of Penalties) Regulations (HMSO, London 1985)
   The Preservatives in Food Regulations (HMSO, London 1989)

The Emulsifiers and Stabilisers in Food Regulations (HMSO, London 1989)

The Food Safety Act (HMSO, London 1990)

The Potassium Bromate (prohibition as a Flour Improver) Regulations (HMSO, London 1990)

Paul, A.A. & Southgate, D.A.T., *The Composition of Foods* 4th revised ed. (HMSO 1978)

Pennant, Thomas, *Some Account of London* 5th ed. (1813)

Reynolds, J., *Windmills and Watermills* (Hugh Evelyn, London 1970)

Victoria History of the Counties of England (Oxford University Press)

Vince, John, *Watermills and How They Work* (Sorbus 1993)

Vines, A.E. & Rees, N., *Plant and Animal Biology* (Pitman, London 1959)

Williams, A., *Breadmaking – the Modern Revolution* (Hutchinson Benham Ltd. 1975)

Index